U6 $125 ok

U6 Roth 55 + 250?✓

Out of the Ether

The Amazing Story of Ethereum and the $55 Million Heist that Almost Destroyed It All

Matthew Leising

WILEY

Published by John Wiley & Sons, Inc., Hoboken, New Jersey.
Published simultaneously in Canada.

No part of this publication may be reproduced, stored in a retrieval system, or transmitted in any
form or by any means, electronic, mechanical, photocopying, recording, scanning, or otherwise,
except as permitted under Section 107 or 108 of the 1976 United States Copyright Act,
without either the prior written permission of the Publisher, or authorization through payment
of the appropriate per-copy fee to the Copyright Clearance Center, Inc., 222 Rosewood
Drive, Danvers, MA 01923, (978) 750-8400, fax (978) 646-8600, or on the Web at www.
copyright.com. Requests to the Publisher for permission should be addressed to the Permissions
Department, John Wiley & Sons, Inc., 111 River Street, Hoboken, NJ 07030, (201) 748-6011,
fax (201) 748-6008, or online at www.wiley.com/go/permissions.

Limit of Liability/Disclaimer of Warranty: While the publisher and author have used their best
efforts in preparing this book, they make no representations or warranties with respect to the
accuracy or completeness of the contents of this book and specifically disclaim any implied
warranties of merchantability or fitness for a particular purpose. No warranty may be created or
extended by sales representatives or written sales materials. The advice and strategies contained
herein may not be suitable for your situation. You should consult with a professional where
appropriate. Neither the publisher nor author shall be liable for any loss of profit or any other
commercial damages, including but not limited to special, incidental, consequential, or other
damages.

For general information on our other products and services or for technical support, please
contact our Customer Care Department within the United States at (800) 762-2974, outside
the United States at (317) 572-3993, or fax (317) 572-4002.

Wiley publishes in a variety of print and electronic formats and by print-on-demand. Some
material included with standard print versions of this book may not be included in e-books or
in print-on-demand. If this book refers to media such as a CD or DVD that is not included in
the version you purchased, you may download this material at http://booksupport.wiley.com.
For more information about Wiley products, visit www.wiley.com.

Library of Congress Cataloging-in-Publication Data is Available:
ISBN 9781119602934 (Hardcover)
ISBN 9781119602958 (ePDF)
ISBN 9781119602941 (ePub)

COVER DESIGN: PAUL McCARTHY
COVER ART: © GETTY IMAGES | JOSE A. BERNAT BACETE

Printed in the United States of America.

SKY10020633_082420

Dedication

*For Rebecca, my life, my love. You always believed
I could do this when I'd convinced myself otherwise.
For that, you have my undying gratitude and thanks.*

Contents

Cast of Characters

Ethereum Cofounders

Vitalik Buterin – Ethereum inventor, ringleader, onetime fashion maven, and lover of bunnies

Anthony Di Ilorio – Created Toronto's first Bitcoin meetup, early and important investor in Ethereum, later pushed out in a power struggle

Charles Hoskinson – One of the first five cofounders, wanted to lead the project from the start, fired after six months for abusive and manipulative behavior

Amir Chetrit – Met Vitalik in Israel working on colored coins project, unclear what he contributed to Ethereum, fired for lack of commitment

Mihai Alisie – Cofounder of *Bitcoin Magazine* with Vitalik, helped set up Ethereum's Zug headquarters, business development

Gavin Wood – Architect of Ethereum, C++ client creator, a bit prickly, took Vitalik's vision and made it real

Jeff Wilcke – Created Ethereum's Go client, sided with developers on power struggle question

Joe Lubin – Early and important investor in Ethereum, former software developer and Wall Street software engineer, true believer, user of strange words, founder of Ethereum development studio ConsenSys

Other important early people

Roxana Sureanu – Helped get *Bitcoin Magazine* off the ground, willing hardscrabble traveler, turned the Spaceship House from a dwelling into a home

Stephan Tual – Ethereum evangelical, ran marketing for the project, has the gift of gab, one of three founders of slock.it, added to Ethereum leadership after Zug purge

Christoph Jentzsch – Helped debug Ethereum code in run up to 2015 launch, theoretical physicist by training, co-founded slock.it, really wishes he could revisit line 666 in the DAO code

Mathias Grønnebæk – Helped establish Zug headquarters, reader of tax laws, worked for Charles Hoskinson, helped craft Ethereum Foundation business plan

Taylor Gerring – Helped secure Bitcoin raised in Ethereum crowdsale, taker of many photos, added to Ethereum leadership after Zug purge

Anthony D'Onofrio – Designer and software developer, helped improve early Ethereum web site, took drugs, saw future, one of the few people Gav Wood likes

Emin Gün Sirer – Blockchain pioneer, first to use proof of work to back a digital coin, Cornell associate professor of computer science, called unsuccessfully for a moratorium on the DAO then found the DAO bug and dismissed it

Peter Vessenes – Bitcoin pioneer, tangled with the Bitcoin Foundation, pointed out smart contract security issues

Ming Chan – First executive director of the Ethereum Foundation, whipped it into shape to keep it within its means, Vitalik favored her though she rubbed many the wrong way

Badass blockchain ninja warriors

Alex Van de Sande – Known as avsa, helped marshal the Robin Hood Group from his apartment in Rio, co-developed the Mist wallet, excellent husband, the one who pushed the button to start the DAO counterattack

Griff Green – The Mayor of Ethereum circa June 2016, hugger, vision-
ary, driver of the RHG, slock.it's first employee, wants a sick jump
shot but it's just not happening this time around

Fabian Vogelsteller – tech whiz who helped the RHG prepare to fight
the ether thief, co-developed Mist wallet

Lefteris Karapetsas – coding guru, replicated DAO attack in a few hours

Jordi Baylina – helped the RHG drain remaining $4 million of ether
from the DAO, coding genius, Spanish freedom fighter

Other really important early people

Dmitry Buterin – Vitalik's dad, supportive father, hater of communists

Natalia Buterin – Vitalik's mom, patient mother, adventurous spirit

Maia Buterin – Vitalik's step mom, patiently waited for Vitalik's cooking

Important people who helped Ethereum go mainstream

Amber Baldet – Hands-on builder, coder, vital within JPMorgan to link
Ethereum to its in-house Quorum project

Christine Moy – Amber's first hire for Quorum within JPMorgan,
finance master in all areas of the bank

Patrick Nielsen – Hired by Amber at JPMorgan, solved the privacy issue
for the bank that gave birth to the Quorum ecosystem

Marley Gray – Microsoft director of blockchain and distributed ledger
business development in 2015, lover of Andrew Keys, delivered on
Microsoft's vision of "a growth mindset" by linking up with Ethereum

Alex Batlin – Ran UBS Labs, a fintech-focused unit at the Swiss bank,
instrumental in creation of Enterprise Ethereum Alliance

Jeremy Millar – ConsenSys executive who helped create the EEA after
realizing competition from R3 and IBM were real and needed a
response

Andrew Keys – One of the first ConsenSys hires, worked for free, loaned
$100,000 to the Ethereum Foundation to ensure Dev Con 1 took
place, great explainer of complicated things

Prologue

The future was broken.

Every person in this story I'm about to tell you knew this. Felt it in their bones. Their views were well known and widely shared, yet nothing ever seemed to change. Capitalism was destroying the planet. Income inequality kept tightening its grip. Tech behemoths like Google, Apple, Amazon, Facebook, and Twitter owned the public square, where once all you needed was a soapbox to voice an opinion. Now any of these monopolists could censor you or shut you down for even clearing your throat. Human beings had ceded their organizing power to corporations that saw them as data to be harvested and sold. The grievances were long and detailed, and yet not many of these people could put their fingers on a way to effect change.

The future was broken.

A global financial crisis had robbed a generation of a decade of productive employment opportunity. The recent graduates in this story who looked out over the years ahead of 2008 saw no hope for economic growth, only job cuts and shrinking industries. The banks that created the fiasco, though, they got off. Hell, they saw their stock prices soar in the years after 2008 thanks to an unspoken but very real US government guarantee – take all the risk you want, we'll be here to bail you out when necessary. The people who lost their homes? Not so much. They'd have to fend for themselves.

The future was broken.

The Canadian philosopher Marshall McLuhan, a giant in media theory who changed the way we look at popular culture, warned us in 1967: "How shall the new environment be programmed now that we have become so involved with each other, now that *all* of us have become the unwitting work force for social change?" he wrote in *The Medium Is the Message*. "All media work us over completely. They are so pervasive in their personal, political, economic, aesthetic, psychological, moral, ethical, and social consequences that they leave no part of us untouched, unaffected, unaltered. The medium is the message. Any understanding of social and cultural change is impossible without a knowledge of the way media work as environments."

Fifty years after McLuhan wrote those words, another writer had also been at work. Here was a rare individual, someone able to put a finger on the dystopia that sprang from so much concentration – concentration of power, of wealth, of media. All of it originated from centralization. The gatekeepers kept making the gates higher and higher and more and more costly. But what if we could create a system without gates, without a central authority and the power to say what is permissible? What if, the people in this story asked, the organizing principle instead was flat and distributed and no one had enough control to stop anyone else?

That's the idea Satoshi Nakamoto gave to the world in the fall of 2008. The creator of Bitcoin had seen the future, knew it was broken, but also knew it could be different. Bitcoin would fix the future, and it would change so much more than how people thought about money. It gave these disconcerted characters the elusive thing they sought – the key to unlock it. Blow up the center. Destroy the middleman. Take the power back. That was the idea, anyway.

And while this story must start with Bitcoin, it is not about Bitcoin. It's the story of what came next. It's about going beyond Bitcoin to use technology to build even more powerful connections among people. It's the story of Ethereum, a global network of computers known as a blockchain invented in 2013 by Vitalik Buterin, a Russian-Canadian genius who'd yet to celebrate his 20th birthday.

Buterin married the digital money aspect of Bitcoin to the almost unlimited capabilities unleashed by what can be written in computer code. If you think about it in terms of contracts, just about everything I can think of can be boiled down to a written contract. Certainly, legal documents, but also financial transactions, commerce, global trade. Now you could take those contracts and in a sense digitize them by bringing them to life on Ethereum's global network. Once there, they could be accessed by anyone in the world at any time of day or night. There's a money feature embedded in Ethereum too, so you can pay for stuff. And it all takes minutes rather than the days, weeks, or months to complete common transactions in the industries I just mentioned. The efficiency gains are on par with what the Internet provided us in the early 2000s.

At its most valuable, the Ethereum network was worth an astounding $135 billion. Its creators became billionaires and millionaires. Ethereum is – slowly – changing the way finance and mainstream corporations think about the myriad tasks they do behind the scenes to make the world work. This is the story of the people who brought Ethereum to life, and how they changed the world.

But it's also about a $55 million heist that threatened to bring Ethereum down. The DAO attack, as it's known, is one of the strangest tales of thievery I know. A group of good-guy hackers who called themselves the Robin Hood Group fought a ninja war on the blockchain to prevent hundreds of millions of dollars from being stolen. Against them was a malicious but ingenious attacker who for the most part remains unknown to this day. And finally, it's about my effort to find out who did it, to unmask the ether thief.

Part I

It is the business
of the future
to be dangerous.
– A.N. Whitehead

Zero

For most of the world the attack began on a Friday in June 2016. The planning and testing and tinkering had been in the works for weeks. Everything would have to be just right or it would fail. What was about to unfold was one of the most elegant, complicated, and weirdest thefts in history.

The clock read 3:34 in Coordinated Universal Time. That's the same as Greenwich mean time, for those who remember. The wee hours in Europe, still Thursday in New York City, and half past 11 in the morning in Beijing. A pair of eyes checked the screen again; a finger hovered over a mouse button. This was a moving machine with many parts: all interacting, all in code, all in cyberspace. It's baffling and complex, and some of the best computer scientists in the world struggle to put into plain

English what happened. Robots attacking robots on the web. That's how one person put it to me, and I've never forgotten it. In this case the reward the robots battled over was immense – a quarter of a billion dollars.

None of this would have been happening if not for a new computer science discipline known as blockchain. While certainly a buzzword, blockchain is simply a new way of implementing databases. Instead of one company or government controlling access to data, the ledger is shared and spread among computer hard drives all over the world. It is what made Bitcoin possible.

Bitcoin, of course, ushered in the era of cryptocurrencies, a time where a new type of money came to exist, one that isn't backed by a government or bank but instead derived from whether people believe it's useful. Bitcoin was the pioneer, but by mid-June 2016, the second-most valuable cryptocurrency after Bitcoin was called ether. Ether is the fuel that allows the Ethereum blockchain to work.

The hacker looked at the contract he'd written one last time, then clicked his mouse. His target: a computer program that held $250 million worth of ether. What it also held was an enormous bug in its code that the hacker believed would let him walk right in and steal it all.

His first try failed. Four minutes later, he tried again. That attempt failed too – a red exclamation point next to his transaction declared "Error in Main Txn: Bad Jump Destination." Shit, he thought he'd nailed this down. He took some time to check all the inputs, the addresses, and codes. Seventeen minutes later, at exactly 3:34:48 UTC, he tried a third time. Then, he saw it. His account had received 137 ether from the computer program that held the $250 million. That was a cool $2,700 he just stole.

The attack had begun. Thousands of these small transactions would accrue throughout the day as the theft continued. People all over the world watched as it occurred, helpless to stop it. Eventually $55 million of ether was stolen, making it the largest digital heist in history at the time.

● ● ●

I remember that day. I'd called in sick to my job as a reporter at Bloomberg News in New York. June 17, 2016. I'd wrapped some blankets around me as I sat on the couch in my Brooklyn apartment and checked my phone for whatever news I was missing.

I'd been at Bloomberg for 12 years, reporting on Wall Street and energy and oil markets, and then, for most of that time, my beat became the financial infrastructure that keeps the whole system humming but that no one talks about. How exchanges work, for example, or the ins and outs of US Treasury bond trading. Then the world went through the worst financial crisis since the Depression. I covered the Dodd-Frank Act's debate and passage: legislation written in hopes of reining in the financial world to stave off another crisis. I never thought I'd end up being a financial reporter – it just sort of happened, and then I found myself involved in one of the biggest stories of the century.

In 2015, all that background brought me to the realization that a new concept – blockchain – could radically change everything I wrote about. I'd dismissed Bitcoin as a fad for years. I didn't understand it. I thought, how in the world could anyone value something that was nothing more than ones and zeroes?

Blockchain, though, was different. Most of the financial plumbing I spent my days talking to people about was antiquated and in great need of updating. Banks like JPMorgan were sitting atop technology systems that would make the mazes of Babylon seem a snap to navigate. That's because they inherit IT systems when they buy other banks. And then they build systems in-house that might be designed according to the whims of a certain part of the bank, which then won't work with a system in another part of the bank. Some of these systems were written in Cobol, a programming language popular in the 1970s that faces the very real possibility that no one who knows how to fix it will be alive in a few years.

The best thing to do would be to rip it all out and completely redesign these systems. Which is impossible, of course. But Wall Street's need to catch up to the twenty-first century in terms of technology systems was critical. Blockchain turned many heads for this reason. Not only could it streamline bank IT systems, it held the potential of speeding up transactions, which would save banks a lot of money.

That's what I realized, thanks to a short article I read in the *Economist* in 2015. Soon after, I told my boss I wanted to include blockchain on my beat. He said, "That's great. What's blockchain?"

As I lay on my couch on that day in June 2016, the news hit that this thing called the DAO had been hacked. The DAO is the computer program I told you about, the one that held $250 million. I didn't use the name at first because I don't want to confuse you any more than absolutely necessary. I'll do my best to make this as painless as possible, but there are still going to be technical details. And names like *decentralized autonomous organization*, or *DAO*. Please — stick with me, hold my hand. We can do this.

So anyway, ether was being stolen, even as I read the story on my couch. I think I remember this vividly because I immediately experienced the pang of guilt any reporter feels when they are out of the loop as a big story is breaking on their beat. I should call in, I thought; I need to help tell this story. But I really was sick, and I didn't have many good Ethereum sources at that time.

In fact, earlier in 2016 was the first time I'd spoken to anyone about Ethereum. I went to visit Joe Lubin in the funky Bushwick headquarters where he'd started ConsenSys, the largest innovation studio for applications that would run on top of the underlying Ethereum network. An Ethereum cofounder, Lubin is quiet and demure. A native Canadian, he has an intense focus that can make you feel you have his entire attention when you speak with him. He shaves off the hair that remains on his head and is strikingly handsome in the way that some men pull off being bald.

Years before I met Lubin I'd lived in Bushwick. The Brooklyn neighborhood had been much rougher in 2004. Restaurants were few and far between. A bar called Kings County was one of the only local gathering spots and was just around the corner from where ConsenSys would later set up shop. I had friends at the bar who told stories of being chased by packs of wild dogs, of returning late to their apartment from the subway to find a tiny slip of paper jammed into their keyhole, put there by the guys in the shadows who demanded everything they had. It was an amazing time.

I knew the building ConsenSys would come to occupy, next to an overpriced natural grocery store. Its facade was forever covered in graffiti long before ConsenSys moved in, a detail no profile of Lubin or his firm has ever seen fit to leave out.

Lubin built ConsenSys in the hopes of fostering the types of digital applications that would make Ethereum indispensable to the world. Think of a blockchain-based digital version of Uber, but without the middleman that is Uber taking 30 percent of every transaction. Consumers pay less, drivers earn more, and hopefully the user experience of clicking an app on a smartphone isn't much different. Or think of an app that directly connects artists with their fans without a record company and lawyers and agents all in the middle taking their cuts.

What's amazing about this idea of a new kind of Internet that's peer-to-peer is that Ethereum has money programmed into it already. Ether is the currency of the realm, meaning that banks can't shut it down. Losing access to banking is almost always a sure way to kill off something you don't like. Here it's impossible.

But what does a blockchain Uber really mean? Let's run through it and call it CarCoin. This is how I first came to understand Ethereum's potential method of mass disruption.

How does CarCoin make money? That has to be the first question. No one wants to build complicated software for free. What you do is create a new cryptocurrency along with the application for your ride-hailing business. CarCoin will be created and sold to the public. Importantly, you must have a CarCoin balance to access the app on your phone.

Now imagine CarCoin hits it out of the park. Everyone wants some. The price of CarCoin goes up. The founders and developers of CarCoin, meanwhile, have made sure to give themselves a lot of CarCoin for free.

They do this in hopes that its value rises; then they're sitting on pure profit and all their hard work has paid off. This is smart contract 101 stuff once you understand the 360-degree nature of the ecosystem Ethereum's inventor Vitalik Buterin and his colleagues created. The app, the coin, and the supply demand dynamics all intertwine. It makes sense, yet I now understand it never really was the vision in the early years.

The people who invented and created Ethereum were flying blind. Very little of how the project became a reality followed any kind of thought-out process. That goes as far as making sure to have a way of making money.

Fabian Vogelsteller was an essential early programmer for Ethereum. Starting in about 2014 he built, with Alex Van de Sande, the Mist wallet, one of the earliest and most important Ethereum apps as it allowed users to access the Ethereum blockchain and hold the different digital currencies they owned.

"There was no business model at the time," Vogelsteller said. The economics are rather limited, as he spelled out. You can't charge for using smart contracts and people are already spending ether to access Ethereum – that's fundamental. A digital application can only hope to earn money if it provides a useful service to people. But that was the last thing on early developers' minds, he said.

"We never thought about business models at all. It was only about what to build, not how to make money," Vogelsteller said. I was speaking to him in 2020 for a story I was writing about his new project, Lukso, an arts, culture, and fashion focused blockchain based on Ethereum. I ran my CarCoin example by him, and he zeroed in on the big problem right away: Why is CarCoin – i.e., the new cryptocurrency – necessary? Why not just use ether for everything? It's taking the money aspect of Ethereum a bit too far to build an entirely new coin on top of it.

While this criticism doesn't blow a hole in the idea of digital applications, it does call into question the nearly two-year-long orgy known as the initial coin offering market that took place from about 2016 to early 2018. Billions of dollars were raised by legitimate and completely fraudulent dev teams alike. Everyone was welcome at this scamfest. And all of it can be seen in hindsight as an enormous waste of time, energy, and the little creativity that went into most ICO projects. It was a folly, but only one of many to come.

"The whole Ethereum community, from the core developers and on, is pure idealism," Vogelsteller said. This sanguine vibe is strongly tied to one of the universally shared beliefs among the people who created Ethereum: the Internet should be free so we can all share it and build cool things, to paraphrase how Fabian Vogelsteller described it to me.

The correct incentives are the next ingredient in this idealism pie. Fabian compared it to a jungle: brutal, yes, but it all works because the incentives line up in favor of keeping the entire ecosystem healthy. Shitty incentives in the jungle lead to death for everything. Blockchain has to believe in incentives because its core function – to date, at least – is tied directly to the network of computers that mine and validate transactions. Making as much money as possible by mining comes with a nifty side effect – it provides the best security for a blockchain network. Greedy miners are wanted.

"In nature we have a lot of these systems" of aligned incentives, Vogelsteller said. "In society we don't believe it's possible, but blockchain shows it is possible."

So does CarCoin work, or not? I wish I could tell you, but advances in crypto-economics aren't exactly whizzing about the industry. As far as I know, as of early 2020 the debate about incentives goes on without a clear answer. There are many problems Ethereum has to face if it's to become universal, not least of which is how people make money from it.

But the middlemen are still there and seem ripe for the taking. The speed at which Uber overtook the taxi industry was phenomenal. It just feels right that they could be disrupted in a similarly brutal and quick fashion.

In the world of finance the applications for Ethereum are particularly ripe, as Wall Street is – at its core – the insanely well-entrenched pure expression of middlemen profit-takers, making their money from other people's money solely by virtue of sitting in between transactions.

Joe Lubin wanted to build a different way of conducting business. He's a great evangelist for Ethereum. He's the one who first explained it to me and made the light bulb go off above my head. I've spoken to many other people who had the same experience with him as he laid out his vision of an Ethereum-enabled financial system. For me, when he kept repeating the words "global computer" I finally saw it and had one of those moments when you think, *Man, that is fucking cool.*

Yet all of this stuff was incredibly speculative. In 2016, the idea that Ethereum could be used in the financial world was only being discussed by a few far-thinking bankers. On the one hand, Ethereum promised the world, it was a hell of a story, but in 2016, in terms of what you could point to as an actual product, Ethereum had nothing to show.

When I cowrote a story for *Bloomberg Markets* magazine in 2015 about Blythe Masters, a former JPMorgan executive who was now heading a blockchain startup, I didn't even mention Ethereum. This is not a knock against Ethereum – I certainly could've known more about it at the time – but it's also true that it was simply too early to be taking Ethereum seriously in a financial markets' sense. So I didn't dig into the story of the $55 million hack when I went back to work. It was fascinating, yes, but for Bloomberg readers it didn't have enough of a connection to Wall Street or finance to justify me chasing it.

In the following months blockchain certainly didn't disappear from the headlines. There was plenty of hype, and I plead "no contest" to the charge that I contributed to it. But at the same time I felt that there was something there. People like Blythe Masters don't jump into things lightly, I told myself. Blockchain seemed to have some staying power.

Masters is what you would call Wall Street famous. She's beautiful and brash and ruthless. She rose within JPMorgan from being an intern in its London office when she was 18 to sitting on a trading desk to running bank divisions. She helped create credit default swaps, the derivative that allowed investors to bet on a bond's price decline. Credit default swaps also ensnared Wall Street banks and their customers in a wicked web of interdependency during the financial crisis that required the Fed to step in and bail out the financial system. Everyone on "the Street" knows who Blythe Masters is.

There were also other big names taking blockchain seriously, like the Bank of England and the World Economic Forum. This helped me take it seriously too, and then near the end of 2016 the editor of *Bloomberg Markets*, Joel Weber, said he was planning a heist issue for the next year. Did I have any good heist stories?

Oh, man, did I.

● ● ●

I love complicated things. I love the process of figuring out how things work and then describing them to people in a way they can understand. I know for sure this trait allowed me to carve out the niche I have within Bloomberg News. When I started learning the details of the ether hack, I realized that I'd stumbled upon one of the most convoluted yet brilliant stories I could ever hope to untangle.

Metaphors will be our friends in this story. Imagine it this way: a bank has been built underground, with a central vault that holds $250 million. The design of this bank is such that once built, nothing about it can be changed. Not its layout or its vault or how any of its banking processes work. Its banking processes are weird, but we'll get more into that in a bit.

This bank has thousands of customers, the depositors, whose money makes up the $250 million. Now, under the rules of this bank, if someone wants to get their money out, they have to tell the bank 7 days ahead of time. During this week the depositor creates a small room underground near the vault. Once that's done, they have to wait for another 27 days. Let's say that it takes the bankers that amount of time to tunnel to the small room so they can deliver the money to be withdrawn.

If all goes according to plan, the money is delivered to the small room, a staircase appears, and after 34 days the customer can climb to the surface with his cash. But what if there is a flaw in the design of this bank? What if once the request to create the small room is made, the customer turns evil and realizes that they can dig a second tunnel from their room that leads back to the vault? Because of the flaw there are no security guards to block this second tunnel and it leads straight to the money in the central vault. Once the digging was done the evil customer could start grabbing as much cash as possible, like a game-show contestant in a chamber with $100 bills flying all around. Because the bank design can't be changed, the flaw that allows for the second tunnel is part of the bank, a glaring hole that customers can exploit.

That's basically what the DAO hacker accomplished, only using computer code instead of a shovel.

I spent months reporting on the hack for the magazine. It was the most fun I'd had in my career. I met and got to know almost all of the people quoted in this book during that period. We called the article "The Ether Thief," a nod to the great *New Yorker* story "The Silver Thief," which Joel Weber gave me to read for inspiration. And yet all through the reporting for the magazine story, no one I interviewed said they knew who had pulled off the heist. The ether thief's identity remained a mystery.

One of the more amazing attributes of blockchain systems is that all of the transactions I'm describing are publicly viewable. This has been the case since Bitcoin was first mined in early 2009, and it's the case with Ethereum. People often claim that blockchain allows users to remain anonymous, but this is wrong. It's pseudonymous, because it's possible to know the identity of the person behind an address. Once that link has been made, a person's activity is traceable for anyone with an Internet connection. But it's rare to know who is behind any given address. And so most of the time we have no idea who is doing what on the Ethereum blockchain. In the case of the DAO, one of the main attack addresses was 0x969837498944aE1dC0DCAc2D0c65634c88729b2D.

But who is that? Even though we can see on the public Ethereum blockchain that this address received 137 ether at 3:34:48 UTC on June 17, 2016, and that hundreds of similar transfers were then made over the next several hours, we have no way of knowing the person behind 0x969837498944aE1dC0DCAc2D0c65634c88729b2D.

It always gnawed at me. The ether thief was out there, and no one knew who they were. It also seemed, after not much time had passed, that no one even really cared anymore. I wanted to change that.

● ● ●

The first time I met the ether thief was two floors above a Foot Locker in Zürich, Switzerland.

That's probably not how my employer would want me to describe our Zürich bureau, but it's true. I felt nervous in a way I'd never felt before an interview. I wondered if the person I was about to accuse would become angry or violent. I wondered if they'd break down and tell me everything, if they'd feel that the burden of their story and what they'd done could finally be unloaded. I didn't know how I was going to ask small questions at the beginning until I was ready to show the person the evidence I had. It was a Tuesday in September, a beautiful day in Zürich, and I couldn't tell if my hand shook from the coffee I'd had or if I was scared.

The man across the table from me wore glasses and a plaid scarf. He was maybe in his late 50s and had lost some hair. Swiss by nationality, he'd spent his career in Zürich or thereabouts. This part of the world is known as Crypto Valley for its early role in many digital token startups, Ethereum central among them. The technical university in Zürich is known as ETH, the abbreviation for ether, which is just a delicious coincidence. The Eidgenössische Technische Hochschule Zürich is a hotbed of blockchain research, and Albert Einstein was both a former student and a professor of theoretical physics there. It made a certain amount of sense that someone who had brought Ethereum to its knees with the DAO attack would be based in its backyard.

We spoke about his background in banking, and how he grew bored with it and wanted out. Bitcoin had enthralled him, like everyone else in this story, because of how it had created its own independent monetary system without asking permission or giving a care about what anyone thought. Ethereum had been smart to base its operations in nearby Zug, he said, as in 2014 or thereabouts the Swiss regulators and tax authorities treated crypto projects very favorably. He told me that he mined Bitcoin back when you could do it with some high-powered hardware. If he'd kept all the Bitcoin he mined, he'd be a very rich man and wouldn't be talking to me right now.

He spoke English well, with a dose of a German accent. The conversation turned to the DAO attack and what he remembered of it. Then I asked him if he had a theory about who did it.

He paused and smiled.

"Next question," he said.

I laughed because he'd been speaking quite freely up to that point. "I have more than a theory," he said. "It's not that difficult to figure out."

This was possibly the first person to ever say that to me about the hack. It was incredibly hard to figure out, in fact, as I had learned in my previous reporting for the magazine story and this book. The ether thief had covered his tracks meticulously.

Yet here I was sitting across from a person who for years had only been described to me as someone who lived in Switzerland. When researching the "Ether Thief" magazine story in 2017, the Ethereum people who suspected this man wouldn't reveal his name to me. It was rather cute, I thought at the time, and indicative of the ethics held by many in the Ethereum community: they wouldn't help spread the rumor that this man had been involved because they didn't really know if he'd done it.

In journalism, however, it's all about finding the right sources – the people who know the story. And I'd been lucky enough to find one such person. Exchanges are one of the only institutions in crypto that know the identities of their customers, and not even all exchanges do: some let people get an account and trade on their platforms with only an email address. But my hunt for the right source led me to someone who worked for an exchange. The names of three people in the Zürich area were shared with me by this person, along with transaction links from the exchange to their Ethereum transaction histories, links that pointed to the DAO attack. The man across from me was thought to be the leader of the group, I'd been told. I was enthralled, and yet knew this was almost certainly unsolvable. I only had a sliver of the whole story as I sat across from him. I would need him to confess to be certain.

Still, there were a few clues to this mystery and I'd discovered one.

● ● ●

There would be no DAO without Ethereum, just as there would be no Ethereum without Bitcoin.

And none of it would have existed without the Internet. Possibly the most tantalizing ingredient missing from the World Wide Web is money in purely digital form. For all that the Internet has enabled, it has fallen short in creating a form of value that can be sent around the world as easily as email. It's not as though no one thought of this, however – there was a realization early in Internet history that digital money should be a feature.

In the 1997 *Internet Official Protocol Standards*, which specifies various aspects of the html protocol that makes the Internet possible, you can find entry 402, designated "payment required." This is the code that would've created a field to fill in on a web page with the type of digital money you'd be using to buy the latest *Sex and the City* DVD. It would have embedded digital payments into the DNA of web pages right alongside graphics and text. Yet for many reasons, it never happened. In the more detailed part of the protocol standards, entry 402 receives a harsh dose of reality: "This code is reserved for future use."

It would take just over a decade before status code 402 passed the baton to Bitcoin. It was not for lack of effort that digital payments hadn't come along until 2009, though – there were many projects over the years that came close. Which is to say, there were people all over the world who craved a form of digital cash. What the mysterious Satoshi Nakamoto did was bring together a set of existing technological pieces into one design that finally solved the puzzle.

Bitcoin looked like freedom. In its purest form, Bitcoin brushed aside any political or social biases when it first gained popularity, leaving its early adherents with nothing but gleaming possibility. Thousands of people all over the world needed Bitcoin for no reason other than it gave them hope for the future again. It made them quit their jobs, invest all of their life savings, or sometimes both, to ensure that this thing succeeded.

What Bitcoin did was to finally present a competitor to the global banking sector. Banks serve a host of purposes, of course, from granting loans and mortgages to making most everyday payment transactions so convenient that a swipe of an ATM card is all that's needed. But for a subset of people, the fact that banks are gatekeepers that can restrict or prohibit certain transactions has always been a big problem. A strong strain of libertarianism ran through early Bitcoin adopters, who wanted to exist outside the traditional financial world.

One of the keys to how Bitcoin works is its hash function. When the latest batch of transactions is sent to the computers in the network for validation – these are the miners – the block comes with a random string of characters associated with it. The miners take this random string and work through trial and error to change it so that it has a certain output value when it's run through the hashing function. In Bitcoin, that output is one that leads with a certain number of zeros. The only way to do it is to add one thing to the input, see how it changes the output, and then try again and again and again until the output has the right number of zeros in front.

Once the input is changed in the correct way, it's a simple operation for the other computers in the network to check the output to see that it's genuine. So it's very hard to produce, but very easy to check. The process also uses a certain amount of electricity to run the hashing hardware, so economic value enters the equation in the form of the cost of that electricity. That's hashing in Bitcoin, and it allows for trusted transactions to take place among users who neither know nor trust each other. And for all their willing effort, the winning miner is rewarded with free Bitcoin.

All of this lives entirely free and clear of Wall Street and government regulators. That's a big key to why Bitcoin is valued as it is. People want it to have value; they want it to work and exist in a world wholly separate from Bank of America ATMs as well as governments and their central banks that set monetary policy.

The big strike against Bitcoin, however, is that it doesn't allow for derivatives. Bitcoin is all Bitcoin is about. It's an amazing thing for what it does, and as of this writing it's been doing it for more than a decade without any person, corporation, or government being able to stop it. But if you want to do more with a global distributed network of computers, Bitcoin can't help you.

That's why Ethereum sprang to life. Ethereum is entirely about the derivative, about being a blockchain system that will support all the weird, amazing, and crazy things people want to build on top of a global digital programmable payment network. As Ethereum cofounder Joe Lubin put it to me, Ethereum's ambition is to be a global computer. In a statement that surely upset Bitcoin loyalists (and there are millions of them), Lubin said that comparing Bitcoin to Ethereum is like comparing a pocket calculator to a desktop.

What I'm about to say now will make some of you laugh, but bear with me. Ethereum is the most successful blockchain in existence. I say that with Bitcoin only a shade behind its younger sibling. Yet in my opinion it's the restrictive nature of Bitcoin that places it second. Ethereum took the distributed security and robustness of Bitcoin and opened a world that allows computer programmers to build whatever they can dream of on top of it. I believe in Ethereum – I'm writing a book about it, for God's sake – but I also know its flaws. I will tell you about them. But as of early 2020, here's what Ethereum has accomplished in brief:

- At its highest price in early 2018 the value of ether was above $1,400, giving the entire network a market cap of $135 billion and making billionaires of early founders like Vitalik, Joe Lubin, Anthony Di Iorio, and others. It made millionaires out of hundreds more.
- JPMorgan Chase, one of the largest and most powerful global banks, is building its blockchain system on a slightly tweaked version of Ethereum and is creating the bank's own digital currency it has dubbed JPMCoin.
- Ethereum didn't allow only for the creation of ether, its own native digital currency, it created a new way for startups to raise money, a process known as an initial coin offering, or ICO. This is an enormous advance in funding, as it allows crypto projects to sell tokens directly to the public, sidestepping any bank or venture capital involvement. While billions have been raised through the ICO market since 2016, it has been rife with scams, fraud, and outright theft.

- It spawned a host of competitors like EOS, Stellar, Cardano, and Ava, which took the smart contract structure and tweaked it to make transaction times faster or added different security protocols. Yet none of those projects can compare with the number of developers working on Ethereum. According to a 2019 study by Electric Capital, Ethereum has four times as many developers working to maintain and improve its network as the number of devs working on Bitcoin.
- Reddit, one of the most popular destinations for US Internet users, integrated Ethereum smart contracts and wallets into its service in 2020 to grant "community points." These can be used as a type of reputation metric, as they're given for posting and contributing to reddit discussions. The points are stored in an Ethereum wallet, which could lead to a significant jump in Ethereum users.
- Financial markets are now using Ethereum in real-world trading and settlement for assets such as stocks, credit default swaps, bonds, and equity derivatives. The Bank of France used Ethereum to replace a key component of its payment system.
- As of June 2020, the value of all ether in existence totaled $27 billion, making it the second-most valuable digital currency behind Bitcoin, with the ether price at about $242.

● ● ●

Ethereum was invented in 2013 by a 19-year-old named Vitalik Buterin. He was familiar to the Bitcoin community at the time as the cofounder and head writer of *Bitcoin Magazine*, where he penned well-written stories on all aspects of the technology. Buterin possesses the type of towering intelligence that forces people to describe him in otherworldly terms, an alien sent from the stars to live among us. He sort of looks like an alien, too. His head is too big for his body, sitting atop an elongated neck. He's long limbed and has a bit of a mechanical gait. His voice can register in flat, almost computer-like tones at times, though when he laughs in quick bursts his voice deepens. His large blue eyes can be piercing if he takes the time to look at you as he speaks, which isn't often. He has an unmistakable presence: you could spot him across the most crowded conference space. His fashion sense for many years led him to lean toward rainbow T-shirts with pictures of unicorns or Doge, the Shiba Inu dog mascot of the cryptocurrency Dogecoin.

There is a whimsy about Vitalik that not many people get to see. He has a sharp wit and is quite funny. We met in Seattle; Ithaca, New York; and Los Angeles to talk for this book. He was incredibly generous with his time, once I could get on his hectic schedule. He doesn't know how to drive and on average is on a plane once a week. Wherever he lands, he tends to stay from between three days and three weeks. He has no permanent home, though his family all live in Toronto. Like any inveterate traveler, he has his routine down to a science. He packs a bag that measures forty liters in volume. Contents: seven T-shirts (a few long sleeved); seven pairs of underwear; seven pairs of socks; sweater; jacket; spare pants; toiletries; a spread of foreign currencies; and public transport cards for Toronto, Boston, Washington DC, San Francisco, London, Tokyo, Seoul, Beijing, Shanghai, Hong Kong, Taipei, Singapore, Bangkok, and Sydney.

He is frugal to an almost ridiculous degree. In high school his dad couldn't convince him to buy a new pair of shoes when his were literally falling apart. Through his early involvement in Bitcoin and then as the inventor of Ethereum, the cryptocurrency fortune he's amassed has at times been in the billions, though he demurs when asked for a specific figure. Yet through the first part of the journey he took across the US and Europe as he formulated the ideas that would become Ethereum he limited himself to a budget of $20 a day. As that level of restraint implies, Vitalik is also fastidious. At one interview we were sitting outside at a café on the Cornell campus, speaking of his fellow cofounder and friend Mihai Alisie. Vitalik peered across the table to my notebook and let me know I'd spelled Mihai wrong.

There is a humility to Vitalik that I find extraordinary and admirable for someone with so much influence and power. He has a joy to him that might come from being independently wealthy – or maybe that's just who he is. After we met at the Washington State Convention Center – Vitalik was speaking at Microsoft's developer conference – he got up from the table, crumpled his paper cup in his hands, and leapt into the air. He kicked his feet out just a touch as he sank the shot in a nearby trash can.

● ● ●

Vitalik wanted to give the world a way to build whatever its heart desired on top of his blockchain. Two things were necessary to make this possible: smart contracts and ether, the cryptocurrency that must be used to pay for every Ethereum transaction.

In the most basic sense, smart contracts are what separate Ethereum from Bitcoin. Bitcoin is used to send value from person A to person B. It's linear. Vitalik wanted to be geometric, to create a system that could involve however many participants were necessary, linking A to B to F to K to G and then back to A. A way to do that is to have computer programs that are tied to and follow the rules of a blockchain system. That allows the various inputs to the program – the data – to change the state of the system.

Okay, wait. What the hell does that mean? Smart contracts are like a store: let's call it 7-Eleven. Think of all the things you can do in a 7-Eleven. We'll call you Electron Girl, because that's what you are – all blue and sparky, sending out lightning bolts from time to time. As you make your way through the store (let's say you're in Tokyo, which has the best 7-Elevens in the world) you can buy some sushi or get money from an ATM or talk to a friend or look at the magazines until the guy behind the counter yells at you. When you pay for your sushi at the register, you might get a receipt, but if you pay in cash there's not much of a record of the purchase.

All the various things you just did at 7-Eleven you can do digitally while interacting with a smart contract. The programming to secure the purchase of the raw fish is written in code that lives within the smart contract – we buy things in such an automated fashion online every day.

Talking to your friend is just a chat function. And the library (maybe the digital Library of Congress one day?) is just over there. Your digitized self runs through this routine by engaging different Ethereum-based applications that use smart contracts. I don't mean to leave the impression that one smart contract runs the entire 7-Eleven; you engage different, discreet contracts for each interaction.

So, what's this part about changing the state of the system? It's simple: it's just the recalibration of funds – for example, when you got cash from the ATM. Your wallet now has $40 in it, while the bank is less the same amount. And, oh yeah, you're reminded that you owe your friend 20 bucks, so you pay up. In Ethereum, paying your friend can be as simple as reading a QR code from his phone. The digital wallet where you keep your ether, where the original $40 value is stored, is now lighter by $20. The state of that environment changed and the blockchain updates to keep track of it.

In this scenario, Bitcoin can only be used to buy your sushi. You can't talk to your friends or read *Moby Dick* while using the Bitcoin blockchain. You can using Ethereum.

Much more complicated systems are also possible. It's not unrealistic to say that almost the entire global oil market could be shifted onto Ethereum using smart contracts. Oil output could be monitored and secured on the blockchain. Private trading would be simple to set up because of the small number of participants. What Ethereum is not yet ready for is the speed at which electronic oil markets, like the crude futures traded at the New York Mercantile Exchange in New York, work. Yet OPEC production cuts or gains would transmit via an automatic information feed to the Ethereum network via what's known as an oracle. The oil tanker industry could move its supply chain to Ethereum as well.

Again, I think about it in terms of generic contracts. You made many contracts in your 7-Eleven adventure, even though we don't think of talking to a friend in those exact terms. But conversation is a contract. Now imagine those contracts are on Ethereum. You engage the blockchain differently than how we go online today, no doubt about it. Yet in many ways it's not that far from what we do today when we interact with the web.

These types of transactions are bread and butter for any computer, but until Vitalik came along they hadn't been coupled with a decentralized network. Smart contracts can handle thousands of inputs and outputs, and as long as the code is clean they can live on indefinitely.

Access to such a system, though, has to have a price. This is where ether enters the equation. Vitalik knew that there would be people who would want to try to overwhelm Ethereum, to slow it down or even break it entirely, by spamming it with thousands of simultaneous transactions. If they wanted to do that, they'd have to pay a hefty fee in the form of ether. Gas was the main idea here, like what you put in your car. No gas, no go.

That means ether would have an inherent value, as it's vital to how Ethereum operates. Whether that value was 10 cents or $1,000 would be up to the people who wanted to use it.

Ether differs from Bitcoin in an important way – one that the Ethereum cofounders were very aware of. In the beginning, ether would be created out of thin air. Some of this ether would go to the founders as a reward for their work on the project, or what's known as a pre-mine. A much larger quantity would be sold to the public to fund ongoing development. Bitcoin never did a pre-mine: every Bitcoin in existence has been earned by the computers on its network that ensure transactions are valid. If ether were to be created, however, it risked falling under the jurisdiction of the US Securities and Exchange Commission, among other global regulators. That's because the SEC could view ether as a security like a stock, which by law is required to be regulated from its moment of creation, whether that's through an initial public offering or a secondary offering.

Yet selling ether to the pubic in a crowdsale is a great way to raise money. So that's just what the Ethereum cofounders did. The Ethereum crowdsale in 2014 was one of the most successful at the time, netting over $18 million. By then the money was desperately needed to continue to develop Ethereum, but we'll get to that part later.

This dilemma of raising money to fund development was hardly unique to Ethereum. What about all the other applications people wanted to build? By late 2015 the crypto world was exploding with new projects that seemed to be sprouting up daily. Every one of them needed to raise money in one way or another if it was going to have a shot at succeeding.

The way the Ethereum community solved this fundraising dilemma circa late 2015 starts with a theoretical physicist named Christoph Jentzsch. It ends with something that sounds straight out of futurist nineteenth-century science fiction – a decentralized autonomous organization, or DAO, which is basically a corporation that runs entirely from a codebase, meaning no humans are involved once it's deployed. DAOs are also very difficult to govern once deployed. In between Jentzsch and the DAO is a startup called slock.it, which Jentzsch cofounded. Their product was called a smart lock, or a slock. (I always think of *Evil Dead II* when I hear the word *slock*, thinking of S-Mart. "Shop smart. Shop S-Mart.")

A slock is an Ethereum-enabled lock, which you could put on your bike, for example. Someone with the slock.it app on their phone could come along and read a QR code that links to the bike's slock. The inter-action is managed by a smart contract on the Ethereum blockchain. If the passerby pays the required amount of ether, the slock unslocks and the bike can be rented for a period of time. This is similar to how Bird scooters and the bikesharing systems that took over American cities in 2019 work, but slock.it preceded them by many years and is decentralized.

It was a clever idea, and Jentzsch and his partners had some fun when they unveiled slock.it at the first Ethereum developer conference in London in November 2015. Jentzsch gave a live demonstration in which he unlocked a slock that controlled a teakettle: pay the slock some ether and the power turns on to heat the water. As the audience watched, miners on the Ethereum blockchain verified the transaction. A few min-utes later the kettle boiled and Jentzsch's partner Stephan Tual came on stage to pour himself a cup of tea. The look on Tual's face as he poured the boiling water was knowing but also held an air of wonder – like, *can you fucking believe what we just did?*

Slock.it hoped to connect the Ethereum blockchain to the Internet of things, or IoT, the catchall phrase used to describe the system that controls your smart refrigerator and smart thermostat.

Yet to make slock.it a reality and not just a demo, the startup needed money. So Jentzsch set the hook.

"I hope those things were amazing to you, but we have just another thing, a really cool thing," Jentzsch said to his London audience. He then introduced his idea for having a decentralized autonomous organization act as a fundraising mechanism. The idea of a DAO wasn't Jentzsch's – that honor belongs to Dan Larimer, another early blockchain pioneer. Vitalik Buterin had also long been fascinated by DAOs, which he mentioned prominently in his 2013 Ethereum white paper, "Ethereum: The Ultimate Smart Contract and Decentralized Application Platform." Now, though, Jentzsch said the way to raise money – not just for slock.it, but for any developer team that wanted to work with Ethereum – was with a DAO.

While the name is rather scary, the premise of this DAO is simple: Create a smart contract that will collect ether from people. In exchange for that ether, they are given tokens. The DAO token holders can then vote on projects that are seeking development funding. Token holders who voted for a winning project can share in the profit if the endeavor succeeds. In the world of finance this is similar to how venture capital works, except a DAO is completely automated and runs exactly as its code is written. Once a DAO is initiated, in other words, the process to change or fix a bug in its programming is complicated and relies on a stakeholder vote. It's asking code to be perfect from the get-go, in other words. And yet anyone who's run Windows will know how unrealistic it is to expect perfect code.

Jentzsch's idea proved to be more successful than his wildest dreams. The DAO became so popular, in fact, that it turned into a nightmare for the German. Instead of collecting the $5 million Jentzsch had expected, ether users poured $150 million into its coffers. Another way of measuring the DAO is that it held 11.944 million ether, which fluctuates in value, meaning the DAO's total holdings rose or fell according to the cryptocurrency's price. By Friday, June 17, 2016, it had ballooned to $250 million. It made Christoph physically ill, and his health and family life suffered. And it only got worse when hackers broke into it on that day.

● ● ●

One of the curious aspects of the DAO attack is that it stopped. The thief was inside, the mechanism for changing the code of the DAO was complicated and risky, and the Ethereum community might not have been able to mobilize in time to save the money that hadn't yet been stolen. Given enough time, the thief should have been able to drain every cent. But he didn't. Sure, $55 million had been snatched, but there was about another $200 million left. Why leave that on the table?

The best theory I've heard is that it has to do with the mechanics of the attack contract used – that is, the smart contract the thief wrote to steal the ether. The theory is that while the contract would work for several hours, it would also have a tendency to break after a certain time. And while you could try to launch the attack again once the original contract had broken, getting all the necessary variables lined up again could take time or simply not work again.

In any case, the original DAO attack lasted a bit more than seven hours. A total of 3.689 million ether was stolen.

The bug that the ether thief exploited was now in the public realm as blockchain sleuths pointed it out on message boards and reddit subthreads. The code itself, in fact, was viewable in the attack contract the thief had used, as it still existed in the Etherscan blockchain records. Not only could the original attacker be readying a second go at the DAO, a host of copycats could as well. And in fact, that's what started to happen.

Four days after the first attack, a second started. The mechanics were all the same; the only difference was the location where the stolen ether was sent.

The Ethereum community didn't take this lying down. From the first moments of the DAO attack on June 17, people tried to discover who was behind the hack and to figure out what to do about it. They would fight this. These were the people who had written the DAO code as well as other developers and programmers who had made a career out of working with Ethereum. A driving force in the group was Griff Green. One of the first employees at slock.it, Griff had realized early on the mysterious power of DAOs. Only he called them decentralized autonomous *corporations* at first, as in a paper he wrote on them for his master's degree in cryptocurrencies from the University of Nicosia.

If you meet Griff and for some reason don't like him, there's something wrong with you. He's a hugger, first and foremost, and an all-around genuine person. He was the mayor of Ethereum at this point in time; he knew just about everyone and was heading up slock.it's communication and community outreach. From the attack's inception, Griff helped recruit other Ethereum community members to form a kind of emergency response team. The beginning days were almost entirely organized via a Skype chat that they named Robin Hood.

"The Robin Hood Group was just a shit show," Griff told me in 2017 when I was writing the magazine story. "I hope the movie portrays it better than it actually was."

He's being modest; what the group did to save the remaining money in the DAO was amazing. Another member was Alex Van de Sande, whom everyone calls avsa, after his online name. While Griff was in rural Germany when the DAO was attacked, avsa was in his apartment in Rio de Janiero.

The Robin Hood Group (RHG) also included a few extremely good coders, like Lefteris Karapetsas and Jordi Baylina. They quickly figured out how to replicate the attack so they could break into the DAO in order to "steal" the rest of the funds to keep them safe (hence the name).

When the second attack began four days after the original attack, the RHG was ready. Avsa took to Twitter to say, "DAO IS BEING SECURELY DRAINED. DO NOT PANIC." My favorite reply to this tweet is "NOTHING SAYS DO NOT PANIC LIKE ALL CAPS."

At the same time, the broader Ethereum community was discussing what to do about the DAO. One thing to keep in mind is that just about everyone who called Ethereum home had bought into the DAO. The pain was spread far and wide. The community really wanted its money back.

Blockchains are constructed to be time ordered; it's crucial that the network knows that block B came after block A. Every transaction is recorded and maintained. So there are ways to change that history if a blockchain community supports such a change. That's because the network is nothing more than software that runs on people's computers all around the world. The people who spend big money to mine Ethereum and get the ether reward for doing so are a huge part of this community. If they all agree to an update to the software that addresses the DAO hack, for example, they can erase what happened. They can change history.

A less stringent approach is to blacklist the addresses known to be involved with the attack. The rest of the computer network could make it so that the ether in those attack addresses could never move, for example, nullifying its value. The first alternative I described (changing history) is known as a hard fork. Blacklisting addresses is known as a soft fork. Each option has its plusses and minuses, and the community seemed willing to go along with the soft fork approach at first.

As public support for a soft fork grew, the second attacker grew angry. He sent an encrypted message to the RHG on June 27, 2016. Here it is, verbatim, including the possibly purposefully broken English and odd syntax.

"This soft fork, and the dao-wars situation is a waste of time for everyone," the ether thief wrote. "I'm supporting the idea that code is law at smart contract, but also the network consensus is law on blockchain." He then pointed to the contract that had attacked the DAO on June 21, and said he'd give the money back if the RHG would as well. "Don't you do it also to see productive future?" the thief wrote.

Usually I would never know what this message said because it's encrypted, and I don't hold the private key needed to decrypt it. A person who does have the private key, however, shared a copy of the unencrypted message with me. This also meant I now knew an address associated with the second attack. I hoped it was only a matter of time until I could connect it to the original attack.

Back in Zürich, sitting across from the Swiss man with his plaid scarf and glasses, I passed him a printout of the message and asked if he sent it.

One

The clock above baggage claim at Toronto's Pearson Airport read 21:45 as Vitalik Buterin, six years old, played with a rubber ducky. A gift from the Lufthansa flight attendant on the long journey from Moscow, it would become one of his favorite bath toys in the years ahead. As the towheaded, blue-eyed boy looked around this new place, he thought about recently celebrating his birthday with his parents and grandparents in Kolomna, the ancient Russian city southeast of Moscow where the Moskva and Oka rivers meet. A few days later, when he was told they were going to Canada, he asked if it was for a week or a month. No, *zaya*, it's for good, he was told. Vladimir Putin would soon be president in Russia, and his parents were seeking better opportunities – as well as some adventure – abroad. There are few bigger changes in a life than moving across an ocean, and like anyone, the skinny six-year-old felt afraid of the unknown he now faced.

He carried fond, but few, memories of Russia with him. He remembered living with his grandparents while his mom and dad were busy with their careers, and as they worked out the details of an amicable divorce. His mother's parents had an apartment in Kolomna as well as a dacha where his grandmother tended a vegetable garden. The nearby forest was his favorite place to play. He remembered it being cold. One time in daycare, he wandered away from the other children who sat in a ring on the rug. His teacher came to collect him and reprimanded him for leaving the circle. In the way of a small child he thought, wait, isn't it normal for me to want to wander around?

While Vitalik had no way of knowing it then, very few things in his life would ever be normal. Now in his first moments in North America, waiting for the luggage to arrive, he only knew that the next stop on his journey would be his dad's apartment. It was a Friday in February, 2000. They took an elevator up to the Toronto apartment to meet his dad's girlfriend. Vitalik thought, again with the innocent rubric of a child, *Oh cool, there's a new person in my life.*

While brand new, Toronto would be where Vitalik grew up and attended school, became obsessed with *World of Warcraft*, and discovered a thing called Bitcoin, a new type of digital money that would propel him on a journey that only a handful of people can claim to have made.

He would change the world.

Before any of that, though, it was time for bed, with his new rubber ducky tucked under his arm.

● ● ●

Vitaly Dmitriyevich "Vitalik" Buterin was born in Kolomna on January 31, 1994, to Dmitry and Natalia Buterin.

His father grew up in Grozny, Chechnya, in southern Russia near the border with Afghanistan. He could read by the time he was three and a half and discovered early that he loved to play with electronics. With the limited materials he could get his hands on he built radios with blinking lights and messed around with sound. His parents had no clue as to what he was doing, and resources were tight in the Soviet era, so keeping his hobby alive was challenging. But then Dmitry got a pro-grammable calculator with 100 bytes of memory and taught himself the machine code to make it work. It was his first computer and he was in love.

But it's a problem for a budding computer scientist if you can't get your hands on any actual computers, and that was the case for the most part in Grozny in the 1980s. "I dreamed of them because in school we didn't have access," Dmitry said. Only in his last few years in Grozny did his class go to a local government office where they were allowed to work with the hulking behemoths of the late 1950s, the ones that take up an entire room. "Russia was way behind in technology," he said, "but I was extremely excited to play with this and learn as much as I could." The lack of hardware was so acute that when Dmitry won a local Software Olympiad, the work wasn't done on a computer. He wrote algorithms to solve the programming challenges with pen and paper, which the judges scored by hand.

Growing up amidst communism didn't sit well with him. He hated the brainwashing and the way that young kids were made to go into the Young Pioneers, a Boy Scout–like group, to prepare them to become party members when they were older. "By the time you're a teenager you realize nobody really believes in this, everybody's pretending and it's corrupt and just a bunch of bullshit," he said.

We were sitting at Dmitry's kitchen table as he told me his life story. He'd just been to the gym and we'd gone to get lunch at an enormous grocery store and deli in the basement of his building in a tony part of downtown Toronto. You can see Vitalik inherited his nose from his father. Dmitry keeps his salt and pepper hair short; he is in good shape and has a tattoo across his left bicep. He wore an Ethereum T-shirt with a turtle and dolphin as part of the green and blue logo. He'd picked up a healthy lunch of salmon and steamed vegetables. As he spoke, he collected any crumbs that fell before him on the table in a tissue. By the end of our conversation he'd amassed a small pile of them next to his plate.

It was odd to think that this man, who was basically my age, had a son who had gone on to such prominence. I sat there thinking, my sons are good at *Minecraft*.

Still, Dmitry knew that all routes to power went through the Communist Party, such as the connections that would help ensure that you could get into the university of your choice. When a teacher advised him to make nice with the Communists so that they couldn't block him from attending the Moscow Institute of Electronic Engineering, he reluctantly went along.

By 1989, Dmitry was 17 and had moved to Moscow to start his first year studying computer science. Two things that he could never have foreseen, however, almost blew him off course: the Soviet Union collapsed in 1991 and war broke out in Chechnya three years later. It amounted to a double gut punch to his parents, who lost all their savings as Mikhail Gorbachev stepped down and Boris Yeltsin took charge of the rapidly changing country. Then war broke out, and his family was forced to flee Grozny. They sold their apartment for peanuts, their financial ruin sealed in only a matter of a few years. In college in Moscow, Dmitry couldn't count on help from his family. "We had to find some opportunities to feed ourselves," he said.

Along with a few friends, they devised a plan to buy Russian souvenirs like Matryoshka nesting dolls and anything cheap that sported the sickle and hammer or other USSR symbols. Then they'd make a few trips over the summer to Prague by train and then bus to sell their wares to people who would in turn sell them to Western tourists. The money they made helped them get by for the rest of the year. But perhaps Dmitry's biggest coup at the time came back to his disdain for communism.

Like all members of the Young Communist League he'd been issued an identification badge. This was the precursor to the official party membership badge that would come with adulthood. But in the immediate aftermath of the USSR's fall, an item of this order had become a hot item. He sold his in Prague for five dollars, an enormous sum at the time, considering his monthly student stipend amounted to only a few dollars. *Spasiba, tovarich!*

But not everything at the Moscow Institute of Electronic Engineering involved scraping by, nations falling apart, and war-torn homelands. He met a girl, Natalia Chistyakova, and fell in love.

Founded at nearly the same time as Moscow, Kolomna is still a wild and beautiful city. It has a fortress and all the churches you'd expect, and when Natalia was a girl she'd race to get her homework done so she could run outside and play until her mother had to yell for her to come home. Her father worked in the military design bureau, her mom in a technical institute. As a six-year-old she spent many days with her mom at the lab, where – like in Grozny 1,800 miles to the south – there were rooms full of computers, each one weighing more than a Chevy.

"Some of my earliest recollections from my childhood are spending time in this lab and printing and using the punch cards and the tape," she said. These were mainframes that ate stacks of specifically ordered cards with holes punched in them to create a program. Her mom wrote code in Algol and Cobol, staples of the mid-1970s that are still in use today at some of Wall Street's biggest banks. For fun, Natalia would enter random commands to see what the computer would spit out. "We'd print large portraits of Lenin, that was a big amusement for the children," she said.

She went on to attend the Moscow Institute of Electronic Engineering, where she first saw Dmitry, whom she calls Dima, amid a group of about 25 people in the gym. They dated throughout university and were married in 1993, when they were both 21 years old. Vitalik was born a year later, and the young family moved into a dorm dedicated to students who were married or had children. Ask Natalia what Vitalik was like as a baby and she'll laugh in the way only a mother can about her child. "We had our hands full, let's put it this way," she said. As a newborn "he was waking up every 45 seconds." By the time he was one or two "he was very stubborn and always knew what he wanted to do," she said. From early on, Vitalik had a sharp memory for what he was taught, remembering the letters of the alphabet or numbers with little effort. He engaged with things so in one sense he was an easy child because she could put a book in his hands and he'd lock in and occupy himself. "I remember the first time he saw a computer, he was fully attached to it. All he wanted to do was bang on the keyboard. He would spend days doing that, just hours," she said.

Back at university, Dmitry worked full time while still a student to support the family, first as a software engineer at a local bank and then for Arthur Andersen as a computer systems consultant in the Moscow office. After graduation, they moved into an apartment in Moscow and Natalia's parents came to help. Natalia got a job as a finance manager at Heinz. "You know, catsup," she said.

In the late 1990s the political atmosphere in Russia was changing, as was their marriage. By early 1998, they had separated. "We were really young, we didn't know what we were doing, so that marriage only lasted a few years," Dmitry said. Natalia had set her sights on moving to Canada, where her plan was to earn a degree at a Canadian school to help her get a good job and settle down in the new country. She attended the University of Alberta for two years while Vitalik lived with her parents in Kolomna.

When Vitalik wasn't running through the forest, stick in hand, or searching out bugs, his grandfather taught him math. He loved Legos and drawing. By the time he was five he was multiplying and dividing three-digit numbers in his head. His parents gave him their old IBM laptop from their university days, which came loaded with Microsoft Office. Excel quickly became his favorite toy, where he learned to draw shapes in the cells and Dmitry taught him to work simple formulas. It was his first exposure to a computer language.

Dmitry left Arthur Andersen in 1997 to help found an enterprise software firm called Columbus with a few former colleagues. They partnered with a Dutch firm to localize the software for the Russian market. But by 1999 the political winds were blowing in a bad direction. "It was clear where Russia was going," Dmitry said. When he saw Putin rise in prominence, he said to himself, "Really? KGB? I don't think anything good can come from this." Russia had defaulted on its debt the year before and Dima knew it was time to get out.

By now, it wasn't hard for Natalia to convince Dmitry that he should move to Canada too. At least that way, the family could be close to each other and it would be less disruptive for Vitalik. Natalia came back to Russia to finalize the move for Vitalik, stuff like taking him to the hospital for tests required by Canadian immigration. He walked around the waiting room in Moscow adding and subtracting three-digit numbers out loud. This was one of the first times that Natalia thought her son wasn't just smart, there was something more to him.

"I remember, vividly, Vitalik running around and calling out the numbers, like 200 by 300 and 25 by 350 and so on and so forth, and he'd come up with all the answers," she said. "He was only five at the time, and I remember the people sitting there and everyone was looking at him going '*awww*' and rolling their eyes in amazement."

● ● ●

As winter turned to spring in 2000, Vitalik now had two new additions to his life to deal with: his new home in the unfamiliar and sprawling city of Toronto, and Maia, his dad's girlfriend. He moved into their apartment and slowly began acclimating to both.

Maia and Dmitry had met while working together at Arthur Andersen. "It was August 7, 1995," Maia said. "I have a weird memory for dates." They moved in together in 1998 after Dmitry separated from Natalia and the talk soon turned to leaving Russia. Maia's mother had emigrated to Canada in 1991 with her 13-year-old brother and she'd been to Montreal and Ottawa many times. When Natalia moved to Edmonton to attend school, all the pieces were in place. Maia had founded Columbus along with Dmitry: all they had to do now was sell the business.

Yet Canada was very different from Russia, and Maia had a precocious six-year-old in her life now. She had to find ways to win him over. She found it fun to introduce him to all sorts of new things, like hamburgers. Vitalik had never had a hamburger in Kolomna. They had a game where they would wrestle and after Vitalik beat her a few times, he said, "You are like a conquered moose." Her nickname was born. From then on, Vitalik called Maia *losik*, which roughly translates from Russian as "little moose."

His creativity and playfulness with language was starting to emerge. When they visited friends in Rochester, Vitalik was given a stuffed dog. He named it *Rastopyry*, which doesn't translate exactly from the Russian but was understood by Maia and Dmitry to mean that the dog's legs were spread. "It was a completely made-up name, but in our family we still use a lot of words that Vitalik created," Maia said. "Vitalik is quirky and very unusual and bright and totally creative."

Vitalik's favorite stuffed animal at the time was a rabbit he'd brought with him from Russia. He'd fallen in love with the creatures and by the time he was seven he'd written a 17-page document called "The Encyclopedia of Bunnies." It contained jokes and pictures drawn in Excel and scientific assessments, such as a periodic table of various bunny qualities.

From the section titled "Bunnies speed":

> On Oct. 19, 2001, 6:07 p.m., the bunnies run 3745.284 million km/sec. Probably on New Year 2002, they will run 0.77 light-years per second.

Two graphs measure the speed progression. If you are wondering, from the section titled "First time bunnies will be seen," the answer is:

> Never! By the year 4000, they will run 1048576.59053
> light-years per second.

Another section details "Bunnies computers" and answers such questions as "What number system do bunnies computers use?" and "What programs are there?" Then there is this exploration of gender differences in his favorite subject:

> How many man and women bunnies are there?
> There are: 8 men.
> There is only 1 woman.
> That is the cat.

Dmitry joked that this was Vitalik's first white paper. "The Encyclopedia of Bunnies" convinced him that his son wasn't just bright, he was off-the-charts smart.

But one thing that never came easily to Vitalik was feeling confident around people outside his family. While still in Kolomna it had been challenging to keep him in daycare, which had worried Dima. He knew his son needed social acclimation. While Vitalik routinely aced his multiplication tests, making friends proved much trickier.

"When people praised me for being some kind of unique math genius, that made me feel isolated," Vitalik said. "I definitely wished I could be more like other people, in both the good and bad ways." While he had people at school he considered friends, who he'd hang out with at recess and lunch, going beyond that sort of forced congeniality eluded him. "I knew that other people had friends where they would even hang out after school and do all those things, and I just never figured out how to get into that."

His mom could see that he felt lonely and like an outsider in elementary school. She helped get him moved into a gifted class in third grade, but then worried that being with other really bright children – who may not have had their own social skills under control – wouldn't help Vitalik get the kind of peer interaction he needed. But she also knew there was a public Vitalik who struggled to make connections and a private Vitalik, the one who loved to draw, who wrote "The Encyclopedia of Bunnies," and who made numbers out of his Legos because math was in his blood. On the computer, he began drawing using the Logo programming language. And it was here too that he first displayed an almost complete lack of interest in material things and possessions that has followed him throughout his life. "He never asked for anything to be purchased for him," Natalia said. "When we'd go to the store, he was really indifferent to that stuff." Buying gifts for him at Christmas and his birthday is difficult to this day because he always says he doesn't want anything.

Yet soon even the gifted class became tedious for Vitalik, and he grew bored. His mom tried introducing piano lessons and tennis, but nothing really clicked. He did look forward to the weekly math classes he took from a local Russian professor. He loved the chance to stretch his brain, and continued with the classes through his senior year of high school.

And then, middle school – Cummer Valley Middle School, to be precise. Like every other human being, Vitalik found himself lost in a confusing, pedantic circus. Canadian elementary schools feature a lot of playtime compared with class time, but that ratio changes in middle school and Vitalik was in for a hard and boring few years. His dad understood his son's innate affinity for computers from the beginning, so he resisted pushing programming on him. He let him find his own way for the most part, with a suggestion here or a nudge there. He bought Vitalik a book on the Allegro graphic programming language and enrolled him in weekend programming courses. Vitalik read extracurricular science books in his spare time. The truth was, though, that Dmitry and Maia and Natalia all knew Vitalik would end up drowning in the tepid sea of Toronto's public high school system. Even if he stood far above all the other 700 students at Cummer Valley, his vast potential would hardly be scratched.

● ● ●

The Abelard School was founded in 1997 by a group of ambitious Toronto teachers who wanted to put already smart students to the test. There are 5 students per teacher, the class size doesn't go above 10, and by graduation Abelard students will have read Sophocles, Oscar Wilde, Zora Neale Hurston, Twain, Seamus Heaney, Shakespeare, the Bible, T.S. Eliot, and many other literary luminaries. Latin is required in the first year; many students continue on with it through graduation. *The Iliad* is taught in Greek. The curriculum is integrated across subjects, with students encouraged to take from chemistry to add to Latin to mix with physics to complement English. The 50 kids who typically make up the student body aren't allowed to use laptops in class; they're encouraged to develop direct interactions with their peers rather than perfect their ability to google. Abelard was about as far away from Cummer Valley Middle School as one could get, and exactly what Natalia knew Vitalik needed.

He entered Abelard in 2008 as a shy, quiet 14-year-old. He carried a book under his arm, either a programming language he was learning or an academic text, which he'd read at lunch. In the beginning, at least, he had no idea how this new school would change his life.

"In the public school system you always focus on the bottom 10 percent, you never get to focus on the top 1 percent," said Asim Sayed, who taught Vitalik math, physics, chemistry, and calculus at Abelard. Kids like Vitalik "tend to get lost," he said. Vitalik soon came to realize he was among peers who shared his love of learning and his work ethic, and that his teachers wanted to hear from him and challenge his beliefs. Mr. Sayed was among his favorite teachers, along with a science teacher, Mr. Maharaj, who passed away in 2018. The holistic approach to subject matter appealed to Vitalik, as did learning new and ancient languages. In 10th grade Vitalik was already burning through calculus – a subject most students didn't get to until senior year. And it wasn't just that he knew how to solve differential equations: Vitalik solved them in ways unlike anyone else.

"He had an algorithmic approach where the whole thing was step by step," Mr. Sayed said. Whereas other students would arrive at the answer using the easiest way they could, Vitalik did it his way. "Whenever I used to mark his math tests, I'm not joking, his tests became my answer sheets because his answers were way more descriptive and in detail than the answers I had written."

It wasn't just math; Vitalik excelled in all his subjects. Michelle Lefolii, one of the teachers who founded Abelard, taught Vitalik English. "He wrote a brilliant essay on formal experimentation in *Moby Dick* in grade

12 that I still use with my students to show them what a good grade 12 essay focused on literary analysis looks like," she said.

Titled "The Nature and Purpose of Formal Experimentation in *Moby Dick*," the essay, which was printed in the 2011–2012 Abelard literary journal, could easily be from the latest issue of the *New York Review of Books*. He began it this way: "Reading Herman Melville's *Moby Dick*, it becomes clear that it is not merely a novel; it is sometimes a novel, sometimes a play, sometimes a sermon, sometimes a textbook, and sometimes a true encyclopedia, encircling the subject of whaling from every side, whether scientific, technical, historical, or cultural." (He knew about encyclopedias by then, didn't he?)

The ability that would propel him into the limelight once he found the Bitcoin world was becoming clear at Abelard: he was a damn good writer.

"His writing always stood out because it was remarkably logical and always beautifully structured, but at the same time not academically stiff," Ms. Lefolii said. With the support of Abelard and the students around him, Vitalik began to grow into himself. "He also just had a lot of fun, in everything, in his class discussions, in his writing," she said. "He always had a great sense of humor."

He wrote short stories too, one of which – "On Christmas Presents and Friendship" – was published in the school's literary journal. In it four friends are exchanging Christmas gifts in a sort of secret Santa fashion. There are echoes of Vitalik's personality throughout the story, such as when his character Ulrich disdains the pursuit of materialism: "How could such trivial things arouse such euphoric happiness, when there was so much more to life than mindless consumerism, more than just money." But he also seemed to enjoy taking diametric sides to the issue, as Ulrich also daydreams of being independently wealthy to the point where he is living off the interest from his fortune and not the fortune itself. By the end of the story, however, Vitalik makes clear that the assumptions each friend has made about the others are off base, that we can't truly know anyone as we know ourselves.

This part of Vitalik's biography might seem incidental, but I find it really illuminating. I think Vitalik is more of a writer than a computer programmer. I mean that as no slight to his coding chops, mind you. He is obviously gifted, to have been able to bring along so many brilliant programmers to make his projects successful. But his ease with fiction and narrative essay is somewhat far afield for many computer scientists. And then there's his affinity for foreign languages. He's a storyteller – and had to be, in many cases, to sell the world on his idea of what Ethereum could be. Paper and pen may be a refuge for him; sometimes in person he can shut down or become terse, such as when conflict arises. He's definitely a writer in that regard, as I recognize the same traits in myself.

Abelard allowed Vitalik to feed his love of language. He already spoke Russian and English, and now he studied French, Latin, and Greek. Brian Blair was Vitalik's teacher for political science and philosophy as well as Latin and Greek. In philosophy, Mr. Blair said he often wanted to give Vitalik more than 100 percent on his tests because he went so far beyond what you'd expect from a high school student. In his 27 years of teaching, Mr. Blair said Vitalik stands alone.

"I've seen a lot of very strong students, but one of the great things about him was that he utilized all the resources the school had, almost like nobody else," he said. In Greek, Vitalik read Thucydides with Mr. Blair, something he hasn't done with any other student. The Greek historian and general wrote *The History of the Peloponnesian War*, and while Mr. Blair often read Herodotus with advanced students, he avoids Thucydides because it's just too hard for most students who only have two years of Greek under their belt. "It was challenging for him, you could see the wheels turning," Mr. Blair said. "It wasn't like the hot knife through butter, which it was almost all the rest of the time."

Freed in this secure environment, Vitalik began to emerge from the shell of social anxiety that had worried his parents just a few years before. "Abelard played a big huge role in his life, that's where he found his own peers," said Mr. Sayed. He trusted Vitalik enough that during chemistry class, he'd let Vitalik sit in the back of the class, programming on his laptop. He always did the chemistry homework, and even with his attention elsewhere, Vitalik earned a 99 percent in the class. He was no longer the shy and awkward kid who'd started at Abelard, but had become one of the more popular kids in the school. He mentored other students and freely gave his time to help whoever needed it. "As a teacher, you see these kids and you know, these are the people who are going to change the world in a positive sense," Mr. Sayed said. "He was one of them."

Mr. Blair made a point that his other teachers repeated – Vitalik was never cocky or a smart-ass. "There was a real humility to him, despite his incredible abilities, and that's really unusual in a high school kid," Mr. Blair said.

Outside of class, Vitalik started entering math and computer programming competitions. These were contests like the Canadian Computer Competition and the National Olympiad for Informatics, where students, either individually or in teams, are given several hours to solve math or programming problems. Vitalik soon made a name for himself. In 2010, he placed in the Metro Division for Toronto in the University of Waterloo's Canadian Computer Competition with his partner, Zachary Devine. The next year, he made the honor roll of the Canadian Open Mathematics Challenge and placed third in the CASCON High School Computer Programming Competition. In 2012, he was selected as one of four students to represent Canada at the International Olympiad in Informatics in Italy.

At Abelard, he won just about every award there is to win. There was the Alexander Award for junior accomplishment in 2009, then the Archimedes Award for excellence in classics his sophomore year. As a junior he earned the Villon Award for excellence in French language and literature; as a senior he took home the Turing Award for excellence in computer science and computational mathematics and the Governor General's Award for the school's top graduating student. At graduation, as Vitalik was called up on stage time and again to collect his accolades, Mr. Sayed happened to be the teacher handing out awards. He gave Vitalik a good-natured hard time and said that the next time he called him up he should bring his backpack on stage since he was being overloaded with medals. The next time Vitalik was called, he brought his knapsack with him.

Vitalik's presence is still felt at Abelard. In a montage of student portraits that hangs on the wall in the main office, a young-looking Vitalik smiles from the very middle of the arrangement, as though at the heart of the kids who have passed through its halls. In 2018, he donated $500,000 to the school, no strings attached. The school is using the money in part to create a scholarship for students who excel across all subject matters, as Vitalik did.

If one document, one piece of evidence, from that time in his life sums up his varied and transformational time at the school, a good bet would be his yearbook entry. It's by turns funny and academic and geeky. In his senior picture, he stares out of the frame with almost no expression on his face – certainly not a smile – his light blue eyes set in a steady gaze, a brush of acne across his cheeks. He is listed as Vitalik – Professor X – Buterin, a nod to his love of science fiction and the charismatic leader of the X-Men.

He lists his superpower as invisibility, "with all the reasonable corequisites as described by Ancient Greek mythology, as well as a passive aura that constantly either adds hydrogen to the universe or decreases entropy."

The yearbook allowed students to describe their future prospects, which Vitalik listed as "computer programmer." The yearbook staff then had their say: "Steve Jobs 2.0 . . . Now with hair!"

Two

Like so many days in Seattle, Friday, June 17, 2016, was slightly overcast with the chance of rain. That afternoon on the edge of town, Dax Hansen left the city on the ferry for Bainbridge Island where he lives. Hansen was one of the earliest lawyers to get involved in blockchain technology and helped shape the early industry though his work as a partner at Perkins Coie. So news of the DAO hack had reached him. When he arrived on Bainbridge Island he saw his friend Peter Vessenes waiting to take the ferry back to Seattle. Vessenes had long been in the blockchain world, and Dax knew he'd have heard too.

"Wow, big day, huh?" Dax said to Peter.

"Yeah," Vessenes said. "I'd already been looking into that and saw some vulnerabilities. I warned people this was going to happen."

Bainbridge Island is about as idyllic a location as you are going to find in the US. If only the cars could be removed it would feel like Cabot Cove waiting for one of Jessica Fletcher's nieces to get murdered. There's wood everywhere. Evergreens come right up to the edge of steep cliffs with houses peeking from between the limbs. Sailboats and motorboats fill a small harbor just across from the ferry terminal. The ferry dock is made of dark V-shaped planks of wood. It all has the feel of another time. Just outside the main terminal, where the taxis line up, Dax and Peter chatted about the DAO.

By 2016, Peter Vessenes had been around the crypto world for a long time. He cofounded the Bitcoin Foundation and started CoinLab, a Bitcoin project incubator that signed a deal in 2012 to handle the US and Canadian customers of Mt. Gox, the largest early Bitcoin exchange, according to Reuters. A year later, a string of lawsuits between the two companies began as CoinLab accused Mt. Gox of not handing over the customer accounts as promised, Reuters said. Vessenes later shut CoinLab down, according to the news agency.

By 2016, Vessenes was a consultant to blockchain firms and did some security work on his own. He became interested in smart contracts and Ethereum and decided to look into why some smart contracts are so dumb. The first one he examined, Ethstick, was a "pyramid scheme which incentivizes participants (donkeys) to keep depositing money to get the payout (carrot)," he wrote in a blog post dated May 18, 2016. "As each payment comes in, a 'lucky donkey' is chosen for payout; the lucky one is chosen from a list of eligible donkeys." But it was a scam; also, about 4,000–5,000 ether were trapped in the contract and he wanted to figure out what went wrong. He identified several major problems in the code that didn't allow the ether to be freed. More generally, he had taken a look at a cross-section of smart contracts that had been deployed on the Ethereum blockchain at that time. He estimated that more than 10 percent of the Ethereum smart contract code he examined had a bug in it. The title of his blog post: "Ethereum Contracts Are Going to Be Candy for Hackers."

The write-up got a fair amount of notice and was picked up by Hacker News. Vessenes was intrigued, so he kept looking for security issues to highlight on his blog. A few weeks after his first smart contract post, he published one called "More Ethereum Attacks: Race-to-Empty

Is Real." Vessenes had noticed a comment online by Christian Reitwiessner, one of the creators of Solidity, the computer language used to write smart contracts. The bug allowed users to ask for money back from a smart contract and end up getting more than they had available to withdraw. While Peter called the bug "race-to-empty," it would soon be known more widely as a "reentrancy bug."

In any event, he wrote this on his blog on June 9, 2016, eight days before the DAO attack, "Your smart contract is probably vulnerable to being emptied if you keep track of any sort of user balances and are not very, very careful."

Vessenes had seen plenty of controversy by then. He'd lost a battle to remake the board of directors of the Bitcoin Foundation and tangled with Mt. Gox in court for years. He said he's received death threats. In one sense, to him, the DAO was just another chapter in the unbelievable blockchain story.

"It's always something in digital currency land," he said. "This was a little bigger, but at the time it wasn't clear it was going to be bigger." In any event, it was impossible to look away.

"Kids get a bunch of money and flamethrowers, so every week, you tune in," he said.

Outside the ferry building on Bainbridge Island, the coincidental timing of meeting Peter Vessenes has stuck with Dax Hansen over the years. "I thought it was really interesting and kind of ironic that I ran into him on that day, and that he had been paying attention to it," Hansen said. Afterwards, Vessenes got on the ferry and headed into Seattle.

Three thousand miles away on the East Coast, another researcher had been looking at security flaws in the DAO. Emin Gün Sirer is an associate professor of computer science at Cornell University. In 2002, he devised a decentralized system for rewarding good behavior he called Karma. It was the first currency system to use proof of work to establish the validity of transactions. Cynthia Dwork and Moni Naor invented the idea of proof of work in 1993 as a means to reduce email spam. The concept was later adopted for cryptocurrencies by people such as Adam Back, and most famously by Satoshi Nakamoto in his design for Bitcoin.

So by the time Bitcoin came around in 2009, Gün – everyone calls him Gün (pronounced *goon*) – was well versed in digital currencies. And then, with its added complexity, Ethereum opened up a whole new vista of possibilities for blockchain applications. With the rise of the DAO, Gün found himself in computer scientist nerd heaven.

"It's a fascinating story," he said. "This is one of the best heist stories I know. It all happened out in the open." He wears his dark hair short and appears years younger than he is thanks to his Turkish roots. He drives his BMW around Ithaca like he's still in Istanbul. There is an earned arrogance about Gün: he rubs some people the wrong way, but I've always found him to be extremely helpful and generous with his time. "People stole from a robot," he said. "It's man versus robot. It's insane."

Every aspect of the DAO was prescribed. It's written in code. The amount of time it was open to collect money had been set to run from April 30 to May 28. This was the fundraising part of the DAO, the time when more money than anyone associated with it could have imagined came pouring in. It was during this period that Gün decided to take a look at its source code along with two friends, Dino Mark and Vlad Zamfir. From the very start they saw it was bad.

"There are like nine different ways of getting money out of this thing," Gün said. Based on the severity of what they found, the three researchers published "A Call for a Temporary Moratorium on the DAO" on May 27, a day before the crowdfunding was set to end.

"These concerns motivate a moratorium on funding proposals to prevent losses due to poor mechanism design," Mark, Zamfir, and Sirer wrote. "A moratorium would give the DAO time to make critical security upgrades."

They'd discovered seven potential flaws in the DAO code, such as inherent biases involved in how DAO token holders would vote on proposals. Another was termed a "stalking attack," and would become important later. A stalking attack is done to someone who wants to withdraw their funds from the DAO. To withdraw their ether, they create a subcontract that's an exact copy of the DAO, known as a child DAO. Remember our underground bank? The bank is the DAO and the room you carved out is the child DAO.

And as you may recall, the person has to wait 27 days to get their money out of the child DAO. Yet because this is done on a public blockchain, a stalker could interact with – or "enter" – the subcontract. They can ride along inside the child DAO. This throws off control of what the contract can do, as the stalker can be evil and vote against proposals such as getting the money out. This is bad. It essentially freezes money in the DAO and encourages blackmail and ransom, the three researchers wrote.

While there was a healthy public debate over what to do about the DAO, no moratorium was implemented. Many people I've spoken to feel that there was just too much momentum behind the DAO for anyone or anything to stop it. Ethereum users wanted the DAO to work. They'd all put their money in. It would work.

The DAO went live on May 28, meaning people could now make funding proposals. Gün continued to watch its progress.

A year earlier, Gün had become a father, and sometime in mid-June his one-year-old son passed on a different kind of bug to him. On the evening of Monday, June 13, 2016, he lay in bed with his laptop on his chest in the second-floor bedroom of his house in Ithaca. His eyes were watering and used Kleenex surrounded him. As sick as he was, he couldn't tear himself away from the DAO. He thought he'd found another flaw.

On the other end of an email chat with Gün was his soon-to-be graduate student Phil Daian. He's skinny and dark haired, not one for a suntan, and possesses an almost preternatural understanding of distributed systems. In his 20s when the DAO attack occurred, Phil seemed to me to be the type of guy who peaks in his mid-50s – so look out. But on this night in June 2016, he sat on a ratty couch in the apartment he shared with friends from college in Champaign, Illinois. He should have been working for the software testing startup he'd joined; they had a deadline approaching. But Gün can be incredibly persistent and had been looking at the DAO code for weeks at that point.

Both Phil and Gün were aware of what Peter Vessenes and a few others had published about the reentrancy bug. This is how it works: imagine there is a line of 20 bank tellers, and you go to the first and ask to withdraw $100. But before you get the money, you go to the second teller and ask for $100. And so on, down the line until all 20 have been visited. Normally you'd need $2,000 in your account to cover all the withdrawals. The reentrancy bug in the DAO, however, didn't allow the code to work that way. If you knew where to focus your attack, you could run the bank-teller trick, asking for more and then more and then more until the DAO had given you millions of dollars even though you only had a few thousand in your account.

But where? Where, exactly, was that vulnerability in the code? The day before, a user on the DAOhub message board named eththrowa had identified a bug. It was encoded in the function that would pay out DAO token holders if they had earned income from their investment. So if you voted for a project that got funded, and that project made money, you got a cut through this payout feature. It's known in the code as the "withdrawRewardFor" function. It came on line 772 of the DAO code. This was a bug, yet it wasn't *the* bug. (Interestingly, eththrowa was never heard from again, he/she popped up once and then disappeared five days before the DAO attack.)

The bug in the DAO code responsible for the $55 million hack, the one Gün stared at on his laptop that evening, lived in a different location.

"Isn't it possible to get multiples of one's RewardTokens and DAOPaidOuts by targeting recursion on Line 666?" Gün wrote in an email to Phil.

I'm not making that up. The bug is on line 666. The absolute ridiculousness of this detail has in fact driven some to believe it was an inside job: certainly someone at slock.it is fucking with us, right? I don't believe this for a second, but as a reporter I became physically stimulated when I first learned this detail in 2017. The devil is in the details, as they say.

It was 7:30 p.m. in Ithaca as Gün wrote to Phil. He wanted to talk about what he'd found. Phil couldn't get on the phone, but wrote back a few hours later that he didn't think what Gün had found was an issue. "We might be up the creek ;)," Phil wrote.

Gün couldn't be sure either. He felt miserable and really wanted to get some sleep.

They'd found the DAO bug – many others came close but Gün had it exactly right. The problem? They didn't tell anyone. Four days before the hack, Gün and Phil went to sleep that Monday night and momentarily forgot all about the DAO.

Three

While Abelard exerted an immense amount of influence on all parts of Vitalik Buterin's life – from helping him open up socially to challenging him academically to allowing him to realize the value in helping others – there would never be a stronger force in his life than his love of computers. Everything up to this point could be seen as minor disturbances to his foundation compared to how his discovery of Bitcoin profoundly changed him.

Security Now is a popular podcast hosted by Steve Gibson and Tom Merritt about computer security issues, software patches, and stuff that appeals to folks who aren't afraid to dirty their hands with a bit of computer code. The February 9, 2011, episode touched on something a bit outside the normal discussions of the latest Firefox browser security upgrade. Steve was keen to let his listeners know about a cryptocurrency called Bitcoin. "It's really, really clever," he said on the show. "I fell in love with this." He went on to describe how hard it is to create money that's not anchored by a central bank since not many people would put value on such a thing. "The goal is to really solve – to offer an honest-to-God, non-hobby level but industrial strength Internet-based peer-to-peer currency where real value can by exchanged between two parties with no intermediary being involved," he said.

For the next 20 minutes or so he describes how Bitcoin solved the idea of digital scarcity. This is a very important part of the story to understand: that is, how do you protect something that is represented digitally, that can be reproduced an infinite number of times? Think of what Napster did to the music industry. Before Napster's decentralized marketplace for digital music files, sure, I could've burned a CD for my friend (and did) or later on been able to upload the new Pearl Jam record and email it to someone (yep). There was nothing protecting those MP3s because of their digital nature; they became a commodity once turned into ones and zeros. Then Napster came along and connected anyone around the world who wanted that new Pearl Jam record, devastating the recording industry.

But when a blockchain is involved in the creation of a digital asset it creates scarcity. I mean, if we could just take a Bitcoin, copy it, and send it to anyone on an email list, Bitcoin would be worthless. To have value it has to be secured by a blockchain, which establishes in a public way the provenance of that Bitcoin. The ledger has tracked it from user to user, so you know the Bitcoin you receive is real and scarce. It allows for trusted transactions with people you don't trust. That's a big idea.

But back to the podcast – one interested listener in Toronto that day was Dmitry Buterin. Afterwards he had to tell his son about this crazy new thing.

"Hey, have you heard about Bitcoin? It's this new currency that's not backed by any corporation or government," Vitalik remembered his dad saying. Dmitry explained to Vitalik how it worked, but Vitalik wasn't impressed. "At first I thought it wasn't interesting because the thing I was worried about was how can it even have value if the currency isn't representing anything?" Vitalik said.

Vitalik soon forgot about it. Until the next month, that is, when he heard a different podcast – which one he can't recall – again talking about Bitcoin. He figured he'd heard about this new thing a few times, so maybe he should reconsider. The second podcast, in March 2011, encouraged people not only to learn about Bitcoin but to go out into the real world and participate in meetups and help create the fledgling Bitcoin community. Vitalik looked online for ways to earn the crypto-currency, as the two ways to get it were unavailable to him at the time. The first was to simply buy it – Bitcoin had hit $1 on the day of the *Security Now* podcast – but Vitalik lacked the necessary funds even at that meager price. The second way was to use computing power to solve the random, trial-and-error problems released by the Bitcoin network to prove that the most recent batch of transactions is valid. This is known as mining, but Vitalik didn't have the type of computer hardware to pull it off. What he could do, though, was write.

In a Bitcoin forum he found a guy calling himself "kiba" – to this day Vitalik doesn't know his real name – who was starting a blog called *Bitcoin Weekly*. He was offering to pay writers five coins per article. Vitalik wrote his first piece about microtransactions – very small transfers of pennies or units even less than pennies that the digital currency allows for. That's because it's denominated out to eight decimal places, or 0.00000001 Bitcoin, a unit known as a satoshi in honor of Bitcoin's mysterious creator. The grand sum Vitalik earned for the article: four dollars. "I calculated my wage and it was like $1.30 an hour," Vitalik said.

Despite the shock known to all writers when they see their first paycheck, Vitalik kept at it. Writing about Bitcoin perfectly combined his desire to get his hands on some of it and to learn about the various aspects of this new type of software protocol. Bitcoin combined many of his favorite things – math, programming, cryptography, and economics. And the people signing on to the Bitcoin belief system were pretty interesting too.

"There were these people with weird political ideologies," he said. "There were a lot of libertarians and there were also a lot of socialists floating around."

His dad had long been a proponent of the economic philosophy of the Austrian School, of people like Friedrich Hayek and Doug Casey who have prophesized the imminent collapse of Western economies for their failure to embrace pure free markets. Dima passed these beliefs on to Vitalik, who took them to heart. For years he thought he had to work extra hard to survive the coming social collapse. He laughs about it today, but said at the time that it "contributed to motivating me to try harder in everything." It also created a soft spot in Vitalik for libertarian thought, and in the Bitcoin community he found these beliefs in abundance.

In another twist that would not surprise any professional writer, *Bitcoin Weekly* soon risked going belly-up. "Despite paying me 15 percent of minimum wage, this kiba person ran out of money," Vitalik said. "To save *Bitcoin Weekly* I came up with this scheme where I would write two articles a week and we would publish the first paragraph of each article, and we would say, 'these two articles are both hidden for ransom,' and we'd put beside each article a Bitcoin address and if this Bitcoin address gets two-and-a-half Bitcoins we would publish the rest of the article," Vitalik said. "This upgraded my wage to maybe two-thirds of minimum wage, so I was very happy."

All the while, Vitalik still had to study for Greek class and get his calculus homework done. Yet he was also a typical teenager in many ways. His dad struggled to get him to clean his room and to eat healthily. He loved video games, in particular *World of Warcraft*. When he was 14 he took a trip to Russia, and when he came back to Toronto he was still on Russian time, so he'd wake up at 5 a.m. "He'd get up and play for a couple of hours, it was a big part of his life," Maia said. "It allowed him to connect to other people around the world."

Then one morning he abruptly deleted the game and never played again. Vitalik described the episode on his about.me web page, "I happily played *World of Warcraft* during 2007–2010, but one day Blizzard removed the damage component from my beloved warlock's Siphon Life spell. I cried myself to sleep, and on that day I realized what horrors centralized services can bring. I soon decided to quit." His dad worried about how much time Vitalik spent playing *World of Warcraft*, but when he came home time and again with straight As, what cause for concern did Dima have? As for the day he quit, his dad said it might've been a bit more complicated.

"Later I found out it was because this girl at school that he liked, she told him that that's stupid," Dmitry said. "Then he stopped."

In dribs and drabs, Vitalik started to open up to the people in his life about Bitcoin. When his mom looked it up online, she immediately found page after page about Silk Road, the online black market for drugs, weapons, and all manner of things meant to terrify mothers – all of it paid for with Bitcoin. Vitalik gave a three-minute presentation on Bitcoin basics to his math class. He advised Mr. Sayed to buy $50 of the digital asset, who, to his eternal dismay, declined to.

Vitalik also continued to compete in the math and programming challenges. Some events were done with partners, like writing code that would send a race car through a virtual course. The individual contests roused his creativity, but he found working with a partner could be difficult. As he would learn in only a few years, the politics and egos and power plays in a group of people can be tough to navigate, and even more so when millions of dollars are at stake. The rewards were nothing like that in high school, but the lesson is one he hasn't forgotten.

"Working in teams was probably the biggest thing I was deficient in," he said, "and team dynamics is the thing that almost killed Ethereum on multiple occasions."

● ● ●

In 2011, Bitcoin still flew under the radar, even among people who were well versed in computer programming. In Romania, a brown-haired guy with glasses in his early 20s named Mihai Alisie had discovered the digital currency through the web site WeUseCoins.com. Intrigued, he tried to research it online to learn more, but found the information available at the time tended to skew to either calling it the biggest Ponzi scheme of all time or the best thing since sliced bread. One writer who cut through the haze was named Vitalik Buterin. The articles Mihai read by Vitalik in *Bitcoin Weekly* were "written in a such a way that I started to take this seriously," he said. Also, how can you forget a name like Vitalik Buterin?

Mihai would never have come to know Vitalik if his father hadn't suffered a stroke the year before. He was rushed to Physiotherapy Hospital II in the Transylvanian town of Sibiu, Romania, an old villa repurposed into a care center. Mihai initially worried that his dad would be paralyzed for the rest of his life, or even worse, but on the second day at the hospital he sat up in bed and moved his hands. A miracle, Mihai thought, and felt enormous gratitude to the doctors who had helped his dad. A nurse told him he was lucky to be there at the time, since the hospital was about to be shut down. After what the staff had done to save his dad, Mihai couldn't let them shut down the hospital. But how do you stop something like that?

He decided to contact the local press to let them know of the hospital's plan to close. Once reporters started asking questions, a local politician who had had a family member treated at the hospital got involved. Within three weeks of raising the alarm, Mihai had helped keep the hospital open. "I was like, whoa, these things just don't happen in the movies," he said. He calls it "one of my proudest achievements."

A year later when he discovered Bitcoin, he had the feeling that for it to succeed, lots and lots of people needed to know about it. He had to get the word out, like he did about Physiotherapy Hospital. If Bitcoin was going to change the world like Mihai thought it would, he needed to shout from the rooftops about it. With that in mind, *Bitcoin Magazine* was born.

"I was coming to this kind of understanding and vision that things happen or don't happen because people know about them or don't know about them," he said. "So *Bitcoin Magazine* was an attempt to make it easier for people to find out about this, to understand, and to increase the chances of this thing happening and touching the lives of billions of people." Mihai worried in the beginning that they would struggle to fill a magazine every month, which gives you a sense of how early in cryptocurrency history this was. "If you look now, what happens in the crypto space in a month, you need like 10 magazines," he said.

First Mihai tried to persuade kiba, the founder of *Bitcoin Weekly*, to become his partner in a new magazine, but kiba wasn't interested. Then Mihai went after *Bitcoin Weekly*'s star writer. He found Vitalik through his Google Plus page and the two of them hit it off. "For me, this was like a promotion," Vitalik said, "I'm going up from a blog to a magazine, so I'm like, yay, I'll do it."

Starting a magazine is no small feat, however, as Mihai soon learned. Besides Mihai and Vitalik, *Bitcoin Magazine* had three other people on its staff in the beginning – Roxana Sureanu, an IT specialist in the UK, and Matthew Wright, who served as the early editor in chief, helped with the layout, and did some public relations. As they worked out problem after problem, by the fall of 2011 Mihai discovered that they actually had something that looked like a magazine. What they didn't have was the money to get it printed. Then Matthew Wright jumped the gun and announced the existence of *Bitcoin Magazine* before they had a product or a printer or any way to ship the magazine to interested people all over the world. The pressure now on: Mihai worried that the whole thing would collapse and he'd be seen as just another Romanian scammer, with the double burden of being involved in the sordid world of Bitcoin.

Then Mihai hit upon the idea of taking preorders to raise the money to print the first issues. They found a printer in the US, then had the magazine shipped across the Atlantic to London. The first cover image is a reproduction of a famous Occupy Wall Street photo of a man in a Guy Fawkes mask, holding a piece of paper declaring "The corrupt fear us. The honest support us. The heroic join us."

The person on the cover is actually Mihai, who bought the mask and took the photo in Bucharest after they couldn't secure the rights to use the existing image. The cover teases articles about mobile money, big hits and misses so far in the Bitcoin world, and a story about the enigmatic Satoshi Nakamoto. Mihai and Roxana wrote the addresses of their worldwide subscribers by hand on the mailing labels.

With Mihai in charge, it's not hard to see why *Bitcoin Magazine* was such a success. His enthusiasm is infectious and he's a great storyteller – even if he does have to stretch for words in English from time to time. He also has put his entire life into the Bitcoin movement and then into Ethereum, taking big financial risks and enduring tough environments to help create the new community he so wanted in the world. It didn't hurt *Bitcoin Magazine*'s chances that it had a star writer on staff either.

Vitalik used the magazine to lure new people into Bitcoin by writing stories that introduced readers to the new terminology or explained how Bitcoin wallets worked or went over the basics of mining. In his first story for the magazine on February 28, 2012 (it was still in digital format) he made the Bitcoin pitch to teenagers, writing, "They are not yet bogged down by the way we currently lead our lives, with our credit cards, loans and mortgages, and some may even choose to lead their lives bank free entirely, using Bitcoin right from the start." Never mind the fact that Vitalik certainly didn't have a mortgage and probably didn't have a credit card either, who better to talk to teenagers than one of their own?

Then in May, Vitalik held a copy of the first printed issue of *Bitcoin Magazine*. Here it was in his hand, proof that he was on to something real, something that had the feel of revolution. For now, at least, there could be no better way to help usher in the changing of the guard than to chronicle it as a magazine writer.

● ● ●

Weeks after holding the first copy of *Bitcoin Magazine* in his hands Vitalik donned cap and gown and graduated at the top of his class at Abelard. His backpack full of awards was testament to the amazing experience he'd had. As for the next step, college, he didn't have a long list of schools that interested him. His first choice, the University of Waterloo, is one of the best research colleges in Canada and was only about 100 kilometers from his family in Toronto. The University of Toronto came in at number two on his list. Waterloo, though, had become familiar to him through the programming and math competitions it sponsored in the greater Toronto area. His freshman class at Waterloo only had about 50 students: not the intimate environment he'd grown accustomed to at Abelard but also not a sprawling state school with 800 kids jammed into Biology 101. He declared as a computer science major.

As Vitalik prepared to move out and live on his own for the first time, his stepmom Maia bought him a beginner's cookbook. Vitalik might have mastered the literary essay and blown away his senior year math final, but he still had a few things to learn. Instead of taking on easy recipes, though – maybe bacon and eggs or pasta – he jumped right into making a whole pizza, including the dough, from scratch. "We'd be waiting for like three hours and it was like 9:30 and dinner is still not ready," Maia said with a laugh. "He didn't perceive the length of time and the complexity of the undertaking. That was very fascinating."

When it was time for him to move out and into the dorms Maia noticed something was off. "He didn't seem happy. He didn't seem like he enjoyed the people around him." Her brother had gone to Waterloo and loved it: it's a well-respected school that many people adore, yet it wasn't a good fit for Vitalik. Toward the end of 2012, Vitalik mentioned to her that he was thinking of dropping out. His passion lay in the digital world.

Even though his relationships with people he'd met through Bitcoin were all virtual – Mihai and Roxana in Romania, Matthew Wright in South Korea, kiba out there somewhere in cyberspace – he felt a much tighter connection to them than the flesh and blood students he knew at Waterloo.

He told his mom that the general classes he had to take were limiting the time he could spend on Bitcoin either writing articles or coding for development teams on the side. His enthusiasm for the cryptocurrency world was only growing, and Waterloo required that he pull away from it. Something had to give.

There were also Bitcoin development projects that needed help and would pay to code. One area was known as colored coins – a term used to describe an application that is connected to the Bitcoin blockchain but that doesn't necessarily run in the same way. For example, a stock or bond can be digitally represented as a colored coin, allowing its owner to sell it to a buyer in the same manner they'd sell Bitcoin. In 2012 and 2013, this area of experimentation was gaining a lot of attention, as it implied that Bitcoin could be used for more than just sending value from user A to user B. Vitalik soon found a project in need of help and earned 30 Bitcoin for the work he did. That translated to between $300 and $900 at the time, based on Bitcoin's wildly fluctuating price. This was no longer minimum wage.

There was an avenue at Waterloo that held out hope for Vitalik. The school's co-op program would either match students with a company for a summer job or help them apply to a company of their choosing. Vitalik wanted to work for a startup in San Francisco called Ripple during the summer after his freshman year, in 2013.

The idea for Ripple was spun directly out of what Bitcoin had accomplished in 2009 when it proved a global computer system could be utilized to send money between two parties anywhere in the world. But Bitcoin was decentralized, meaning no individual or group controlled it. Ripple envisioned itself as a central party in the network it wanted to create to compete with the global correspondent banking system. That's the network of banks that every day send $76 billion zipping around the world as companies and individuals need to make payments in foreign currency. A company like Toyota, for example, has to pay its suppliers in different currencies and return profits to Tokyo from all around the world. To do so Toyota uses its correspondent banks. It's an expensive and slow process, yet still it's a business fiercely guarded by giants like Bank of America and Barclays. Ripple's proposition was to speed up the process of sending money around the world and make it cheaper to boot. To do this it had to convince banks that they should use the cryptocurrency it had invented, known as XRP.

Ripple created 100 billion XRP out of thin air for the purpose of using it as a gateway to change how cash shoots around the world. The idea is that a company in Tokyo, for example, would convert its yen into XRP then send the XRP over Ripple's blockchain to (say) another company in Berlin. In Berlin the XRP would be converted to euros and the second company would be paid. Ripple said it could accomplish this in a matter of minutes, as compared to the days or even weeks that the correspondent banking system can take to do the same thing. In theory, it would save companies millions of dollars in fees every year.

Jed McCaleb is a cofounder of Ripple, and he'd come to know Vitalik's work in *Bitcoin Magazine*. He remembered Vitalik as eager and smart and he was excited to have him work for him over the summer. At that point, however, Ripple had only officially been a company for nine months, and to get a work visa for a summer intern, a company needs to have been in business for at least a year. The tantalizing prospect of what would've come from Vitalik and McCaleb working together will have to be left to a footnote in crypto history. "The world could've turned out quite differently if he'd come here to Ripple," McCaleb said.

Vitalik continued to write extensively for the magazine. In the first five months of 2013 he averaged more than 12 stories a month, publishing about every two days. He wrote about the hacks and thefts and fraud that seemed to be a near-constant fact of Bitcoin life (which have continued to this day), about the digital wallets users needed to send and receive coins, and a rebuttal to *New York Times* op-ed columnist Paul Krugman's argument that Bitcoin is antisocial. All the while he was making contacts, expanding his knowledge of the ecosystem, and earning $500 a month in salary.

In May, he traveled to San Jose, California, to report on the Bitcoin 2013 conference, a rare chance for him to meet with his subjects and sources face-to-face. In one of his dispatches he echoed what Maia had picked up on during his unhappy times at Waterloo.

"Events like this are particularly emotional; here, for the first time, we are able to see fellow Bitcoin users, whom we have loved, worked with, and had heated arguments with over forums or Skype/IRC chat for many months or years as something more than just a username," he wrote in a story titled "Bitcoin 2013: Day 1" on May 18, 2013. On a less poignant note, he also had another job to do – sell magazines. He's remembered by many in the Bitcoin world during those early days carrying stacks of *Bitcoin Magazine* into conference sessions and trying to unload copies. He ended the San Jose post with this: "Everyone who is at the conference can feel free to talk to me personally or buy issues 7, 8, or 9 of the magazine at *Bitcoin Magazine*'s corner of the BitPay booth." Those copies weren't going to sell themselves.

● ● ●

Something profound occurred to Vitalik in San Jose. As he alluded to in that dispatch, the experience of meeting the actual people behind Bitcoin had a big effect on him. Real businesses taking risks with real money filled the exhibit hall – all for Bitcoin. "The realization I had is that, wow, this space isn't just a bunch of random people on the Internet, it's real, it's people doing serious things and people making a really serious effort of pushing the space forward," he said.

The time had come to tell his family that he wanted to drop out of Waterloo and travel the world in search of Bitcoin. Not the currency, but the people behind it who were doing new and unheard-of things. He wanted more of the in-person interaction he'd so enjoyed in San Jose. Dmitry remembered that day in his apartment. Natalia was there too. Vitalik sat them all down and told them what he'd decided.

"He was a bit tentative, so kind of excited, but hesitant, anxious," Dmitry said. His parenting philosophy had always been to allow Vitalik to do what he wanted. Even when Dmitry disagreed with a decision, he made a practice of talking about the things that were upsetting to him so

Vitalik could make the choice to do something different. "He always knew the decision was his; it wasn't like we were going to say, 'No, you have to do it.' That's not how we work in our family," Dmitry said. He was also proud of the way Vitalik had thrust himself into the Bitcoin community. He wanted the world to know what his son could do. But he knew striking out on his own wouldn't be easy for Vitalik. "I'm a big believer that through hardships and challenges, you learn," Dmitry said.

As his mom listened to her son, she thought of her own journey when she left Kolomna as a 16-year-old girl to attend university in Moscow. How could she deny Vitalik a chance to see the world when her own journey away from home had been so helpful? "You can only control your child so much, right?" she said. "At some point you need to set them free and let them go and hope that the way you brought them up, and the values you taught them, are going to stick with them and they're going to do the right thing."

What struck Maia as Vitalik spoke was that just two years before he'd barely wanted to leave his room, and here he wanted to go and travel the world. "He seemed very serious, he had thought it through, and you could sense the depths of it," Maia said.

By May, Vitalik had given up on interning at Ripple, and as luck would have it, another opportunity came his way.

Mihai had his hands full putting out a monthly magazine, but he also wanted to dive into the more technical side of the Bitcoin world. Bitcoin wallets – the interface where users buy and sell coins – were still cumbersome in 2013, and Mihai wanted to make the process of actually buying something with Bitcoin simple and easy. His idea was to create Egora, a sort of eBay where only digital currency was accepted, and he knew just the person to help him develop it. Here was a chance for Vitalik to help build a project from the start and not to just jump into an existing one as he'd done as a work-for-hire on the colored coin project.

But how could they differentiate Egora from eBay? This became an important issue to Mihai, and to solve it Vitalik said he wanted to write the code so that the shopping platform wasn't just decentralized but autonomous.

This appears to be one of the earliest times Vitalik discussed this idea of a blockchain-based entity that requires no further human maintenance once deployed. The concept would come to haunt the Ethereum community in a few years, but in May 2013 it was simply a vision in Vitalik's mind. A DAO – a decentralized autonomous organization – is a system of code that runs entirely on its own once released onto a blockchain. In the case of Egora, that means an online shopper looking to buy shoes with Bitcoin would interact with Egora's computer code through some kind of application. No salesperson – or anyone associated with Egora, for that matter – would be on the other end of this deal. As long as the buyer chose the item and sent the correct amount of Bitcoin, the shoes would be theirs. Nothing like this had ever existed. The vision was clear; now Vitalik just had to build it.

● ● ●

With the prospect of Egora before him, Vitalik agreed to join Mihai in Spain that summer. But first Vitalik wanted to take a trip to New Hampshire to experience the Porcupine Freedom Festival – PorcFest, for short – the annual gathering that bills itself as a "liberty camping event" organized by the Free State Project, a libertarian group that seeks to lure like-minded people to New Hampshire.

Vitalik hit a trifecta with PorcFest. The festival was an early adopter of Bitcoin – he paid his rent in Manchester with it – and vendors at the event had started accepting it. It allowed him to be among fellow thinkers in the libertarian pure-market economics camp, who were a huge reason why Bitcoin had such a presence there. And he could commune in real life with the people who were spreading the Bitcoin gospel.

Erik Voorhees was one such evangelist. He lived in New Hampshire at the time and was a member of the Free State Project. He came from the world of marketing and communications, so when he discovered Bitcoin he soon brought the two together. By early 2012, he headed marketing at Bitinstant, a Bitcoin payments company cofounded by Charles Shrem, who later pleaded guilty to a federal charge of aiding and abetting an unlicensed money transmission service and served two years in jail. These were the wild early days of Bitcoin and almost anything went at all times. Voorhees, though, had left Bitinstant by that time, having cofounded Coinapult in January 2013. Coinapult offered digital wallet services and allowed users to buy and sell Bitcoin. (On his LinkedIn page, Voorhees offers this advice under the Coinapult section: "If you haven't heard of Bitcoin, drop what you're doing and go research it, for it is the most important project on the planet.")

Erik had come to know Vitalik through his writing for the magazine, and they hung out together that week at PorcFest. "We spoke a lot about Satoshi Dice, which was fun, that was the gambling site I ran back then," Voorhees said. "He was telling me things about it that I didn't even know, like how the mathematics of the rolls worked and things like that." (A year later, Voorhees would settle charges brought against him by the SEC that he had sold shares in Satoshi Dice and another site he controlled without registering them as securities with the government. He paid a bit over $50,000 in fines and returned profits.)

They were sitting in the grass at PorcFest and what Vitalik said next stuck with Erik. "It was a tangent about Bitcoin's importance in human liberty and how intertwined those things were, and he went on this tangent that was fascinating and strange." Vitalik twirled a blade of grass around his finger as he spoke. "He was in a zone, and it was strange and weird and brilliant all at the same time. It was one of those moments where you realize you're sitting with someone who has a very amazing mind."

As can so often be the case with brilliant people, while Vitalik continued to amaze those around him with his intellect and focus, internally he struggled with thoughts of inadequacy. The hangover of his restless time at Waterloo seemed to shroud him emotionally. The money he earned from *Bitcoin Magazine*, starting back in December, had helped some. And then at the San Jose conference about 30 people had approached him to say how much they enjoyed his writing, and slowly he began to accept that he was actually worth something. He described it in a Google Plus post as feeling "like I was in love again." The Bitcoin community had embraced him when he needed reassurance, and he wanted to return the favor. He resolved that upon setting foot in New Hampshire he'd start actually enjoying his life.

Even early in his travels he missed his family and urged them to write to him. In long emails he sent home he described his new awakening. "No more putting life off until the future," he wrote in an email from New Hampshire in June 2013, "no more complaining; if I want to make my life interesting, the keys are in my hands to do that right now."

● ● ●

If only it were that easy: to write what we want in an email and have it be so. Vitalik stood at a crossroads. In his very recent past he'd utterly dominated in all his subjects at an elite high school – not in a cocky or boastful manner, but with the humility that he carries with him to this day. Still, he had mastered Abelard and everything the academic realm could throw at him. He'd also made a fast and strong impression on the nascent Bitcoin community with his combination of deft writing and mastery of the software's technical details. Before going to San Jose, all of his early friendships and professional accolades had come in the form of messages on his laptop. San Jose changed that, and he knew what he needed more than anything was to go see the world, to meet the people trying to make Bitcoin mainstream and see how he could help.

Now that he was in New Hampshire to do exactly that, the qualms set in again. Once he'd settled in Manchester the week before PorcFest, he felt a familiar tinge of loneliness. It disconcerted him and he became afraid that he'd already failed in his new goal to have fun in life. The problem, he discovered upon arriving, was that he'd planned on setting out to meet cool and interesting people but hadn't actually figured out how to do that. It left him worried that he'd end up holed up in his room with his computer all day.

He'd also never spent this much time in the US, and certain aspects of the country added to his unease. The first was the difference between the US health-care system and Canada's. The omnipresent blizzard of television ads and billboards for every kind of prescription drug was new to him. Every third building seemed to have something to do with doctors or insurance companies. Yet none of that meant people in the US were healthier than Canadians, and he realized that the American approach was to think of health care as a product that you buy from corporations, as opposed to the Canadian approach of choosing to be healthy in day-to-day life. In an email to his friends and family he compared health to computer security, and said the best approach was to be holistic and attentive to it yourself instead of relying on the latest version of McAfee antivirus software protection.

The state of repair of many buildings and homes in Manchester also reminded him more of Russia than of Toronto, which intrigued him. He had the impression that everything in America was on par with other developed nations. He bristled at the police-state aspect of the US post–September 11. Nineteen at the time, he was asked to leave a bar where he was attending a Bitcoin meetup because he was underage. He had to show identification to board buses and became annoyed at the Homeland Security messages that seemed to be everywhere: "If you see something, say something."

He traveled to the New Hampshire town of Keene to attend the trial of several people who, in the spirit of the free-state libertarian ideal, had been caught feeding expired parking meters just ahead of the meter maid. They hadn't broken any laws, and their aim was to deny the state more revenue from parking fines, but nonetheless these six "Robin Hooders," as they were known, were being served with an injunction to stay more than 50 feet away from the police. The first trial he'd ever witnessed left Vitalik drawing different conclusions, but like most things in his life at the time he related it to an aspect of the Bitcoin ethos. While the trial left him feeling that the US justice system was horribly inefficient, he realized government intervention in some cases can be a good thing. Like how law enforcement had been stepping up efforts to find and prosecute Bitcoin scams and thefts. People weren't being as careful as they should've been about their own security and protecting the private keys that unlocked their Bitcoin. He thought that maybe relying on personal responsibility wasn't enough, and that the long arm of the law could be an advantage in dissuading thieves and scammers.

However, seeing government in action made Vitalik recoil a bit. Watching the machinations of the Robin Hooders trial reminded him of 11th grade, when he was part of the Abelard delegation to the model United Nations in New York City. Vitalik and his classmates represented Malta that year in the debates and other activities. Even though it was a mock government gathering, it left him with the vivid impression of the types of psychological pressures that can create the need to do busy work. In his electronic missive home he described it as the impetus that drives "government diplomats to write up big long 600-page documents" that get made into legislation that "never gets seen again until someone decides to use them as a legal bludgeoning club."

In Bitcoin, of course, there are no laws, no one to stop a user from accessing the network. There is some inefficiency – it's the trade-off for the security the protocol has achieved – but in this digital thing Vitalik must have seen an ideal of sorts. And not a personal ideal, either, but one that had participants tapping into its power from all over the world. For a budding libertarian the Bitcoin ethos becomes an intoxicant – a rare example of their foundational aspirations made real.

Part II

We're half awake
in a fake empire.
– The National, "Fake Empire"

Four

Ethereum is a gamble. It always has been, from the moment it sprang to life inside the mind of Vitalik Buterin. But to the people who built it, who dedicated their lives to it, it wasn't a gamble. It was clear. And in many cases, it felt as though the future depended on their success.

Decentralization is the lever. Bitcoin showed the world an alternative path for organizing institutions, communities, companies, and self-governing bodies. But decentralization isn't just about how a computer network is set up, how it's organized. It's about data and who controls it. Decentralized systems have the ability to wrest your data from corporations that are using it to shape the world in ways that are completely outside of your control or consent. That's where Ethereum's most powerful potential lies. Deleting the middleman. Your Internet usage can be yours again.

It's a funny quirk of history that the Internet began this way. The lack of system-wide infrastructure meant many pioneers hosted their own servers in order to put web pages up. It was decentralized by necessity, networks jury-rigged all over the place.

By 2013, centralization in social media and Internet service providers had changed all of that. It can be argued that a company like Facebook allows its algorithms to be gamed, that it's a feature and not a bug that allows for dire outcomes such as subverting elections. The same argument can be made about Twitter, that it allows hatred and divisiveness to spread on its platform while at the same time it bans its critics. Real-world consequences can be directly linked to the concentration of power and data accumulation that the Internet era made possible.

Here's a slightly less heady example, but one that I find personally compelling. As I was writing a section of this book, I wanted to play the new National album. But I only had access to it on Spotify; I hadn't bought it yet through iTunes. I opened Spotify and I got a notice saying that Spotify wants to control access to my computer. I am being told to change my security settings if I want to use it. I have no idea what that means, but I don't like the sound of it. I don't want Spotify to have control over my computer: God only knows what it would do with all the personal information I keep on my desktop. But yet I don't have a choice – if I want to use Spotify, I have to give in to what feels like a security lapse.

In contrast, a decentralized version of Spotify using Ethereum would likely be built such that I interact with a smart contract to play the music I want to hear from the contract's music library. It's peer-to-peer in a way that Spotify isn't, so the decentralized version would never ask to reconfigure my computer or have more access than I allow. I would be in charge, not the program.

It doesn't have to be this way. Gavin Wood, one of the Ethereum cofounders, certainly thought along these lines when he discovered the project in late 2013. In the years since, he's honed his beliefs on how decentralization can help restore personal freedom, and he's one of the most articulate speakers around on this topic.

As Marshall McLuhan predicted, we have come to an era where "*all of us have become the unwitting work force for social change.*" We have all become *users*, and in the Internet era the number of users translates directly to profits.

Microsoft and Facebook and Google, as well as the corporate interests that benefit from them, like advertisers, all want the biggest user base they can get, Wood said in a Third Web podcast recorded in 2019. The number of users a company has equates directly with how much it will be valued by venture capitalists, for example. A social media company with five million users might get a $50 million valuation.

"In fact, it's increasingly not so much about that, and increasingly about the data these users generate," Wood said on the podcast. The idea that user data is valuable on the Internet is still an idea many people don't understand. The scale of data now being generated and the ability to harness it has opened up new opportunities and huge economic incentives to companies that know what to do with the data.

"This can be things like targeted advertising, but it can also be other things like just learning better about how the world works," Wood said. "You can start to predict what people are thinking. You can start to understand the political changes afoot in a country. You can certainly predict things like the outcome of elections." Social media companies can then be used to refeed and recycle this data to the same set of original users after it's been manipulated or skewed, or what Wood referred to as "memetic feedback loops."

"Basically, the sorts of clever shenanigans that Russia and Saudi Arabia, and probably a lot of other countries, are using to better control other country's populations," he said.

Facebook has been a main engine of this disinformation. The US Senate Select Committee on Intelligence report on Russian interference in the 2016 US presidential election has an entire volume dedicated to the country's use of social media. The report noted how social media has changed the very nature of human interaction. During the 2016 campaign 128 million Facebook users in the US engaged in nearly nine billion interactions related to the presidential race between Hilary Clinton and Donald Trump. Fake accounts were created by Russian agents to sow discord and promote false news stories. The report notes that a 2016 analysis done by BuzzFeed stated, "In the final three months of the US presidential campaign, the top-performing fake election news stories on Facebook generated more engagement than the top stories from major news outlets such as the *New York Times, Washington Post, Huffington Post*, NBC News, and others." Two of the biggest fake stories the analysis uncovered were about Hillary Clinton selling weapons to ISIS and about the Pope endorsing Trump.

While Facebook has made efforts to limit the spread of disinformation on its platform, many people feel it hasn't done nearly enough. Gavin Wood doesn't even want a Facebook in the equation to begin with. But preventing this type of misuse of Facebook and other Internet companies is an exceedingly hard problem to solve.

"It comes down to centralization," Wood said on the Third Web podcast. "It comes down to there being a relatively limited number of organizations that have access to data and that are used to get access to data. The fewer search organizations – and the greater level of individual control within those organizations – the more they are able to be gamed, gerrymandered, and utilized to the desires and the needs of third parties that may or may not have the world's best interests at heart," he said.

Ethereum is a gamble, but its creators wanted very much for it to be a bold gamble that could help solve this real problem in the world. Ethereum isn't some force for moral good: I don't mean to leave that impression. It can't be when Vitalik designed it specifically to allow all manner of applications to be built on it. There are gambling sites and scammers and frivolous endeavors on Ethereum, just like in any industry. The libertarian ideal is very much expressed by the free-for-all nature of what can be done with Ethereum. But the core of the Ethereum ethos, the guiding principle laid out by Vitalik and Wood and Lubin and Green and many others, has always been the idea of creating a better future.

Listening to Gavin Wood lay out his vision, I had the thought that he, like a lot of futurists, has the ability to be dystopian and utopian at the same time. He said he didn't want to sound like a doomsayer, and then laid out his thesis that most people are motivated by greed or power. On an individual level this is understandable to Wood, but he noted that on a larger scale it becomes a problem. The "magnifying glass" of social media and our Internet-based lives are combining to create "societies that are malfunctioning," he said.

"What we need to do is restrict these nexuses of power to the point where they no longer suck in all that information and no longer give out all that information," Wood said. "And any information they do suck in and give out should be transparent in its origin."

Wood is standing on the shoulders of earlier thinkers like Lawrence Lessig. *Code and Other Laws of Cyberspace*, Lessig's 1999 book, has become a Bible to many in the cryptocurrency world. In it, the former Harvard professor and founder of Creative Commons argued that the dawning Internet era need not be regulated to death by government red tape. Instead, if code is treated as a form of law, cyberspace can be allowed to blossom into a new kind of social commons.

"The space promised a kind of society that real space could never allow – freedom without anarchy, control without government, consensus without power," Lessig wrote. "In the words of a manifesto that will define our generation: 'We reject kings, presidents, and voting. We believe in rough consensus and running code.'"

Lessig saw government agencies as the oppressors of online freedom, and in 1999 that made sense. Skip ahead 20 years and the scrappy startups Lessig wanted to protect – tech giants like Google, Amazon, and Facebook – have become the oppressors. A point he makes about the importance of how systems are built concerning decentralized systems and their ability to alter the power balance and about limiting government control of cyberspace is as apt today as it was when he made it.

"But as a culture we are just beginning to get it," he wrote. "We are just beginning to see why the architecture of the space matters – in particular, why the *ownership* of that architecture matters. If the code of cyberspace is owned," he said, "it can be controlled; if it is not owned, control is much more difficult. The lack of ownership, the absence of property, the inability to direct how ideas will be used – in a word, the presence of a commons – is key to limiting, or checking, certain forms of government control."

Andreas Antonopoulos lived through the early days of cyberspace and the debate about control. One of the sharpest minds in blockchain, he's written books on how to understand the technical aspects of Bitcoin and Ethereum, as well as on the "Internet of money." He wants Ethereum to "re-decentralize" the web.

"I was around for the first round and it was very decentralized at first," he said, referring to the years around 1993–1994. "Everybody ran their own web server," he said. "If you wanted to have your own personal

Facebook page you ran your own web server where you put up your face."

But it can't end with decentralized data; the code itself must be decentralized too.

"Until now we couldn't decentralize trust, so the trusted code ran in the hands of a trusted custodian," Andreas said. That could be about how you log in to a web site or how much of your personal information is shown to someone else whom you don't trust.

"If you control the code, you control where the data is being processed," Andreas said. "It therefore doesn't matter if the data is decentralized at first, it will centralize to the places where it's processed and manipulated."

"With Ethereum, what we're talking about is breaking that control," Andreas said. A key element here is the payment function embedded within Ethereum. It always comes back to the money. Because ether can be used as payment for smart contracts that control escrow operations, for example, a company like PayPal could be made unnecessary since it only exists to ensure payments are made. If you remove the problem of payments, lots of companies can be cut out of their middleman role, Andreas said.

"We couldn't re-decentralize the web without digital currencies," Andreas said.

The control exerted by custodians has real-world consequences. Geoffrey Golberg knows this firsthand. In his own telling, he's been "at war" with Twitter for a long time over fake accounts and the real people who use them to amplify false news on the social media web site. In 2018, he exposed thousands of fake accounts in North Carolina that were working together to sway public opinion ahead of Congressional elections. One prominent account was @greensboro_nc, which in many ways tried to pass itself off as the official Twitter account of that city. It wasn't. And not only that, but the fake account dwarfed the real one, @greensborocity, in many ways. The first was in its number of followers: according to a news article in the Raleigh *News & Observer*, the fake account had about 256,000 while the real one was followed by about 46,200 people. Then there was the number of tweets sent out. The fake account logged more than one million while the real municipal account had tweeted 22,700 times, the newspaper reported. The fake account was also followed by prominent people in the state, including accounts associated with North Carolina's two senators, according to the *News & Observer*.

The fake account fooled people into believing it was authentic by posting things like local content, pictures of new restaurants that had opened, and announcements about local events. The problem is that the fake Greensboro account made a habit of sending out far right-wing news articles and retweeting similar messages every so often.

"They're trying to set a condition where you expect a certain type of content and then over time they'll start to increase the frequency with which they'll start to inject the stuff that they're truly trying to get your head around, to essentially impact your perception," Golberg said. As an example, he wondered what would have happened in the November election if the fake account had said that polls were closing early. It didn't do that, but the potential to spread disinformation had been established.

Surely this is a problem Twitter should fix. Except it didn't. The *News & Observer* noted that the official Twitter account for Greensboro hadn't been able to get the company to remove the fake account, even though it violated Twitter's rules. Twitter didn't even respond to the reporter writing the story about its nonresponse to this fake account.

This is what Golberg is trying to expose. It's sometimes called astro-turfing, and it shows up in many ways online. On Twitter, Golberg has battled tweets relating to US–Iranian relations and with the thousands of accounts – fake and real – that rally behind a divisive cryptocurrency project like Ripple (#XRPArmy). While it was hard for Golberg to quantify whether the fake North Carolina accounts had an effect on the congressional elections of 2018, real effects on the 2016 presidential election have already been seen.

Golberg became interested in analyzing the metrics of social media followers after he'd amassed about 40,000 people who followed his video blogging on Periscope. The data of his own group of followers was there for him to explore. He'd created a nice income for himself and had a deal with Heineken to create content during the Rio Olympics. But then he was alerted to some of the extremely disturbing ways in which Periscope, which is owned by Twitter, was being used.

He sought to expose "the rampant nature of these pedophile net-works within the Periscope, the Twitter, live video ecosystem that were preying on and grooming children," Golberg said. "I felt compelled to leverage my audience and status within the community" to do something, he said.

Golberg took an aggressive tack by livestreaming one of these videos to his followers while on a smart phone he searched for what other users were doing on Periscope at that same time. That meant that when he found disturbing content, like an underage Periscope user being encouraged to take off their clothes, it was shown in part to his own audience.

In April 2017, Golberg was kicked off of Periscope by Twitter. He tried to get an explanation of why his livelihood had been taken away, but to no avail. The most he was told was that he'd violated the service's rules. "In many ways I felt helpless, at the whim of some big tech that operates unaccountably, without any recourse."

Moving to a peer-to-peer system is a step in the right direction, Golberg believes. Yet it's a challenge to say blockchain can fix the problems presented by monopolistic tech companies that can censor – or not – at will. What may be the deciding factor is whether Ethereum can benefit from the network effect. People need to use its platform, it needs to become something they can't avoid, and it needs to be easy. No one really needs to know about the blockchain or smart contracts that are working in the background. But they will notice that a ridesharing app based on Ethereum is 30 percent cheaper. And they might notice that they have more control over their Internet lives if they can pick and choose the social connections they make on their own, without a Facebook or Periscope or Twitter being able to impose their rules and allow their platforms to be abused without consequence.

Ethereum is a gamble. For sure. It could very well fail entirely. But for many of the people involved in building it, failure is a worthy risk if they can put a dent in the way the current technology landscape is fracturing lives and making it easier for hate and discord to spread. They'll gladly fail trying to right that wrong.

Five

The refrain that Bitcoin will change the world is almost universal when you talk to early adherents. For one thing, it's unstoppable, and appears to many to be an honest arbiter compared with a system of commerce they view as broken – that is, the existing financial system with central banks and commercial lenders like JPMorgan and Citigroup in charge of the money supply. Bitcoin's hardcore followers are known as maximalists because they are unwilling to accept any other cryptocurrency as valid. Bitcoin, to a maximalist, is where the digital token conversation begins and ends. The vitriol is real and most often unleashed online. It even extends to subgroups of Bitcoin supporters, who tore each other apart between 2015 and 2017 debating how much information a Bitcoin block should contain.

Such tribalism is rampant in crypto. The community that supports Ripple and its digital token XRP are notorious for this. I'd been the focus of their attacks in the past after I wrote stories for Bloomberg News questioning the company's claims that it was just on the verge of mass adoption by global banks. The Ripple/XRP pitch is that XRP can replace the US dollar as the dominant currency in the enormous correspondent banking system. As noted before, that's the bank network needed to move national currencies like dollars or yen across borders. Banks have no interest in switching to XRP for their correspondent banking, as I reported. That critique unleashed a Twitter flame war on me that was rarely elevated beyond ad hominem attacks on my looks and intelligence. (One of my favorite milder jabs was from a Twitter user who took a picture of me speaking on Bloomberg Television and added a gold chain around my neck, a cigarette hanging from my lips, and some sunglasses. I'd gone on TV wearing a black, collared shirt with the top two buttons open – a grave sin, I know, but maybe it was my Magnum, P.I. moment. I laughed at that one.)

But crypto trolls also made my work in-box unusable for a week or two when someone in the XRP Army signed me up for every email newsletter in the world. The spam that inundated me was insane: lumberjack newsletters from rural Canada, cooking newsletters from Korea. There was also a threat made to unmask my personal and financial details on the dark web, the illicit part of the Internet used by identity thieves, drug dealers, and child pornographers. I didn't think that was funny.

But back to Bitcoin. Its code is seen as honest by maximalists, as having established clear and simple rules that must be followed if transactions are to be validated. Another rule caps Bitcoin's issuance at 21 million, meaning there will only be that many in existence once the limit is reached. The inability to print more Bitcoin is anti-inflationary, and very unlike traditional finance where the ability to print dollars or euros is seen as a benefit of issuing a national currency.

In Bitcoin, there are no gray areas of banking or usurious interest rates or shady deals. The code is all; it is your guide. It allows value to be sent from one person to another anywhere, anytime, with no one who can stop it. It's the anti–Wall Street solution to a problem many people had a hard time putting their finger on, and it elicits a powerful response in a certain type of person. That problem, for those who have trouble articulating it, is that as I said earlier Wall Street exists for almost no other reason that to be the ultimate rent seeker, to sit in the middle of every transaction taking a cut of the capital that is created around the globe. (My favorite example of this is a group of interest-rate swap traders who worked for a brokerage called ICAP in New Jersey. These traders became known as Treasure Island because they made around $20 million a year each just for sitting in a chair and picking up a phone. There would be one bank on the line, and the ICAP trader's job was to find another bank to complete the swap trade. The amounts of money we are talking here on a yearly basis are in the hundreds of millions, and corruption on the Treasure Island desk led to US government investigations and hundreds of millions of dollars in fines.)

As far as grievances go, wanting to be anti–Wall Street is not a small one in the Bitcoin world, nor unjustified. Vitalik certainly held many of these convictions. He explicitly linked the new type of monetary system Bitcoin enabled to the cause of human freedom as he was sitting on the grass talking to Erik Voorhees at PorcFest. And he wrote about ways to help promote mainstream adoption of Bitcoin in several of his magazine stories. He wanted to give people the option to know this freedom. The more people he met in the community, the more entrenched his beliefs became. He'd even found one such group of like-minded souls in Toronto, led by a then 30-something man named Anthony Di Iorio who is fond of tracksuits and baseball caps.

The Bitcoin bug bit Di Iorio in 2012. Before that he'd had a peripatetic career in lots of different fields, not unlike many of the early digital currency adopters. His family owned a patio door company in Toronto where he worked for a few years, but when they sold it in 2008 he left because he didn't want to work for the new owners. He started a company called CityDrill Inc. and purchased an Italian rig for $1 million that allowed him to drill enormous holes into the earth to convert buildings to geothermal heat. He bought and sold properties around Toronto. In 2010, in the aftermath of the financial crisis, he became interested in economics and the seemingly simple yet quite complicated question of *what is money?* This quickly led him to economic thinkers from the Austrian School and libertarian ideals.

He never liked being told what to do and hated school. Growing up, his family expected their children to be normal, and that was the last thing Di Iorio wanted. The one thing that came easily to Anthony was technology. When he discovered Bitcoin in 2012 it was as though all the previous difficulties in his life aligned to point him in the direction of this digital savior.

"I really thought the solution to a lot of the world's problems was this thing called Bitcoin," he said. Unlike many of the people in the early years of Bitcoin – who lean toward the very young – Di Iorio could remember the world before the Internet. Bitcoin would prove a more important innovation, he believed. "I understood right away this technology would allow me to be my own bank."

He locked himself in his bedroom in his apartment in the Richmond Hill section of Toronto, reading everything he could about Bitcoin. Then it came time to emerge and meet others in the Bitcoin world. He looked around the city but couldn't find any meetups. Oh well, he thought, I'll do it myself. He'd been to a few libertarian meetings at a bar called Pauper's Pub, so he created an invitation on meetup.com advertising beer and wings and an opportunity to "talk all things Bitcoin."

It was Saturday, November 3, 2012, when the seven or so people filed in to sit in the bar's red booths. It was the first Bitcoin meetup in Toronto that any of them was aware of, and in attendance was one Vitalik Buterin. On the invitation Anthony had asked that attendees tell the group what appealed to them about Bitcoin, be that investing in it, mining, or development. Vitalik, who in his meetup.com profile picture is sporting some seriously hard Terminator sunglasses, replied (maybe in a Schwarzenegger voice), "All of it."

Vitalik and Anthony struck up a relationship that would prove pivotal to the development of Ethereum. Vitalik, though, was still unhappily attending Waterloo. He wanted more face-to-face contact with his Bitcoin brethren and thought pushing the limits of blockchain software was possible using the code Satoshi Nakamoto had created in 2008.

Nothing he'd reported on for *Bitcoin Magazine*, nor any of the conversations he had at the Toronto meetups – not even his revelations at the San Jose conference – made him doubt this conviction. By the time PorcFest ended in late June 2013, he was set to travel to Europe for the most ambitious part of his plans, and to test his theory firsthand.

Six

The train went through Barcelona, then another 60 kilometers to the station at Vallbona d'Anoia. From there they'd have to go on foot, first through the town and then on dirt roads with Vallbona at their backs. Mihai and Roxana followed Pablo, the developer they'd hired to help build the Egora project, over yellow dusty roads that led down to a valley and a stream. The surrounding brush was similar to that in the southwestern US and much like the foothills and chaparral of my hometown, Los Angeles. Pine trees were grouped in clumps here and there and hardy wild herbs grew naturally. Earlier that summer Pablo had sat with them in a third-floor apartment with no air conditioning in the Spanish city of Castellón de la Plana. He said, "What are we doing here? We can take Egora to *Calafou*."

The word has a magic to it, doesn't it? It certainly rolls from the tongue. Calafou.

On the road to Calafou, Roxana looks like maybe she just came from a rave. Skinny black jeans, a furry top with a hood, and mouse ears. She's got the Minnie Mouse bow with dots like a pair of dice. The only thing bringing her glamour down a notch is the grey pleather roller suitcase she's got at her side. She is off-the-charts cute as she heads to the anticapitalist collective started by Enric Duran – the Robin Hood of Spain.

As the trees grow thicker and the town recedes farther into the distance, Mihai turns to Pablo to ask, "Is this the spot where you take us out in the woods to shoot us?" Unlike his girlfriend, Mihai looks 100 percent hacker. Colorful sneakers, black jeans and hoodie under a black leather jacket. Backpack? You bet.

Pablo was involved in helping to establish Calafou, the commune Duran has created in the abandoned buildings of a burned-out textile mill. The main work here has been on Duran's environmental projects, but it's also known as a gathering spot for talented European computer programmers with a bit of anarchy in them. A few years before, Duran had become famous in Spain for taking out several bank loans that totaled nearly half a million euros, giving the money away, and then promptly and purposefully defaulting on the debt. An anticapitalist, Duran had used the money to fund alternatives to what he saw as a broken and corrupt system. One of the main vehicles he used to do this was the Catalan Integral Cooperative. At the time of Mihai's, Roxana's, and Pablo's approach to the CIC compound, Duran had already fled Spain and was hiding from the authorities.

Two footbridges had to be crossed over a river that could smell awful in the summer. A factory upriver that made cigarette rolling paper had apparently polluted the water something fierce and its sulfur smell was worst when the weather turned hot. After half an hour they came to some buildings. From one side they looked like new construction, but if you kept going around the picture was much different on the other side – graffiti-covered walls, burned-out rooftops. The factory had caught fire after being struck by lightning.

"If you want an image," Mihai said, "you know in *Terminator*, when there's ashes and the buildings are collapsed and it's like the resistance trying to rebuild humanity to its former glory?"

They also met the tiger mosquitoes on their trek from Vallbona: merciless aerial monsters. They had citronella candles to ward them off, but the tiger mosquitoes landed on the candles freely, as though mocking them. Maybe still in *Terminator* mode, Mihai described the pests as having "target-locked" homing skills. "They hunt you," he said.

Vitalik, Mihai, and Roxana had come to the collective to work on *Bitcoin Magazine* and Egora. What they got in return was so much more.

"It was about 30 people, some back-to-the-land hippie-type people, and some free-software developers," Vitalik said. The developers at the commune tended to devote their time to projects that helped keep the Internet free and private. They worked on things like alternative ways to structure and process network information that don't rely on a centralized authority like an Internet service provider such as Verizon. Such structures are known as decentralized mesh networks and they make it impossible for users to be censored or restricted from using the Internet, which ISPs have been known to do. Or restricted from accessing the Bitcoin network, for example. Other coders worked on cryptocurrency development or privacy protection: projects to help people keep control over how they interact with the web.

There were separate buildings for sleeping and working. Mihai, Roxana, and Vitalik stayed in Pablo's three-bedroom apartment in the old factory workers' quarters. Across the way was a set of stone stairs and the outdoor shower.

The factory seems to have been a little community of its own before lightning destroyed one of its main buildings. If you weren't feeling generous, you might say it looked a bit like a work camp: more penitentiary than pension. There was a long hallway in the apartment where Pablo hung bundles of tea leaves from the ceiling to dry. Mihai and Roxana slept on a double mattress on the floor. Their room had no window. After a while they got a second mattress and weren't so close to the floor anymore.

Most days (which started late as everyone typically went hard into the wee hours) were spent in "the hack lab," where a variety of computers were connected to guifi.net, the local mesh network. The compound generated its own electricity and had secured a water supply; some of the people worked on agricultural projects or with animals. They grew their own tomatoes and onions and kept chickens for eggs. While the compound was largely self-sufficient, the denizens had struck a deal with local shopkeepers, who gave them overripe fruits and vegetables. Everyone had jobs to perform to keep the place running, and most meals were communal.

The other coders at Calafou who were testing and stretching the limits of what Bitcoin could do fascinated Vitalik. "For Vitalik it wasn't so important about the luxury or the conditions or how the place looked," Mihai said. "It was mostly about the intellectual challenge and the people who were there." Vitalik met Amir Taaki at the compound, who was working on a project to make Bitcoin transactions and addresses impossible to track. Dubbed Dark Wallet, Taaki had partnered on the project with Cody Wilson, who had already gained fame for the 3-D printed gun design that wildly divided opinion about limits on technology available on the web.

They debated the merits of the various projects meant to allow Bitcoin to do more, like colored coins, and a new idea called MasterCoin, which sought to use the underlying infrastructure of the Bitcoin network to allow for more complicated operations. There was also the Ripple approach, and a host of other new cryptocurrencies were being created every week as well.

Although they'd worked together on *Bitcoin Magazine* for almost a year, the first time Vitalik met Mihai and Roxana in person was at Calafou. At first Vitalik struck Roxana as shy, and very smart, the kind of person you could start a conversation with but not someone who would break the ice himself. She also liked how he lived his life. He ate well, and unlike many of the others at the compound he went to bed early and got up early. He liked to run and came across as down to earth. "We became friends and he got to open himself up more to people around him after some time," Roxana said.

She felt she was in another world at the compound, with its still-visible burned-out roof beams. Surrounded by hills and forest, there wasn't anything around for miles. Roxana spent her days helping to keep *Bitcoin Magazine* on track by answering reader emails and making sure new issues were going out on time to their growing number of subscribers. The Spartan lifestyle had a big effect on her and the others. "It changes you, because you see the material world is not necessarily important," she said.

There were two working showers and two working toilets, one of each inside and outside. The outdoor toilet was a certain kind of abomination you find in communes and in other places hippies gather. It was a dry composting toilet, a polite way of saying that you will be going on top of a giant pile of shit and piss. Once you're done you throw sawdust onto the pile, which in time will be compost for the garden. When I first met my wife she lived in a quasi-commune in Marin County that doubled as an educational farm for city kids to visit. They had a composting toilet and I can still feel the sting of that smell in my sinuses. It is like nothing else I've ever smelled.

In Calafou, the residents christened the outdoor toilet *cagafou*, after *cagar*, the Spanish word for shit.

Every so often there would be a party at night, and some nights they'd watch movies in the hack lab. But for the most part they were there to work. Here Vitalik encountered marijuana for the first time in his life. Before this, weed had been some abstract thing that you bought on Silk Road; now the people all around him were smoking it. At least they weren't smoking cigarettes, he thought, which he abhorred. His feeling was that it wasn't a big deal because weed is less harmful than alcohol, but still he didn't partake.

● ● ●

Of course, sometimes they just needed to get away and touch a bit of civilization again. One Sunday they took a day trip to Piera, a town just past Vallbona. Life at Calafou was rewarding, sure, but hard. They could have built the Egora project almost anywhere in the world. They didn't need to be living hand to mouth. But the people they wanted to be with, the inspiration Vitalik, Mihai, and Roxana needed, was here, so it was the place they needed to be.

They hadn't had a hot shower in weeks and to flush the indoor toilet you had to pour a bucket of water into the bowl. A wall in the hack lab was covered in a sort of graffiti made up of a swarm of bats, which flew inside at night through the open windows near the ceiling. No one really knew if they ate bugs while they were flying around up there inside the hack lab, but it was a thing. "You can live in it, but if you're a person who would go to a three-star hotel and complain, you would leave," Mihai said.

That Sunday in Piera they found a *kebap* place and had a sumptuous lunch. Morning and evening meals at Calafou tended to be rice based. There was a lot of couscous. All of them were losing weight. Piera and its Turkish wonders came as a delight. "We were so hungry," Roxana said.

At Calafou dinners, the group who was eating would take a moment to applaud the cooks as a way of saying thanks. (Later in their Swiss headquarters, the Ethereum cofounders would adopt this same ritual as communal dinner was served.)

Vitalik felt like his head was spinning. In just over a month he'd gone from living in his family home in Toronto to sleeping in a tent at PorcFest. Now he'd become just another squatter at the compound of a Spanish revolutionary on the lam from the law. (Not to mention the night he'd left Boston for Spain, when he slept for two and a half hours on a bench and the homeless guy he spoke to told him that wasn't a smart thing to do.) Through all these changes, he couldn't deny this amazing phase of his life. He could deal with the flies in the dry toilet and with the harsh sleeping conditions (he did wish for better fruit). "I've pretty much stopped caring," he wrote home.

But on the other hand he fretted about his lack of productivity. He questioned the amount of time he spent on the Internet and what he was reading there. Working hours at the compound had become a challenge, as most of the other developers slept until late in the day. The work he was getting done on Egora often felt more like a slog than a passion. At one point he spent the majority of three days battling with the idiosyncrasies of the CSS programming language as he worked to develop the Egora web site. The interesting projects seem to come and go too quickly.

What really had hold of him, what his mind kept returning to, was how Bitcoin had built itself into a box. Well, two boxes: box A and box B, and you could send a coin from one to the other. Couldn't Bitcoin do more? Or, more saliently, why couldn't Bitcoin do more?

Mihai described all the projects like colored coins and MasterCoin as trying to add "buttons" to Bitcoin. Here, you want to do this new thing? You need our button! You want to do something else, well, here's a different button for you! It led to a bit of an "aha" moment for Vitalik.

"Vitalik was able to look at these initiatives and draw his own conclusion," Mihai said. "Adding the second button, then adding the third button. What's the end conclusion here? And I think that helped him leap to this idea of programmable blockchain," he said. "Blockchain now becomes this platform of sorts, rather than just a ledger tracking transactions from A to B, now it's tracking more. It's sort of the infrastructure layer of a whole new ecosystem."

The wheels were turning in Vitalik's mind, but it was only the wisp of an idea at the time. Ideas have a great power, however, and Vitalik knew he needed to chase this one to its end.

"When I was starting, I thought I'd just go to Spain for a couple of months and then come back," Vitalik said. With the revelations that came at Calafou, however, Vitalik made the decision to extend his hiatus and delay returning to the University of Waterloo. "I thought, okay, I'll take a full 12 months off, so I'll have this 6-month trip around the world where I'm learning about all the Bitcoin communities." Then he'd take the remainder of his time "to do something else." San Jose taught him that the people of the Bitcoin community were real and doing good and serious work. Actual businesses were being created and money was on the line. What Spain had shown him was the next level, that not only did he belong with these people, he also had something profound to give them in return. What exactly that might be wasn't yet clear to him at the time, but the chance before him was too good to pass up.

"I realized there was this one-time opportunity to get involved in something incredibly interesting," he said.

● ● ●

As the summer of 2013 wore on, Vitalik embarked on a month of itinerant travel across Europe. He accompanied Amir Taaki to a squat in Milan, Italy. There, Taaki introduced Vitalik to Mike Gogulski, whom Vitalik referred to as a "stateless political activist." Gogulski had renounced his US citizenship years earlier and was living in Slovakia at the time. In 2011, Gogulski announced on a BitcoinTalk forum that he'd acquired and remade BitLaundry, a service that allows users to mask their transaction histories. Vitalik went from Milan to Bratislava, Slovakia, where he stayed with Gogulski for a week. The natural beauty and language reminded him of Russia, and the cheap eats were a plus as well.

From there it was on to Zürich, Switzerland, where Vitalik knew exactly no one and used an online booking tool to couch surf for the first time in his life. It was one of the most expensive cities he'd ever visited. He had to pay to use the toilets and most everywhere the Wi-Fi was locked. But a Bitcoin meetup was taking place that he wanted to attend, with the purpose of getting to know two of the most important core developers of the cryptocurrency. The first, Pieter Wuille, is among the most active programmers around in terms of the number of changes he has made to the Bitcoin code. In 2012, he added a feature that made wallets easier to use by requiring far fewer backups. The second, Mike Hearn, began working on the Bitcoin code in 2009 and corresponded frequently with Satoshi over email. A former Google executive in Zürich, Hearn gained notice in 2016 when he announced that he had sold his Bitcoin and would no longer work on the project due to the constant infighting and personal attacks leveled by developers against fellow developers.

Vitalik also met Carl Lundström in Zürich, who invited him to stay with him for two nights while in town. Lundström, an heir to the Wasabröd crispbread fortune, had helped finance Pirate Bay, an Internet site that let users download songs and movies for free. In 2009, a Swedish court convicted Lundström and others of violating copyright law, sentencing them to jail and fining them millions of dollars. An appeal reduced the sentence but increased the fine.

"It's interesting the kind of people that Bitcoin brings together," Vitalik wrote in an email at the time.

In the wider world away from Vitalik's travels across Europe, the Bitcoin community found itself split on many issues. Since its inception in 2009 this has almost always been the case, as the fractious and digitally connected group of adherents are spread across the globe and do a lot of debating online, where it's easy for comments to turn acrimonious. One of the main issues facing Bitcoin users in September 2013 was whether they should engage with government regulators in an effort to educate them or stay true to their anarchistic, libertarian roots. On the pro-anarchy side were projects like Dark Wallet and BitLaundry, services that wanted to keep the law's prying eyes off of whatever people wanted to do with their Bitcoin. On the education side a new group called the Bitcoin Foundation had met in August of that year with US government agencies including the FBI and Federal Reserve, according to an article in *The New Yorker* magazine.

The article describes Cody Wilson, Amir Taaki's partner in the Dark Wallet project, as wanting to "use technology to remove government intervention from his life, and from the lives of like-minded people." The idea that Bitcoin users would want to meet with law enforcement ran counter to everything Wilson thought Bitcoin stood for. "The public faces of Bitcoin are acting as counterrevolutionaries," Wilson said to *The New Yorker*. "They're actively working to try to diffuse it and to pollute it."

Another debate centered on the get-rich-quick schemes that pervaded the Bitcoin world. The scams and hucksters were taking away needed energy and momentum from the people trying to make Bitcoin into an alternative economic system. As Vitalik wrote in *Bitcoin Magazine* at the time, a Bitcoin conference in Amsterdam was attempting to address the rift.

"The sentiment is common among Bitcoin users in mainland Europe that the Bitcoin community in the US is focusing too heavily on integrating with mainstream finance, securing large profits and investments and, some would add, bending backwards to regulatory authorities to make Bitcoin seem more friendly to established institutions," Vitalik wrote. He quoted Matthew Wright, one of the organizers of the conference, who explained in Amsterdam what they were trying to do differently, "It's not a money grab and tap dance of self-importance by those who seek to centralize and 'get rich quick.'"

The constant infighting and antagonism – the cliques that formed and the internecine brawls among developers who may have had only the slightest difference of opinion – are almost as hardwired into Bitcoin's ethos as the hash function. Vitalik now saw it firsthand and even met some of the combatants. The hostility of the community toward itself was beginning to make a mark on him.

What Vitalik faced as he delved deeper into the guts of what Bitcoin could be, how its engine could be rearranged or made to fit another purpose, is one of the central paradoxes related to the digital currency. Its greatest strength is also its main weakness. That is, Bitcoin is a wonderful vehicle for transferring value from one person to another, anywhere at anytime in the world, almost for free. Barring a complete shutdown of the Internet, no government or corporation or bank can stop it. This is exactly its design, as the title of Satoshi's white paper blatantly spells out: "A Peer-to-Peer Electronic Cash System." The code has worked for more than a decade, and has never been reversed, which is theoretically possible if someone – a rogue state for example – devoted enough computing power to overwhelm the network and change the transaction history for the purpose of stealing Bitcoins that have already been spent.

Yet as many people in 2013 were discovering, this strength of Bitcoin also limited its adaptability. This is not a criticism. What Bitcoin does, it does extremely well. Yet for someone like Vitalik who wanted to harness the power of a globally linked system of computers to do more than send money, the limits of Bitcoin became a frustration.

That Bitcoin emerged when it did is a bit of a mystery. An intriguing essay from 2011 titled "Bitcoin Is Worse Is Better" examines the confluence of events that led to Satoshi's breakthrough. Written by Gwern Branwen – a pseudonym for a writer and researcher who likes cats and lives in Virginia – the essay makes the case that all of the elements needed to bring Bitcoin into the world existed long before 2008.

"The ugly inefficient prototype of Bitcoin successfully created a secure decentralized digital currency, which can wait indefinitely for success, and this was enough to eventually lead to adoption, improvement, and growth into a secure global digital currency," Gwern wrote. The essay notes that Satoshi didn't invent anything new that unlocked some long-unsolved puzzle. Peer-to-peer networks dated to 1999, according to the essay, with the most familiar probably being Napster. The proof-of-work paradigm had been created in the early 1990s, originally to thwart email spam, and the public key cryptography that authenticates and secures the privacy of the Bitcoin network had been around since 1980. "All that was lacking was a Satoshi to start a Bitcoin," Gwern wrote.

The essay also makes an astute point about the "truth" that's determined by a network of computers. The network has to be in consensus, or agreement, at all times about its state. It's a global ledger, recording the movement of Bitcoin from one address to another. To achieve consensus, the proof-of-work system is used, where computers race to be the first to solve an arbitrary but extremely difficult computational problem. The method used is known as cryptographic hashing, where an input consists of a string of random characters. On the output side, the hash function transforms the input into a new string of characters that other computers can easily verify as being correct. It can only be solved by trial and error, so the fastest, most souped-up computers usually get the answer first. And when they do, the reward is free Bitcoin. Yet, Gwern asked, is this actually truth?

"So they adopt a new scheme in which the reality of transactions is 'whatever the group with the most computing power says it is'? The hash chain does not aspire to record the 'true' reality or figure out who is a scammer or not; but like Wikipedia, the hash chain simply mirrors one somewhat arbitrarily chosen group's consensus."

All of this is to point out that Bitcoin – for all its success – is limited in how it can be adapted to other uses. It's far from perfect: it's clunky and uses an enormous amount of energy to secure its global ledger. In the end, it relies on whatever 51 percent of the network computers say is the truth to determine if Joe actually sent Mary five Bitcoin.

A lot of these issues were front and center in the Bitcoin community in 2013, as colored coin projects sought to push the boundaries of what a blockchain can facilitate. From Amsterdam Vitalik traveled to Israel, where he spent the remainder of his trip. For a week he worked out of the Tel Aviv office of a project imaginatively called Colored Coins.

If the prior part of his journey could be summed up, it might be called the "info gathering" phase. Now in Israel, he moved into the "kick the tires" phase. He pulled and stretched and prodded the Bitcoin code to get as much out of it as he could. "I definitely started thinking a lot about the other things a blockchain can do," he said. "I guess I was always looking for what was the next step in the technology."

Working with several members of the Colored Coins team, including Yoni Assia and Meni Rosenfeld, Vitalik wrote a white paper to describe their project, which they named BitcoinX. The general idea of colored coins is that the Bitcoin network is utilized for digitizing real-world assets like stocks or mortgages, so that they can be transferred from one owner to another in the same way you'd send or receive Bitcoin. There's just one problem, as they noted in the paper: "Bitcoin does not include any facilities for doing this by default; to do any of these things, an additional protocol is required. And BitcoinX intends to accomplish just that."

They planned to split Bitcoin into two layers. The underlying layer would act exactly the same way as it did for moving Bitcoin. On top of that, they'd create "an overlay network of issuance of distinct instruments encapsulated in a design we call 'colored coins.'"

But what if you wanted to do more than just send a digital copy of something? What if you could use the Bitcoin network to create a transaction that depended on the outcome of a future event? Colored coins couldn't handle that kind of complexity, but another startup with a presence in Israel was hard at work on just that kind of development.

Known as MasterCoin, Vitalik immediately understood its potential. "When I learned about MasterCoin it was definitely clear to me that MasterCoin was more powerful than colored coins," he said. Initially, MasterCoin allowed its users to specify trades on future dates, a slight improvement on the immediate transactions that Bitcoin users are limited to. The next step was to develop multistep processes that could be executed on top of the Bitcoin protocol: you'd be able to place a bet with someone that relied on the future outcome of an NFL football game, with the winner paid automatically from the contract based on the code it contained. This got Vitalik thinking, which meant he was writing. In this case, he wrote a proposal for how MasterCoin could become even more powerful by shifting to a more generalized approach to allow a wider variety of transactions.

"Up until this point MasterCoin has been taking a relatively unstructured process in developing these ideas, essentially treating each one as a separate 'feature' with its own transaction code and rules," he wrote in the introduction to his proposal. "This document outlines an alternative way of specifying MasterCoin contracts which follows an open-ended philosophy, specifying only the basic data and arithmetic building blocks and allowing anyone to craft arbitrarily complex MasterCoin contracts to suit their own needs, including needs which we may not even anticipate."

Once he started examining the MasterCoin code, he realized all of it could be replaced to accomplish his goal of expanding its capabilities.

"I wrote this document and I presented it to the MasterCoin team, and what I expected was that I thought this was really cool and the obvious next step of where to take MasterCoin," Vitalik said. The response he got didn't quite live up to his expectations. The MasterCoin team told him they liked the idea but weren't willing to rip up all their current work to make the changes he envisioned. With a bit of a chuckle in his voice, he recalled his reaction. "Uggh, guys, are you insane?" Vitalik said. "Do you not realize that this is so good that you should immediately drop everything and switch your entire road map to this?"

This was the man who had written "The Encyclopedia of Bunnies," of course: an expansive work that included sections about the bunnies' calendar – including holidays – and details about "how long does it take them to eat one ship" and "when was the discovery of how bunnies make children." He loved variety and thorough documentation. When confronted with limits he wanted to buck the system. But as the idea of Ethereum began to crystalize in his mind, one of the smartest decisions Vitalik made was to generalize his approach – to give people the tools they needed so they could build what they wanted to on top of the system he sought to create. A clue to his thinking can be found in the last section of the MasterCoin paper, "Possible Extensions." Here he detailed the next steps MasterCoin could target, writing, "Allow contracts with one party, more than two parties, a coalition of parties, etc., and allow scripts to look at who donated to the script and how much. It might be possible to encode an entire distributed autonomous corporation that proportionally pays out dividends to investors."

That's Vitali-speak for *do whatever the fuck you want, I'm out*. That shouldn't diminish what he built. The protocol layer is what crypto nerds call this part of blockchain tech. It's a bit boring but essential to the enterprise (rather like my beat at Bloomberg; no one really wants to know how the plumbing in the financial world works until it breaks). Vitalik was becoming a master plumber and dreamed of bringing whole groups of people together online in his blockchain world, like when he'd first become enmeshed in the community of rebels and scoundrels who populated the early Bitcoin scene.

Vitalik knew the beauty of what Bitcoin had given the world. He wanted it to be adopted far and wide and had been doing his part by living off of it as much as possible as he traveled. Bu necessarily agreed with Gwern's statement that Bitc initely for success." He didn't want to wait indefinite envisioned. He knew where he wanted to go.

Nineteen at the time, Vitalik had done all he could to test Bitcoin's limits. The MasterCoin experience, and being rejected by its management team, helped him reach a decision.

"I'm like, fine, I'll just do this myself," he said. "So that's when I started pushing the idea forward on my own."

Seven

The town of Mittweida in the state of Saxony in Germany escaped being bombed in the Second World War. In the middle of town, old stone streets divide rows of brightly colored buildings. If you leave the town square and walk for about 10 minutes you'll come to a quiet street with a police station; next door is a mint-green house with brown trim and shutters. On Friday, June 17, 2016, just after 8 a.m., Christoph Jentzsch lay on the beige carpet of the first-floor office inside. He tried to still his breathing, to take deep breaths, to not let the world get away from him. Thieves were inside the DAO, his creation, robbing it at the rate of about $8 million an hour.

One of the first things Christoph felt was relief: finally the DAO saga would come to an end. It had overtaken his life for the past six months.

He'd battled anxiety and depression and exhaustion; he'd neglected his wife and five kids. There had been moments when he froze at the thought of releasing the DAO code, because once it was out in the world it couldn't be changed. There could be a bug in the software, or maybe terrorists could figure out how to use it to fund an attack he'd be power-less to stop. The pressure made him physically ill several times. He'd puked under the strain. God, please, let this be the end of all that.

But Christoph also felt a strong sense of responsibility. It shook him that he'd messed up so badly and that people were losing money because of it. He believed in the ideas underpinning DAOs. (The language gets a bit confusing here as there were other DAOs around at this point, MakerDAO among them. DAO is a generic term for the structure that smart contracts fit into, but because of its eventual size and high profile, Jentzsch's DAO became *the* DAO.)

A DAO is what got him into Ethereum in the first place, the moment he realized its potential. Vitalik's white paper had outlined a vision for how DAOs could democratize corporate structures to replace owners, employ-ees, and investors with users who directly managed the firm's affairs with smart contracts encoded on the blockchain. That breakthrough is what made Christoph pause his PhD studies and start working for Ethereum in 2015. And then, improbably, he built one: the biggest DAO ever built, in fact, which made it a fat target. After all the security checks, Christoph couldn't understand why no one had found the right bug in time.

He got up from the floor of the office and went back to his IBM ThinkPad laptop. Christoph knew the cops next door couldn't help him. No, this was his mess and he'd have to clean it up.

● ● ●

In one sense, if toasters and door locks were allowed to have bank accounts the DAO never would have happened.

At least, that financial discrimination against appliances and hard-ware had stirred Christoph's imagination when he first encountered Ethereum. Now that the cryptocurrency ether had been created, the question that plagued Christoph's mind was: How could it best be used? Not as a straight cryptocurrency like Bitcoin. Rather, ether seemed per-fectly suited to be a form of micropayment for what Christoph likes to call the "economy of things." Airbnb had become popular around this time, and when Christoph looked at the company thorough his Ethereum lens he saw nothing but a middleman to be eliminated. What if with a smart lock on your front door connected to the Ethereum blockchain, you could rent out your apartment directly to someone else? There would still be a web site like Airbnb's to let an apartment owner find a renter, but the Ethereum version would differ in one key way: the web site would connect people peer-to-peer and there would be no Airbnb in the middle taking its 30 percent cut of the profits. Where does Airbnb's business model account for that kind of disruption?

This is exactly the kind of simple but very powerful idea that overtakes Ethereum followers. It made me realize its potential on the day in Brooklyn that Joe Lubin explained it to me. Put a similar type of lock on your car. How does Hertz feel about that? Look at Uber in this way too: it could be as easy to move in on their ridesharing market as it was for them to take on the taxi industry.

The promise for Ethereum, in my view, is in large part intertwined with this sort of reimagination of the world wide web. If Vitalik and friends can offer an alternative Internet that is peer-to-peer – where middlemen are shunned, things cost less, and privacy and data security are taken seriously – that's a killer combo. I would sign up for that. Yet it's far from assured that they will pull it off. For years now, this doubt about whether Ethereum can really deliver on its promise has been in the background of all my work on it. That's not to say anything about the thousands of people working on Ethereum as developers, entrepreneurs, and salespeople. They are all doing amazing things. But maybe it'll turn out to be a neat diversion that captured people's imagination for many years but ultimately came to nothing. It will have to fight for any gains it makes, that's for sure.

Airbnb, Hertz, and Uber aren't going to let Ethereum just roll into town and eliminate their businesses. These are global corporations with billions of dollars backing them. Then there's the state of the actual technology. Ethereum is a long way from having the scale and robustness needed to support millions of users. Regulatory issues are another hurdle. But although the odds are long, there are plenty of people like Christoph, a theoretical physicist, who are willing to drop everything to work on Ethereum and willing to bet on the payout.

While researching his dissertation, Christoph needed to amass a cluster of computer hard drives to simulate his work on generating very long molecules. What worked better than CPUs, he learned, were graphics processing units, or GPUs, which would be faster and more efficient at crunching the data. He looked into buying a bunch of GPUs and ran straight into Bitcoin, as GPUs were the preferred hardware for Bitcoin miners. Soon he was down the rabbit hole, and then in January 2014 he came across Vitalik's white paper.

"I was totally blown away," Christoph said. "Now it made sense. Bitcoin was just a cryptocurrency, but this was a decentralized application platform." The possibilities of what you could do on Ethereum seemed endless to him.

Christoph has so many kids that he can forget how many he had at a particular point in his life. But in the summer of 2014 he needed to earn some extra money – and it doesn't matter if he had three or four children at the time. He'd seen a presentation where Ethereum cofounder Gavin Wood talked about the money Ethereum was raising in a crowdsale and that it hoped to open a Berlin office and hire C++ developers. That's exactly what Christoph knew how to do, and Gavin soon hired him.

He became the lead tester for the blockchain protocol. Ethereum was written using three programming languages: C++, Python, and Go. These are the clients that made the blockchain work. But if they don't talk to each other so that an action on C++ is interpreted in exactly the same way on the Go client, the whole thing breaks down. The blockchain must be sequential above all, so if there's a breakdown it causes what's called a fork. When there's a fork two strings of blocks are created and it can be hard to know which string is the official transaction record. Christoph made it his job to attack the three clients to try to make them fail: to fork. He worked most closely with Vitalik, Gavin, and Jeff Wilcke.

"They were all trying to pass my tests," Christoph said.

After about 10 months working on Ethereum, Christoph wanted to take it to the next level. He'd been pondering the best use for ether and decided it would be for micropayments to Internet-connected devices. He formed slock.it with his brother Simon and Stephan Tual, who each controlled a third of the company. At a BitDevs meetup in New York City on June 13, 2015, at the offices of venture capital firm Union

Square Ventures, Christoph publicly unveiled the idea for slock.it for the first time. Joe Lubin was there that day. Christoph used his phone to connect to Ethereum and unlock a door handle he'd brought with him. This was so early in the company's history that they called themselves EtherLock.

Christoph received warm welcomes as he went around introducing people to smart locks. The idea gained a following, and now he had to figure out how to fund its development. He soon realized that his desire to build a DAO could be fulfilled, and he began to figure out how it would work. But he not only had to figure out the mechanics of the smart contract. There were thornier issues, like would the slock.it team be legally responsible for what the DAO enabled?

They had lawyers working on this question in New York, Switzerland, and Germany. "They actually said, well, if you are not very attached to the project, you just write the contract and publish it, and you will later on ask to work for this company, it will be legally fine," Christoph said. This was a mark of how decentralized the goal was here – even the people who would bring the DAO to life imagined that they'd have to ask to work for their own creation. How the heck do you do that? Easy; it's like any other proposal to the DAO – it gets voted on by DAO token holders. Christoph and the rest of the slock.it team felt comfortable with the idea that DAO token holders would vote to fund their startup, out of courtesy to the creators of the DAO, if nothing else.

Then they had to contend with what a regulator like the SEC would think of the DAO. Would a DAO token be deemed a security? If so, they'd need to go through a strict registration process and provide potential investors with all sorts of information about the business plan, risks, and other details meant to enhance transparency for investors.

Their lawyers had an answer for this too. "Even if it is a security, the formation of a company is not something you need to ask the SEC for approval," Christoph said. "We saw the DAO creation as the formation of a company, but not with 3 founders, with 23,000 founders."

Let's fast-forward here for a moment and ask an interesting question. According to slock.it's lawyers, the token sale wouldn't be considered a security offering in part because the DAO had thousands of founders. What does that say about what Ethereum did with its ether crowdsale? Remember, these are distinct events. The Ethereum cofounders – including

Gavin Wood, Vitalik, and Mihai Alisie – sold ether to the public in mid-2014 to raise money to fund development of the Ethereum blockchain. A discrete, small group of people earned a lot of money through the Ethereum token sale. Doesn't that imply that ether is a security? The ether sale raised $18 million; cofounders such as Joe Lubin and Anthony Di Iorio were adamant that ether was not a security, but really all they had to back that up was their own opinions and the legal opinion from a lawyer in a situation that hadn't been vetted by a government agency like the SEC.

Then the DAO comes along and slock.it's lawyers say that if its executives are not attached to the project and everyone who buys DAO tokens is considered a founder, *boom!* You're not a security. See the inconsistency? Under this logic, either a DAO token or ether is a security, but both of them can't escape the designation.

On the US front, at least, the reality is that in 2014–2015 the SEC was asleep at the switch. No one in the government was paying attention to what was going on with the nascent ICO market. The SEC wouldn't start bringing enforcement cases until years later, and it didn't get around to writing its opinion on the DAO until a year after it blew up. We'll get to this a bit later in the story.

Now, back to the DAO. The people who bought DAO tokens never gave their money to Christoph or anyone at slock.it. They were in control of it the whole time and only interacted with a smart contract that exchanged their ether for DAO tokens. They could get their ether back if they wanted to.

The brightest minds in Ethereum at the time also gathered to act as a sort of fail-safe mechanism to prevent an attack against the DAO. Known as curators, group members included Vitalik, Vlad Zamfir, Alex Van de Sande, Gavin Wood, Taylor Gerring, Aeron Buchanan, and others. The group was meant to signal that the smartest people in the room had looked at the DAO and implied a type of seal of approval. The curators were exposed as nothing more than window dressing, however, after a number of security flaws were found in the DOA code.

After presenting the idea of the DAO at DevCon 1 in London in November of 2015, excitement only grew around the project. The DAO public slack channel soon boasted 5,000 members. Christoph thought if each of them bought $1,000 worth of DAO tokens they'd be dealing with $5 million. That seemed manageable.

But as the months came and went, a new concern began to gnaw at Christoph. Now that he was into the guts of writing the DAO code, he couldn't escape its fundamental nature. Once released into the world, it was unstoppable. That was a hell of a lot of pressure to handle when the code you are writing in has only been in existence for a few months and bugs are being found in it on a seemingly constant basis.

In March of 2016, slock.it paid $10,000 for a security audit of the DAO code to the Seattle firm Deja vu Security. The company specializes in examining and testing software meant to power the IoT. Christoph went to Seattle for a week to work with the Deja vu Security team.

"I was staying in an Airbnb and feeling almost sick, like do I really want to do this? I was really nervous, what did I get into here?" Christoph said. There was still time to say no, he thought.

But Christoph couldn't quit, not on his partners, not on his brother Simon, the CEO of slock.it. They'd maxed out their credit cards, the bank account was empty. They paid Deja vu Security out of their pockets, and Christoph knew he couldn't keep asking for one more month for testing. Then there was the wider community, who were watching every development.

It's important to note here that the DAO had a huge part to play in the early history of Ethereum. It's not overstating it to say that the DAO *made* Ethereum. There were smaller projects here and there but nothing with the scope and ambition of what the DAO wanted to do. You can see its influence on the price of ether. As 2016 began, the only things the Ethereum community had to look forward to in terms of progress were new versions of the base layer software being released. Put another way, there wasn't much of a catalyst for the digital currency ether to go up in value. And while work on the underlying Ethereum network was important, no one would use a network that doesn't have applications on top of it. This is why the DAO was vital.

As the months went by in 2016, ether's price began to rise. Aside from the network upgrades I mentioned, I can't find any other reason than the imminent deployment of the DAO for the gain in ether value. By mid-March it traded at $15. The demand to become part of the DAO was the fuel. You first had to buy ether to then buy DAO tokens, so it's easy to see that thousands of people were converting Bitcoin to ether to then buy DAO tokens, sending the price of ether to a record high.

Everyone was in on it. There wasn't anything else to do with ether at the time, to be honest. That's a big reason the DAO grew to $150 million in pure ether purchases.

Soon Christoph didn't feel like himself anymore. The stress was winning. This wasn't like him; he came from a large, stable family. The Jentzsch clan had lived in the Mittweida area since the 1500s. His parents have 36 grandchildren. Christoph also had a strong connection to his Mormon faith. His grandfather had brought the religion to Mittweida when he'd started the first Church of Jesus Christ of Latter-day Saints in the small town. Christoph's wife was another calming influence on him and had supported him through the DAO rollercoaster. And still he felt he was getting sucked into the chaos: he went up and down in depressive fits. Like the DAO code, it seemed unstoppable once deployed.

Griff Green was in Mittweida on the day of the attack. He woke in the spare bedroom of Christoph's mom's house to his smart phone blowing up with messages that the DAO was being hacked. He called Simon and Simon called Christoph.

Griff hadn't seen Christoph is such bad shape before. Before becoming slock.it's first employee, Griff had done Thai massage in Beverly Hills.

"I didn't have a license to do it, because you know I'm not the kind of guy to get a license," he said. "There was this very intense moment that day when [Christoph] was like, 'I don't know what to do.' He wasn't crying, but he looked like he was on the verge and he just had to lay down. He was having kind of a panic attack." Griff went to work on his boss and friend, giving him a massage to help calm him down. "Germans aren't the most touchy-feely guys," Green said.

"There were so many fears," Griff said. "Does this destroy Ethereum? Does this destroy DAOs? What's going to happen to all this money?"

Not a cent in the DAO belonged to Jentzsch. This was other people's money, and for a religious, family-oriented man, a good man, that made the theft all the more troubling.

"Dealing with other people's money fucking sucks, you know?" Griff said.

As the May 28 DAO fundraising deadline had approached, the amount of ether in the DAO just kept going up. No one could ignore the magnitude of what the DAO was becoming right in front of their eyes. The $5 million Christoph expected became a drop in the bucket and he began to freak out.

"I was really not a good husband or father at this time," Christoph said.

He lay in bed that Friday morning when the phone rang. His wife answered and then told Christoph that his brother had said something was wrong with the DAO and he needed to log on right away. In his home office Christoph checked Etherscan, the Ethereum blockchain block explorer (kind of like Google for a blockchain). He saw money leaving the DAO through the split function, which existed in case a DAO user wanted to get their money back and leave.

"In the beginning I thought, well, it's just someone leaving the DAO," he said. "But then it's very weird, it's always the same amount coming out all the time. And it was one transaction, so one transaction and many payouts. But it should be only one payout per transaction."

Something was very wrong. He lay on the floor of his office then, trying to keep the world from slipping away. Yet he felt a mix of emotions.

"There were two kinds of feelings in me," Christoph said. "One feeling was – I felt released – because this was clearly the end of the DAO." This insane, amazing, stressful chapter in his life would finally be over. His responsibility would cease.

"On the other side, there was shock and a feeling of, I basically messed up the whole system. I need to fix this now," he said. "I need to find out what's going on, people are losing money. I could go to jail. This kind of fear."

He got up off the floor and started to fight back.

● ● ●

Two other people who had heard of the DAO disaster by now were Emin Gün Sirer and his soon-to-be graduate student Phil Daian. After finding the bug and then dismissing it earlier that week, Gün and Phil had gone about their lives. And now the bad code on line 666 had roared to life. Soon people would find out that Gün had made his discovery and not alerted anyone, and there would be hell to pay for the Cornell associate professor. Griff Green, for one, was incensed, and Gün doesn't look back on this particular part of the story with any glee.

"I found a lot of bugs, I found *the* bug," Gün said. "That was a case of misclassifying what was clearly a bug not being a bug." For Phil's part, he wrote a detailed dissection of the DAO attack and how exactly it was put together. Gün was among the people he thanked for help at the end of his paper, and Phil had this message for his new professor: "Gün, we were so damn close – sorry it wasn't quite enough this time ;)"

●　●　●

Christoph Jentzsch didn't fight the DAO attacker on his own; he had Griff Green at his side from the very beginning (though they took different tacks as to their approach to stopping the ether thief). The thing about Griff is, he probably wouldn't have been in Mittweida the morning of the DAO attack if not for his love of the Seattle Supersonics.

He grew up in Spokane, Washington, as the type of kid who did better at school as it got harder. He describes himself as "a people pleaser," but at his Catholic high school he went a bit irreverent. He'd shave his head in strange patterns: one time he looked like Bozo the Clown, with a bald crown and hair that went past his shoulders, and another time he wore what he called "a shooter mullet" because "I should shoot myself in the face with a shotgun."

Basketball has always been a love of his, though he's not very good; his height of about six feet two doesn't translate to the court. His large Catholic family has some interesting twists and turns: He says he has six parents because his mom and dad weren't married when he was born, then his mom married his stepdad when he was 2 years old. He didn't meet his biological father until he was 12, who married, then divorced and married again. His mom and stepdad also split up and then his mom got a new partner. Three moms and three dads, by Griff's calculus.

But basketball and a billionaire would soon turn Griff's life in a strange direction.

"I was obsessed with the Seattle Supersonics," Griff said. "We're talking next level." He carried the rookie card of Supersonic legend Gary Payton in his pocket every day. The only days he didn't wear Supersonics gear was after the team lost, because he'd be in mourning. Then when he was studying chemical engineering at the University of Washington in Seattle, Howard Schultz, the billionaire founder of Starbucks and owner of the Supersonics, sold the team to a guy from Oklahoma City. While the new owner said he wasn't planning to move the team, Griff didn't buy it. With two friends he started Save Our Sonics.

"I was basically third in command, I was general of the fans," he said. "This is where I cut my chops in community organizing." After two years of fighting to keep the team in Seattle, it all hinged on a court case, which the fans thought they were going to win. On the day of the court decision, the mayor of Seattle cut a deal with the Oklahoma investor and let him take the Sonics two years earlier than a city contract allowed in exchange for $60 million.

"I'd fought for two years, we're talking this was a second full-time job," Griff said. "And it was all ripped out with one signature." Griff was devastated.

"I couldn't believe it. I was already, I wouldn't say a full-on anarchist, but I've always been pretty irreverent since high school and I never thought the way the government worked was anything special," he said. "After that I was like, fuck this, fuck Seattle, fuck the system. In a parallel universe, where the judge makes that reading, I'm just like an obese dude hanging out with courtside seats watching the Sonics as a chemical engineer in a cubicle."

After college he worked for Amgen in a biotech lab that was producing a genetically engineered form of mouse ovary cells. "Amgen sketched me out, man. I didn't like that gig," he said. "I've always been kind of a hippie." Then he went to work for a renewable energy company, but the 2008 financial crisis affected one of the projects he was working on and layoffs were imminent. Through all of this, he'd been buying physical bars of silver and gold coins. A deep distaste for the banking system made him want to be off the grid as much as possible. "Bankers allow governments to borrow money to go to war. I've always thought that was one of the biggest problems with the world," he said.

Once his job at the energy company was over, he took to the road in a van. He went to Thailand and South America and attended Burning Man in the Nevada desert for the first time. Through it all he'd been funding his travels by selling the silver and gold. Which is kind of a pain. Enter Bitcoin.

"I traded $3,000 of gold and silver for $3,000 worth of Bitcoin," he said. Soon Griff was buying all sorts of new cryptocurrencies on the exchange BTC-E. His best investment was in Litecoin: he turned $500 into $17,000. Money had been running low, and now he had enough for another year. He was hooked.

"I was obsessed, it was like the Sonics all over again," he said. He enrolled in the online University of Nicosia, where he earned a master's degree in cryptocurrency. For a class that assigned a white paper, he proposed a bikesharing startup that had a very similar setup to what slock.it was doing in Germany. Once he found out about the company he sent them his white paper over and over, but got no response. Finally, he got through to them and said he'd work for free. Ethereum was still very new at this point, and Griff thought at first it was a fad. But once he worked for slock.it, which is based on Ethereum, he had to figure it out. For a different class he had to write a will contract, and he did it in Solidity, Ethereum's programming language.

"I don't even know how to code," he said, "and I did it in like four hours. It was shit code, but it worked. I could create a will and save the hash on Ethereum and prove that it was this will." He started writing blog posts about Solidity for slock.it's web site and reaching out to Ethereum community members, whom he found to be helpful and kind, which can't always be said for Bitcoin followers.

"The Ethereum community is just another level," he said. "Ethereum made this really important choice, and at the time it wasn't common." Most of the community stayed in touch over reddit threads, like r/ethereum. "R/ethereum would not talk about the price," Griff said. "That totally changed the vibe of Ethereum. If there was one choice that the Ethereum community made, it was to take the price conversation out of it at the early stage and just focus on the technology. That changed everything."

While that is true, by June 2016 there was one project that was very much about the money, and it had been hacked. Griff was in deep with the slock.it team and the broader Ethereum world by now, and when the attack began, he jumped into action.

His job had always been to rally the community and keep people up to date about what slock.it was up to. Now, he logged in to the DAO slack group and announced the attack, alerting people in 30 time zones with one message. "Transparency was a big part of our campaign," he said. His years of experience in rallying public support for causes were about to be tested like never before. Was he ready?

"I was excited," he said. "This is the craziest thing that's ever happened to me. This is the craziest thing that's almost ever happened to anyone. I thrive in chaos."

• • •

Once it was understood that an attack was in progress on the DAO, the first thing that occurred to everyone is that they could spam the network to try to slow it down. Maybe that way the thief's efforts would slow too, so they'd have time to develop a more direct approach. Griff got the message out to overload Ethereum. Vitalik was in Shanghai at the time and spent 20 ether to spam the network he'd invented. It must have been infuriating to watch as transaction after transaction drained ether out of the DAO. A heist in broad daylight.

The slock.it team now could also see the exact way in which the attacker had exploited the DAO bug. There had been many weaknesses found with the DAO up to this point, but none of them had found this exact defect before the ether thief had. The attack had started in the split function, the command used to begin a withdrawal from the DAO. The "split" here refers to leaving the DAO with the ether you originally invested. There are a host of reasons to be leaving the DAO: it isn't some kind of nefarious activity. The split was part of its design. But still, it had been coded by Christoph to take time, just like everything related to the DAO. You had to make a proposal to split, then wait seven days before the next step could be taken.

During that week others can "join" your split. When your split leaves the DAO, those new passengers go with the contract; they're linked to you in a way. That meant that the group of good-guy hackers that formed that morning, the Robin Hood Group, could check to verify everyone's identity in the splits that were in their waiting period. Maybe they could identify the attacker if they got lucky. This was one of Griff's jobs.

"Everyone who wasn't us, we assumed to be malicious," Griff said.

That meant asking some people to take a picture of their driver's license and send it to Griff. Requesting that kind of exposure, a link between an Ethereum address and a real-world identity, would usually be severely frowned upon. Circumstances seemed to call for some flexibility here, though, and Griff was happy with how many people revealed their identity to him.

Another member of the slock.it team, Lefteris Karapetsas, began to recreate the hack contract. They could copy the attack, in other words. But would that even be necessary? As that Friday wore on, the DAO continued to be drained of ether. Not surprisingly, the price of ether also tanked, falling 51 percent in three days, from $21.52 on June 17 to $10.52 on June 21.

Eight

November is a generally wonderful time to be in San Francisco, and that's where Vitalik found himself in late 2013. Known for its fog and cold summers, the city transforms for a few months toward the end of the year and offers clear skies and warm days.

These are fertile technology grounds, having given life to Hewlett-Packard and Cisco, and to Google and Apple and many other giants. It made a fitting place for Vitalik to stand on the threshold of his break-through. The City by the Bay had already established itself as a center of cryptocurrency activity. Ripple had its headquarters there, as did Kraken, one of the first digital currency exchanges in the US. Vitalik was staying in the spare apartment of Jesse Powell, the bespectacled founder of Kraken. After almost five months of communal living, going from living

among the freedom-loving PorcFest attendees to the Spanish compound
to a hostel in Amsterdam, the peace and quiet of having an apartment all
to himself felt like a precious luxury. Powell's apartment was in Noe
Valley, one of the nicest neighborhoods in a gorgeous city. There is a
freedom to living alone that he'd missed while on his European adventure, and he found himself buoyed by the rise in Bitcoin's price. Even as
he was trying to not remake Bitcoin, but to make something more than
it, he still relied in large part on his stash of Bitcoin to live.

On November 28, 2013, its price passed $1,000 for the first time.
Not only was that an astronomical gain from the $0 where Bitcoin had
started, it was a huge jump in value over that month alone. Bitcoin
had traded at just over $200 at the beginning of that November and had
jumped fivefold in only four weeks. When Vitalik had worked for kiba
to earn Bitcoin by writing for *Bitcoin Weekly*, his coins had amounted to
80 cents each. While it's impossible to say if Vitalik had held on to them,
at $1,000 he would have been sitting on an increase of *125,000 percent*.

Money occupied his thinking more and more that November. "If
you didn't realize it, I have quite a lot of the stuff now with the Bitcoin
price going up," he wrote in an email home. His windfall led him to
increase his daily spending allowance to $20. "I'm actually enjoying life
more this way," he wrote, adding for anyone who didn't know, "$20 per
day is really not all that much."

His frugality had always been a part of his personality. He'd never
asked for toys or other things when out shopping with his mom. At
Waterloo he'd often skipped going out to dinner with friends or visiting
his family in Toronto due to the cost. In his new life, though, those
choices seemed unwise.

"Now that gaining and losing a thousand dollars is just a matter of a
few clicks on the Bitcoin price chart, I'm starting to somewhat regret
making that choice," he wrote. "Maybe I would have been considerably
less lonely had I been willing to let myself spend another $50 a month
on those kinds of things."

Vitalik now found himself in the situation his character Ulrich
dreamed of in the short story he'd written in high school. Bitcoin represented financial freedom for him: not only did this thing he loved
rouse his intellectual curiosity and expand what he thought possible in
terms of human organizing principles, it was also making him rich. He

now knew a freedom he'd never known, and it became clear to him that his ideas about expanding Bitcoin's possibilities were linked to giving others this freedom. Not freedom in a financial sense, not directly at least. His dream was to give people the freedom to do whatever they wanted within the confines of a global network of linked computers – the freedom to unchain activities and business decisions from centralized authorities and their ability to censor or prohibit actions. He didn't know what people wanted – who does? – but he could provide the infrastructure for them to turn their ideas into reality.

He'd bunked with anarchists and radicals, and had healthy doses of libertarianism and Austrian School economics sprinkled throughout his upbringing. He lived off of less than $20 a day but was still thrilled at the rising price of Bitcoin. A multidisciplinarian in almost every sense of the word, Vitalik excelled at bringing together disparate threads of math and science and economics to create something new. As he once told his father, what he loved most about traveling was talking to smart people all over the world and then connecting the dots among them. All these factors added up to Vitalik realizing that he wanted to give the world paint and canvas, but to leave the art up to the people.

So. He set to writing. The solitude afforded by Powell's apartment was exactly what he needed to finally synthesize the thoughts and experiences of his travels. But there was still one hang-up he couldn't get around. All the additions Colored Coins and MasterCoin had made to Bitcoin's capabilities only involved two parties. Vitalik knew he needed to open up the platform to as many people out there who wanted to engage with a contract as possible, but he hadn't yet cracked how to do it.

As any writer will tell you, a lot of the time spent creating is actually spent sitting and thinking. For Vitalik this meant walking. He'd always been an avid walker and runner. At university, he'd once wanted to walk the roughly 100 kilometers to Toronto to visit his family. He made it halfway but then had to turn around because his decrepit shoes had fallen apart. Now in San Francisco, he headed north from Jesse's apartment toward the Presidio, an old Army base and parkland that overlooks the Golden Gate Bridge. For over three hours he meandered through the park and other parts of the city, mulling how to open up a blockchain-based system to a multitude of users while at the same time ensuring that the system couldn't be overwhelmed by a deluge of demand.

Here, on this day in mid-November in San Francisco, the spark that would become Ethereum came to him.

He called it "gas." He had no better name for it then — the name *Ethereum* hadn't yet occurred to him — but what he did know is that any computation running on this new system would have to require a very small amount of cryptocurrency. That's because whoever wanted to harness the power of this global set of linked computers would have to pay for it. It would also make it very expensive if a bad actor wanted to send millions of messages into the network to slow it or stop it entirely. In the Bitcoin world, transaction fees are paid by one of the two parties engaged in the trade. But if you have 20 or 50 or 1,000 people engaging with a contract on a blockchain, who pays for that? You need a way to manage that demand, and gas was it.

"When I came up with the idea, I went back and just started writing the white paper," Vitalik said.

His thinking on the generalization concept now crystalized. He could allow users to write any kind of computer program on top of a blockchain. An unlimited number of people could interact with it. The potential seemed limitless for what could be done in a distributed system that's beyond the reach of governments or corporations. The programs would come in the form of smart contracts deployed on the blockchain. Vitalik designed them to be Turing complete, which means the programs could execute commands and process logic according to their code as long as the correct inputs and resources were made available.

He captured his ideas in the form of a white paper, yet what he created in November 2013 is just as much Vitalik Buterin's manifesto. It was a bold and focused path forward to leave the limitations and prescriptive nature of MasterCoin, Primecoin, and colored coins in the dust. It was the next step beyond Bitcoin. He added flourishes of humor to the writing and knew with every word what he intended Ethereum to be.

"The Ethereum protocol's design philosophy is in many ways the opposite from that taken by many other cryptocurrencies today," he wrote in the conclusion to the white paper's first draft. "Other cryptocurrencies aim to add complexity and increase the number of 'features'; Ethereum on the other hand takes features away." He wanted radical simplicity so that smart contracts could do the work of whatever programmers wanted. "Everything is a contract," he wrote in one section.

That meant users could create new cryptocurrencies in Ethereum, or derivatives or crop insurance or voting mechanisms for corporate governance. Want to set up a full-scale Skynet, the computer network in *Terminator* that destroys humanity by launching a nuclear war? No problem, as long as you have the resources. "Maybe you might want to have a few thousand interlocking contracts, and be sure to feed them generously," he wrote. "The sky(net) is the limit."

In the white paper Vitalik also proposed the creation of ether, the cryptocurrency that would be required to fund any transaction sent to the network. The idea of gas that unlocked the whole project now had a name. He also described the issuance of ether as involving different methods of "fundraising" that were yet to be determined.

The power of Ethereum "can be used to build up literally any feature that is mathematically describable," Vitalik declared. "As a result, we have a cryptocurrency protocol whose codesbase is very small, and yet which can do anything that any cryptocurrency will ever be able to do."

He proposed, in essence, the creation of the first global computer. Once this door was open, it meant anything that can be put into a contract could be deployed on the Ethereum blockchain and executed by the code inside a smart contract. The life cycle of a bond payment could be automated. A pharmaceutical company could authenticate the sources of its drugs. Gambling and dice throws could be trusted and verified with no central authority in charge, eliminating suspicions of unfair play. And it theoretically meant entire companies could be coded and automated in "decentralized autonomous corporations." His autonomous vision finally lived before him.

Once the idea of gas unlocked the generalized approach Vitalik had been searching for, he wrote the white paper in two weeks. The only thing he didn't have was a name for what he'd created. He'd always been a fan of science fiction, of writers like Peter F. Hamilton and television shows like *Star Trek: The Next Generation* and *Enterprise*. As he sat in Jesse Powell's apartment thinking about what to call his invention, his mind turned to the books he'd read in high school.

"I remember reading a list of elements from science fiction. And I remember liking Ethereum because it has this connection to this nineteenth-century scientific theory of, like, ether, this medium where if water waves travel through water, sound waves travel through air, the hypothesis would be that light waves move through ether," he said. "It's this medium that permeates the entire universe that is this kind of substrate that everything is based on. And I thought that was something nice to name Ethereum after."

● ● ●

On November 27, 2013, Vitalik sent the first version of his white paper to a group of about 15 people. He had no idea how it would be received and nervously waited for the scathing comments to arrive. Erik Voorhees received a copy of the white paper with an email from Vitalik explaining what he hoped to accomplish with Ethereum.

"I think you might appreciate the fact that this essentially allows people to create financial and data-based services that are impossible to regulate, since they operate on a decentralized computer network without anyone actually running them, so no bank, corporation, or government can shut it down," Vitalik wrote to Erik. Vitalik's message of giving power back to the people came through like a shot. Removing the gatekeepers – the Googles and Facebooks and Apples of the world – had become more than just a wish in what Vitalik described as "cryptocurrency 2.0."

Erik didn't get the technical details. "It was frankly over my head," he said. But he had enormous respect for Vitalik and knew to take Ethereum seriously.

The Ethereum white paper also landed in the in-boxes of Mike Hearn, Anthony Di Iorio, Mihai Alisie, Amir Chetrit, Elizabeth Ploshay, Meni Rosenfeld, and Virgil Griffith, and was sent to several other people as well. It then pinged around the Internet as the initial recipients forwarded it to people they thought should see it. All the while, Vitalik still wasn't sure he could build an entirely new blockchain on his own. But, crucially, the criticisms never arrived. Everyone seemed to love Ethereum.

"The number of people interested in Ethereum clearly got big enough that it made sense to do it as an independent thing," Vitalik said. "Originally I thought I'd have to write the thing myself, and writing my own chain was just too daunting." But now other developers contacted him, wanting to be a part of the project and help build it. That allowed Vitalik to have the confidence to make Ethereum an entirely new blockchain system, independent of everything else. "Now with more resources I'm like, cool, there's other developers who could be relied on to make a blockchain client, so let's actually do it properly," he said.

Vitalik Buterin invented Ethereum on his own, alone. To build it, however, he needed comrades.

Part III

And did we tell you the name of the game, boy?
We call it "Riding The Gravy Train."
– Pink Floyd, "Have a Cigar"

Nine

The quest Vitalik had set out on in June of 2013 ended that November the moment he pushed send to deliver his white paper. He'd braved the unfamiliarity of Europe and the Middle East on his journey to make Bitcoin better, arrived in the US with Ethereum on his mind, and in the end had invented a way to create distributed organizations that went light years beyond what Bitcoin had achieved four years earlier.

From its inception, Ethereum has been about – and for – the people who use it. To do what, exactly, no one can say. That's the point. Bitcoin excels at being a means of sending value directly to anyone. Vitalik created Ethereum to be a vessel for the world to fill.

Yet while people are Ethereum's strength, they've also proved to be a weakness. As the coming years would show, egos and backstabbing and incompetence and greed would all come to the fore in the group of people Vitalik started to assemble around him. He needed them, as they needed him. Yet it can be argued that the rather loose fashion in which Vitalik introduced his peers to Ethereum would in time come back to hurt him. That's because it led to an almost communal way of deciding who would become founders of the Ethereum project. Vitalik gave little thought to who would take on these important early roles other than choosing people who were excited and eager to help right from the start.

Looking back on the experience, as Vitalik spoke to me in 2019 at Seattle's convention center, he mused that "team dynamics is the thing that almost killed Ethereum on multiple occasions." As 2013 became 2014, however, he didn't have the benefit of hindsight, and he was about to find this out the hard way.

●　●　●

Organizing Toronto's first Bitcoin meetup in late 2012 marked the beginning of Anthony Di Iorio's involvement in the digital currency world, and he's been a busy boy ever since.

He created a Bitcoin gambling site called Satoshi Circle with a partner he met through a Reddit post. He had in the works a plan to create Decentral, a coworking space in Toronto that would offer people who wanted to jump into the digital-asset world a place to congregate and share ideas. And in 2013 he cofounded a Bitcoin wallet company with Steve Dakh called KryptoKit, which worked as an extension on the Chrome web browser. Wallets were as important to early Bitcoin users as web browsers had been to the Internet, Di Iorio believed; just as browsers made the Internet much easier to use, wallets would unlock Bitcoin for the general population.

KryptoKit came to market before its main competitor, Dark Wallet, which was still in its fundraising phase. Vitalik had a hand in both projects, as he had spent a few hours working on a JavaScript prototype of the Dark Wallet when he was hanging out with Amir Taaki. He also served as an adviser to Anthony on KryptoKit and later took an ownership stake in the company, according to an article in *Entrepreneur* magazine. (Vitalik didn't disclose that he'd worked on KryptoKit to readers of his *Bitcoin Magazine* story on the project in December 2013; he did disclose his association with Dark Wallet when he wrote about that a month earlier.)

The whole while Anthony had been buying Bitcoin, beginning with an $8,000 investment in 2012 when it traded for about $13. That would have given him around 600 Bitcoin. In early 2013 he sold Satoshi Circle for 3,000 Bitcoin, which he had to share with his partner, yet his stash had grown impressively. As the price hit $1,000 in late 2013 he found himself, like Vitalik, becoming a rich man from his passion project.

"I was the only one who had money of the founding five," Di Iorio said. "I put a lot into the early days of Ethereum and it was a crapshoot."

Also in 2013, Di Iorio started an educational and policy-focused group called the Bitcoin Alliance of Canada. As chief executive officer, he often traveled to conferences around the world, where he'd cross paths with Vitalik. When the Ethereum white paper landed in his email, Anthony quickly discovered the technical details were above his head. He turned to another developer he knew, Charles Hoskinson, for help.

The two had a lot in common. Hoskinson had also helped Anthony with KryptoKit, and he provided the Bitcoin Alliance of Canada with educational material he'd created through his association with the Bitcoin Education Project. Charles saw right away that Vitalik was on to something with his idea for a programmable blockchain. His first question was what Anthony and the others were planning to do with Ethereum. Anthony said they weren't sure but that they were discussing how to move forward in various Skype group chats. He invited Charles to join the weekly meetings they were holding.

"I joined the informal meeting, which became the Ethereum founders' group," Hoskinson said.

Amir Chetrit was also among the group of early Ethereum supporters who would go on to fund and organize the development of the Ethereum ecosystem. Vitalik had met Amir in Israel, where he was working on colored coin projects. Chetrit has a light presence on the web and couldn't be reached to talk about his part in the history of Ethereum. To distinguish between the two Amirs in his life – Amir Taaki and Amir Chetrit – Vitalik came up with nicknames for them. Taaki became "Anarchist Amir" while Chetrit was "Capitalist Amir."

By early December 2013, the four people who'd joined Vitalik's inner circle were Mihai Alisie, Anthony Di Iorio, Amir Chetrit, and Charles Hoskinson. For the first few weeks the group Skype chat consisted of debate over how they could actually go about creating a cryptocurrency. They batted around ideas, but it soon became clear that they needed to meet in person to hash things out. Anthony planned to attend the North American Bitcoin Conference in Miami in January, and he suggested to the group that they all rent a house together. The cast of characters was about to get much larger. As they descended on the Miami house, the buzz about this new Ethereum thing started to build within the blockchain world.

•   •   •

The two-story house on Bay Harbor Drive opens onto Indian Creek Lake from its backyard and is only about 10 miles from downtown Miami. There are five bedrooms, a pool table, a bar, and 4,500 square feet, which makes the house a prime destination for bachelor parties and other large gatherings. You can swim with dolphins and manatee in the water just a few feet from the backyard. The Ritz-Carlton, the Palm restaurant, and Saks Fifth Avenue are all a short walk away, as is Surfside Beach on the Atlantic coast. But this wasn't a bachelor party, it was Ethereum's coming-out party, and Anthony had found the perfect place to host the newly formed group of supporters.

They turned it into a kind of nerd heaven: Whiteboards, laptops, and charger cords snaking away in every direction. Coding and coding and more coding. Debates late into the night about consensus protocols and proof-of-work. All of it fueled by pizza and beer and a fridge full of cold cuts. "The Ethereum House" quickly became the place to be for a certain set of attendees at the Bitcoin conference, most of whom had incidentally become rich thanks to Bitcoin's skyrocketing price.

In a wider context, the North American Bitcoin Conference in January 2014 can be seen as perhaps the first halcyon days of the Bitcoin world. It had been nearly five years to the day since Satoshi Nakamoto had mined the genesis block of Bitcoin, and many of the conference attendees had been dealing with bouts of self-doubt and a hurry-up-and-wait impatience. When was the rest of the world going to catch on to this unbelievable new thing they'd discovered? How many times did they have to explain to friends and family that yes, this thing made of ones and zeros actually *does* have intrinsic value? They were told over and over again that they were fools for throwing their money away. They were dismissed. And then, the price began to rise, and it didn't seem to be due to speculation alone.

In November 2013, the US Senate had held hearings on Bitcoin that were seen as largely positive in terms of how regulators and law enforcement viewed the digital currency – the attitude had changed from hostility or mockery to curiosity, according to a report on the industry news site CoinDesk. The chairman of the Federal Reserve at the time, Ben Bernanke, wrote in a November 12 letter to Senator Thomas Carper that Bitcoin "may hold long term promise," CoinDesk reported. Well-known businesses like Overstock.com and the NBA basketball team the Sacramento Kings announced that they would start accepting Bitcoin for payment.

Four days before the Miami conference began, Marc Andreessen, one of the earliest and biggest Bitcoin bulls (his venture capital firm Andreessen Horowitz had invested about $50 million into Bitcoin startups, including the San Francisco–based crypto exchange Coinbase), wrote a *New York Times* op-ed extolling the virtues of Bitcoin. One of the features that most intrigued him was that Bitcoin allowed for strangers anywhere on Earth to trust each other – or, put another way, that Bitcoin now enabled transactions to occur in a trustless environment.

"Bitcoin gives us, for the first time, a way for one Internet user to transfer a unique piece of digital property to another Internet user, such that the transfer is guaranteed to be safe and secure, everyone knows that the transfer has taken place, and nobody can challenge the legitimacy of the transfer," Andreessen wrote in the *Times*. "The consequences of this breakthrough are hard to overstate."

The largest Bitcoin exchange in the world, known as Mt. Gox, still hummed along at this point in early 2014, processing over 70 percent of all Bitcoin transactions in the world, according to the *Wall Street Journal*.

There had been black eyes, of course, such as the seizure of the black market bazaar Silk Road and the arrest of its founder Ross Ulbricht. Bitcoin had been the coin of the realm on Silk Road. Then on the second day of the Miami conference, before he was scheduled to give a presentation, Bitcoin pioneer Charlie Shrem was arrested at JFK airport in New York for allegedly laundering $1 million worth of Bitcoin on behalf of Silk Road users and operating an unlicensed money-transmitting business.

Yet these shadows were dismissed for the most part. As the Miami conference commenced, the state of the Bitcoin world was one of increasing faith and optimism about what the future held. Not to mention wealth. This novelty that so many had dismissed as ephemeral for most of its existence was trading for over $800, making many of the early adopters – that is, the people who strode the Miami convention halls – very, very rich. It was one hell of a time to be introducing Ethereum to the world.

Of the original members of the Ethereum inner circle only Mihai hadn't come to Miami, as he couldn't obtain a Romanian visa in time to travel. But there were many new faces about, as Vitalik's white paper continued to pull people into the Ethereum orbit. Almost to a person, these new acolytes immediately understood the expansive possibilities that Vitalik had unlocked. These were the people – quite distinct from the Bitcoin diehards – who'd always known something more was possible, but maybe hadn't been able to put their finger on *what*, exactly. Joe Lubin fit this description perfectly.

Lubin had spent several decades in software development, working on varied projects like an automated composition tool for musicians and an early idea to let banks validate digital transactions using public- and private-key cryptography. A graduate of Princeton University, he later worked for Goldman Sachs as a software engineer, helping the bank build asset allocation and portfolio management tools to handle its clients' money. He started a hedge fund with a partner, where they bought and sold mutual fund shares. In a 2017 speech he spoke about experiencing the September 11 attack firsthand and recounted how he looked up as the Twin Towers were engulfed in flames, his eyes burning from the jet fuel in the air. "Curious fool that I was, I walked toward the event," he said in the speech. "I was about to be chased down the street by the pyroclastic flow that results when a very large building collapses on itself."

By the mid-2000s Lubin had begun to despair about the state of the global economy and society in general. September 11 had served as a wake-up call to many, he believed, and created a movement of people trying to rouse their fellow citizens from their slumber. Yet for whatever reason, it wasn't working. As the decade progressed, he grew increasingly depressed about what he saw all around him. He came very close to buying land in South America as an "escape plan."

"I felt we were living in a global society and economy that was figuratively, literally, and morally bankrupt," he said in his speech.

Then, in early 2011, he read Satoshi's white paper. "I had the epiphany so many in our space have had – decentralization was a game changer." What Bitcoin allowed – the way it cut out middlemen and gave power back to its users – was the salve Lubin's soul needed; his mood turned back from gloomy to its more natural optimistic state. "There was no reason to consider exit or escape, we could now focus on building, building better systems for a better future," he said.

While Satoshi gave the world the promise of decentralization, it took Vitalik's vision for Lubin to grasp the potential of creating scalable systems based on distributed blockchain networks. Now that promise could be about so much more than money. A native of Toronto, Joe had met Anthony Di Iorio and Vitalik at Decentral in early January 2014, around the time Anthony had unveiled one of the first Bitcoin ATMs in Canada. Soon after, like snow birds, they'd all flown south for the warmer climes of Miami.

About 10–12 people were living at the Ethereum House, and at any given time 15–20, or as many as 30, other people would be hanging out. "It was pretty electric," Joe said. "There was the general awareness that something big is happening." They planned to sell ether to the public the Tuesday after the conference ended, which would explain a good part of the enthusiasm of the Bitcoin adherents who flocked to the house. But others came too: people who wanted to be involved with helping to build the Ethereum ecosystem.

One of the guests at the Ethereum House was Morgen Peck, one of the best journalists around covering Bitcoin and blockchain technology. She'd met Joe in New York through LocalBitcoins, a way for people to buy or sell the cryptocurrency in face-to-face transactions rather than over the Internet. A week before the Miami conference, Joe emailed Morgen to tell her she had to come to Florida to learn about "the next big thing that's about to happen." Problem was, she was totally broke and could only afford airfare, so she asked if she could crash at the house.

"My poverty was what got me a seat in the front row," she said. She knew of Vitalik through his writing for *Bitcoin Magazine* but said, "he wasn't like some big name at all at that time." It became clear to Morgen right away, however, that power plays were already emerging among the people who surrounded Vitalik.

"It was pretty clear that everyone was trying to have their own sort of 'in' with Vitalik," she said. "They were treating him like their oracle." While there were other projects competing to push the boundaries of blockchain, the combination of Vitalik's extreme intelligence and thorough understanding of those projects set him apart. "He was it, you know?" Morgen said. "There were other people trying to bring big ideas into the mix. Vitalik was like the magnet. Totally. There was a special halo around him already."

In a wonderful story for *Wired* magazine in 2016, she recalled her time in Miami. She woke up to a quiet house after sleeping in a back hallway with a couch pillow and found the living room "blinking and whirring with technology." No one was awake but Vitalik. "He was sitting outside in a deck chair, working intensely," she wrote. "I didn't bother him, and he didn't say hello. But, I remember the impression he made on me at the time. This skeletal, 19-year-old boy, who was all limbs and joints, was hovering above his laptop like a preying [sic] mantis, delivering it nimble, lethal blows at an incredible speed."

Another new face at the house belonged to Anthony D'Onofrio. Better known in the crypto world by his social-media handle "texture," D'Onofrio for years dismissed his roommate's pleas to get into Bitcoin when you could buy it for a buck. Then he did some work that paid in Bitcoin, the price tanked, and he lost about $10,000. Still, he knew there was something to this weird kind of money, so on a four-hour road trip to see his girlfriend he ate some edible pot and binged on episodes of the *Let's Talk Bitcoin* podcast.

"I had a fully downloaded vision of the future. I just saw it," D'Onofrio said. Before his eyes, a world emerged where human beings coordinated in brand-new ways that had never been possible, all because of the decentralized nature of a blockchain system. "It was biblical," he said. In December 2013, he tracked down one of the hosts of the podcast, Adam Levine, who told him to check out Vitalik's white paper.

"That's how I got into Ethereum," D'Onofrio said. "I took drugs and saw the future."

Soon he was in a Skype chat with Vitalik, Charles Hoskinson, Levine, and others. A designer before he became a computer programmer, D'Onofrio took one look at the early Ethereum web site – a yellow background with text on top of it – and knew he could help the project's aesthetics. "In the beginning, I made sure Ethereum looked like a project worth believing in," he said.

He'd been involved with startups for 12 years before he discovered Ethereum and had seen a lot of failure, so he approached Vitalik and the new crew with some seasoned caution. He arrived in Miami a few days later than everyone else, but the energy in the air was noticeable. "This was the best time, feeling Ethereum was going to be something," he said. "We still trusted each other."

The first time he saw Vitalik was in the kitchen as he was intently studying his phone. "Okay, we all come here to hang out with you but you're fucking studying Chinese on your phone in the back room," texture said. "Cool. Guess we don't have to worry about you going to parties."

When he met Joe Lubin, D'Onofrio wondered if he was someone's dad because he came across as so quiet and calm.

Pretty soon, however, texture knew something was different at this startup. "It was supercharged," he said. "There was a moment I felt like I was tripping, like I was high on drugs, because the energy was so crazy."

As the cofounders met one another for the first time, an easy vibe developed. The Ethereum House was the place to be and they were at its center. "It felt like one big happy family where everyone was just chilling and getting along," Charles Hoskinson said. "We were all very hopeful." No agendas had yet emerged and no one was dug in, which made for an exciting atmosphere. "When you're in that kind of social dynamic it's like a party, everyone is having fun," he said.

When not studying Mandarin, Vitalik had several roles to fulfill in Miami. The first was to wrangle the programmers, designers, and others who had gathered at the house into working out exactly what Ethereum stood for and how it would be organized. For his second act, he was to unveil Ethereum for the first time to the public in a talk at the North American Bitcoin Conference in only a few days.

They played pool and drank beer and ate pizza and threw a party the first night they were in the house. The vibe seemed more social than anything, a chance to meet all these new people and see if they could make a go of it. When Anthony Di Iorio invited Charles Hoskinson to the Miami house, he'd said, "Let's try to bring as many people as we can, let's just meet up, see if we're assholes or if we like each other. If we like each other let's go ahead and try to do something."

Only a few blockchain projects at the time had built entirely new software systems to support their work. BitShares, created by Dan Larimer, was one such system. NXT was another. But most work at the time was either done by taking the Bitcoin code and changing it somehow – known as "forking Bitcoin" – or involved adding layers to the Bitcoin protocol (like MasterCoin had done). In early 2014, starting a blockchain from scratch was daunting.

"The white paper was very raw, there wasn't a lot of information about how to do things," Charles said. The team debated whether they should follow suit and build Ethereum on top of an existing blockchain or go all in and build their own. And they debated the philosophy of Ethereum. What did it stand for? Would it be a world computer or simply a better Bitcoin? "We were trying to find our bearings as a project and decide what we wanted to build," Charles said.

One strong voice in this debate came from Gavin Wood. A British computer programmer (who, you may recall, has very strong opinions about how decentralized applications can bring more trust and freedom to society), Wood initially dismissed Bitcoin as merely a new type of currency, before realizing in 2013 that blockchain technology could affect deep change. He contacted Vitalik in December to offer his C++ coding abilities after reading the white paper. This was exactly the type of person Vitalik had hoped to attract. As the Ethereum team at the Miami house debated what they wanted their new blockchain to stand for, Gavin coined the term *alegality*. Charles explained the definition as, "It can't be evil, basically. The code has to follow the instructions. So there was a lot of that, of philosophical fact-finding."

Gavin had mixed feelings as he arrived to meet the group. On the one hand, he met some cool people like Anthony D'Onofrio. On the other, he wasn't impressed with the level of technical ability he encountered.

"Others were enjoying the house and cracking more than a few beers," he said. "I was mostly working on writing code to get the thing built." It also seemed that the leadership roles were a bit soft. "There was a rather substantial lack of alignment on quite fundamental issues, like who was a 'founder,'" Gavin said. The surroundings, though, were pretty sweet. "That beach house with a pool table and dolphins to swim with was pretty impressive, even if there were 16 people stuffed into it," he said.

The team also soon discovered that selling ether to the public required far more care and attention to detail than they had anticipated. Several nuts-and-bolts issues stood in their way, such as how could people buy ether with Bitcoin? Would they just post a Bitcoin address for people to use?

"It didn't take us very long to realize that we didn't have a sales mechanism," Joe Lubin said. They also hadn't figured out how to store the Bitcoin they would receive, which is one of the trickiest and most dangerous security issues to confront when using Bitcoin. One wrong move and a hacker could steal it all. Finally, and crucially, both Joe and Charles raised the specter of US regulatory authorities like the SEC. Its lawyers are very picky, it turns out, about companies issuing unregistered securities to American investors.

"That launched a fairly long process," Joe said. They ended up hiring law firm Pryor Cashman to advise them, and spoke to Joseph Grundfest, a law professor at Stanford University who is a former SEC commissioner. Grundfest recalled receiving a few phone calls from the Ethereum team, but he doesn't remember who they were. While he declined to take Ethereum on as a client, he did offer some advice.

"I emphasized that they would have to either comply with SEC rules or avoid US jurisdiction," he said. "There is no other way to operate, in my view." Grundfest noted that the challenge for startups in the crypto world – whether in 2014 or now – is that "the law is less than clear in many but not all respects." He said the Ethereum team took the news well and didn't try to argue with him. "They seemed genuinely interested in understanding the relevant law, and that's the reason I gave them more time than others that called me in that same time period," Grundfest said. "Many of the others were either just talking nonsense or trying to sell something that they should have known would never fly."

At the end of their conversations, Grundfest said he was offered to be paid in ether for his time. He declined.

All this legal stuff meant the team wouldn't be hitting pay dirt as soon as they expected to. The ether sale would have to wait until they had confidence that the SEC wouldn't come after them; they also needed to build the infrastructure to hold the actual sale. Anthony Di Iorio and Joe would need to reach into their pockets for several more months to keep the project afloat financially.

That's not to say real cash hadn't already been spent. Anthony and Joe had already pledged huge amounts of their own money to subsidize Ethereum development. In the beginning Anthony had loaned the project about $400,000 worth of Bitcoin and paid all the expenses at Decentral in Toronto, which had become the temporary home of Ethereum. The terms he received were eye popping – as long as Ethereum went on to be a success. For every Bitcoin he lent the foundation, he would receive 3,000 ether. In the first investment phase Anthony loaned around 4,000 Bitcoin to the effort, giving him the right to 12 million ether.

Considering what everyone had seen with the recent spike in Bitcoin's price, Anthony understood that while he was taking a large risk with the money he lent to Ethereum he stood to make a huge payoff. Even if ether only traded for $10 once it was created, his stake would be worth $120 million (on paper, at least). At its highest price in January 2018, ether topped $1,400. Do the math: that's $16.8 billion in Anthony Di Iorio's bank account. He had no idea it would go that high in 2014, but you could say he had billions of reasons to push as hard as he could to ensure the commercial success of Ethereum.

But Anthony wasn't the only one funding Ethereum's early development. Joe Lubin had a huge role as well. Joe loves to talk about the technical details of decentralized systems as much as he hates to talk about himself. Getting him to open up about his personal life and family is incredibly hard. Maybe it's his nature as a Canadian to be polite and reserved and to refrain from speaking about how he financed early Ethereum development. But he declined to give me details about how much actual money he put up.

Anthony has his own ideas about Joe's involvement. Di Iorio estimates that in total, between $850,000 and $1 million was spent developing Ethereum before the ether sale in mid-2014. According to Di Iorio, Lubin's deal wasn't quite as good as his own: Di Iorio said Lubin received 2,000 ether for every Bitcoin he lent the project. That means Anthony's capital contribution equaled about 40 percent of the total and Joe put in about 55 percent, but even at the lower ether-to-Bitcoin loan ratio, Lubin was in for billions as well.

To be fair, filthy lucre pervaded every aspect of the crypto world in 2014. The stakes of the potential wealth involved with the Ethereum project would have been lost on no one at the North American Bitcoin Conference in Miami. Outrageous displays of riches seemed like a rite of passage. Morgen Peck remembered seeing a car being auctioned in front of the hotel where the conference took place. A year earlier she'd attended the Bitcoin conference in San Jose and it had had none of this flagrant, conspicuous consumption about it.

"Miami was so indulgent," she said. "It was like nothing, too, they hadn't like called an event, it was just an impromptu auctioning in front of the conference center," she said. Here was another face of the Bitcoin world: spending $300,000 on a sports car on a whim.

● ● ●

On Sunday, January 26, 2014, Vitalik Buterin took the stage at half past 10 in the morning. Listed in the program as "head writer at *Bitcoin Magazine*" he strode to the podium in a black T-shirt that read ethereum. org in white lowercase letters. Before this, Vitalik had always been part of the audience at conferences, listening to the kinds of speeches he was about to deliver. Sure, he'd been on a panel discussion here and there, but nothing like this, where he alone had to explain this entirely new blockchain he'd invented to a curious audience. He got off to a rocky start to boot. He had to be shown how to move his presentation slides forward. Then his microphone didn't work. "One two three, okay," he said. Now the audience could hear him. So, he began.

Visibly nervous, he gave an introduction to what Bitcoin had enabled in terms of trustless global transactions. His eyes cut from side to side as though he expected at any moment to get rushed off stage. *Sorry, sir, this Ethereum thing is all a big hoax.* Yet as his talk progressed, he warmed to the material. He had a friendly audience. Joe Lubin, Charles Hoskinson, and other Ethereum supporters sat in the front. By the end of his talk, his demeanor had changed. As he had in the white paper, he listed the potential uses for Ethereum – crop insurance, decentralized exchanges, and DAOs. In the flow, and like a far more seasoned speaker than the 19-year-old novice he was, he echoed the *Terminator* joke he'd made in the white paper. Ethereum could be used to build all these things, he said, "and, perhaps, maybe even Skynet."

In just under 25 minutes he was transformed from a respected member of the Bitcoin community into something much larger.

"There was incredible pressure on him, you could feel it," Morgen Peck said. The heroic nature of Vitalik's speech and the atmosphere surrounding it has gained quite a bit of mythos and grandeur as the years have worn on. I've been told countless times that he received a standing ovation and that there wasn't an empty seat in the house; that it was three people deep at the back of the room. Those are great details, but they aren't true. As a YouTube video posted by user "thales" shows, many seats were empty, and while the audience did clap and cheer for Vitalik when he was done, they stayed seated.

The audience, though, had questions. So many questions that when Vitalik went out into the hall, he was surrounded by people wanting to know more. He'd caught their attention. And in the case of Dan Larimer, the founder of Ethereum competitor BitShares, that meant it was time to pose some tough questions to Vitalik.

The back and forth ended up on YouTube a few weeks later. Clearly, Larimer had a bit of a setup in mind for Vitalik. But his questions were good and tough and homed in on problems with Ethereum that it's still dealing with today. For Larimer, who coined the term *decentralized autonomous corporation*, to pick up on those issues so quickly is a testament to his own understanding of how hard it can be to build blockchains from scratch, as he'd done with BitShares. He wanted to know how Ethereum could handle the scale of the number of transactions Vitalik had said it would be able to do, like supporting gambling sites and verifying digital identity and maybe allowing Skynet to end humanity.

Larimer pressed Vitalik on his statement that some of the data Ethereum would access would be stored offline, away from the main blockchain network. Vitalik stumbled through an answer that wasn't too convincing. Vitalik has a hard time making eye contact with anyone, even when he's feeling unstoppable. Here, his eyes reverted back to the nervous shifting they'd exhibited at the beginning of his talk. His mojo had been knocked back. Joe and Anthony Di Iorio stood next to Vitalik as he spoke to Larimer. Lubin looked like he wanted to be anywhere in the world other than in that spot at that moment.

Vitalik knew Larimer was gunning for him, and the two don't see eye to eye to this day. But still, Larimer's questions allowed that internal voice within Vitalik to pipe up.

"I definitely had some doubts. Maybe he's right in that it's more efficient to have specialized blockchain features for specialized applications," Vitalik said. He'd come too far by then, though, to let a few hard questions dissuade him from his approach. "If I had to bet on one thing or the other, I'd still bet on the generalized approach."

Vitalik was learning tough lessons in public, a hard thing for anyone, let alone someone who would celebrate turning 20 in a few days. His youthfulness is maybe the strongest aspect of Vitalik's mythos. It was impossible to read anything about him back then – or since – that didn't mention his astoundingly young age right away. He's one of those blessed people who know very early on what they want to do with their lives: like a novelist in their early 20s, or Trent Alexander-Arnold, the footballer who started at right back for Liverpool at 19, the same age Vitalik was when he invented Ethereum. I have always had a special kind of envy of these people, a jealousy within all my other selves: why hadn't I known what to devote myself to through the turbulent but creatively powerful teenage years? It very well may have taken the invincible assurance of a teenager to dream up Ethereum and then make it happen.

And then, along the way, Vitalik and all his friends and colleagues got incredibly rich. When your idea not only succeeds but adds many new zeros at the end of your checking account – or, come on, to your digital wallet – what does that do to the bravura of a someone who can't legally enter a bar in the US? The fact that Vitalik handled that pressure with such aplomb is testament to how grounded he's always been – to how Dmitry, Maia, and Natalia raised a son who was radically equipped to draw from many different disciplines to achieve his goal. That's not to say he always knew what he was doing, or that it was easy.

"I was definitely inexperienced," he said. "And I totally did not realize the scale of the project. When I started Ethereum I thought I would just do it for a couple of months and then go back to university."

The world was in on the Ethereum secret now, though. There was no going back.

Ten

Afew hours after my meeting with the Swiss man I was back in the room in the apartment I was renting in Zürich. It was a modern building in a quiet part of the city and had a good view of the street three stories below. It was raining that evening.

I remember the pause in the conversation while the man read the encrypted message. I'd stopped taking notes, but my digital recorder was on.

He said he'd never seen the message before. When I asked him if the address the message was sent from belonged to him, he said he couldn't remember all the things they were doing back then. Fair enough: it had been over three years. And yet he didn't strongly deny that he had something to do with the message and the theft. I was accusing him of stealing a rather large amount of ether and at first he mostly seemed reticent. Like he didn't want to say something wrong.

He began to warm up a bit when he said I really should be looking into some of the people in the Robin Hood Group. They knew more than anyone about the DAO and the attack. This was a suspicion I'd heard from many people, that the DAO was an inside job. It had to be, right? Look how complicated it was. Surely the guys at slock.it or their associates planted the bug. It was on line 666, for Pete's sake: that can't be a coincidence.

I'd always rejected this theory and had never come across any evidence to make me think it was true. But he was talking a bit more now, so I listened.

"I actually feel humbled that you give me so much credit," he said. He thanked me for thinking he could pull off such a sophisticated attack. He asked to see all the information I had gathered, and I said I'd email it to him. Then, he left.

I didn't know what I'd learned, to be honest. It seemed like a weak denial at best. As I stared out the window of my room on the Zürich street below, I noticed a man standing outside of the Italian restaurant across the street. He looked like the man I'd interviewed earlier that day. I went to the living room, which led to an outdoor terrace, and looked from that vantage. It could be him, I thought. He had a common Swiss build for an older man. *Stout* is the term, I believe. And he wasn't going into the restaurant but standing under its awning to get out of the rain, just looking across the street.

I'd been warned that there were some unsavory characters linked to the DAO attack. One of my sources told me that there were a few people who held enormous sums of DAO tokens, but said it would be dangerous to name them. Their money came from scary and shady places, I was told.

I went back to my room and turned off the light. Hoping to see better in the dark, I still couldn't tell if the man across the street was the same man that I'd accused of being the ether thief. I had to go and see for myself.

Once at street level, I could see from across the way that it wasn't him. I crossed the street and walked right past the person, just to be absolutely sure, and because I was hungry and wanted to get dinner.

I'd been wrong about the man, just as I was wrong about the person I'd interviewed earlier that day at the Bloomberg bureau. In the coming weeks I learned that he wasn't actually associated with the Ethereum address that had sent the encrypted message. While this happens from time to time in journalism, it's still devastating. My source had gotten it wrong, and only after looking at a fuller transaction history in 2019 did my source see how the mistake had been made. There were many more links between accounts as ether or other crypto was moved around both before and during the DAO attack. What had looked simple in 2016 was now significantly more complicated. The capability of blockchain forensics was significantly less advanced in 2016, and so I had questioned an innocent man.

But just because I'd been wrong didn't mean I stopped looking. With better data comes better clues, and the original ether thief, the one who stole $55 million, and the copycats, were still unknown.

Eleven

The original DAO attack stopped after about seven hours, and by that time the thief had 3.69 million ether in his account, which was now being called the Dark DAO. That equaled about 30 percent of the digital currency held in the DAO right before the attack. No one understood why the thief had stopped, whether it had been intentional or if the attack contract had stopped working. What everyone did know, however, was that the thief could start again, or copycats could try their luck. That's because the attack contract that held the lines of code the thief had used could be viewed on the blockchain by anyone who knew where to look. The blueprint for the hack had been left in the public domain.

No one was more aware of this threat than members of the Robin Hood Group. They'd all been working against the attack in various ways since its first moments; on Sunday, a group of five or six of them gathered for a call using the voice chat app Mumble. They called in from South America, Germany, and the UK.

It was mid-evening for Alex Van De Sande, or avsa, as he jumped on the call from his apartment in Rio de Janerio. Like everyone else he had bought DAO tokens. He wanted this thing to work, wanted it to help fuel the growth of Ethereum and prove that decentralized systems could be a match for any centralized model. When he found out that the DAO was being attacked, he turned to his wife and said, "Remember when I was telling you about that huge unhackable pile of money?" She nodded. "It's been hacked," he said.

In fact, one of the first things he thought about when he saw the DAO being hacked was that he should get his 100,000 tokens out. That amounted to about $15,000 at the time. Avsa was the lead developer on the Mist wallet, the Ethereum application that let everyone interact with the blockchain. He'd need to be in his Mist account to do anything, in other words, yet as he tried to log on there was a glitch. He couldn't imagine the frustration that everyone in the Ethereum world would be feeling right now if they were being locked out from moving ether or initiating other functions on the blockchain. That's when he realized he needed to help fight the DAO attacker or to do something for the larger community, rather than worrying about his own pocketbook.

The attack was only a few hours old on the Friday in June when avsa reached out to Griff, whom he knew would be in the middle of any response effort, and the RHG began to take shape. This was when Griff was asking DAO users in the split contracts to identify themselves. The idea the group agreed upon was to find a friendly split, join it, and then launch the same attack the bad guy had used. That way, they could "steal" the remaining ether in the DAO and protect it until they could give it back to everyone. They would use avsa's 100,000 DAO tokens to fuel their attack. The more tokens you have, the faster the drain is, and they wanted to get the ether out as quickly as they could.

Griff found a guy in Germany who was willing to identify himself, so at least Griff could put a name with a random Ethereum address. The German said he'd be willing to let the RHG use his split to begin their attack. By this time Lefteris had been able to replicate the attack con-tract. Then the question of who would actually initiate the attack came up, and the group had its first debate.

"But who pushes the button?" Alex said. "Because someone has to push the button." They realized that if they used Alex's 100,000 DAO tokens it could easily be traced back to him, so he should be the one to go public. Lefteris created the attack contract they would use if they suc-cessfully got into a split. All the while the clock was running. That's because the German guy's split function would close when its time ran out (remember, all split functions only ran for a certain amount of time). If Alex wasn't in it by then, they'd lose this chance.

With 25 minutes remaining until the split closed, Alex loaded their account with the DAO tokens and the attack contract. The good-guy hackers coordinated over Skype in a group call named Robin Hood. Then they were finally ready to go.

"Okay, everyone, let's go rob a bank!" Alex said, as he was about to execute the attack. "Not everyone really appreciated the humor," he told me later.

As he stood ready to execute the good-guy attack, his Internet failed. His router was dead. The split was set to close in mere minutes.

"I was like, what the fuck is going on here?" avsa said. His Skype connection still worked, so he told the group what was happening. Someone else needed to take over and finish entering the split. At the same time he was on the phone with his Internet provider, speaking to a robot.

The robot said in a mechanical voice, "We see there's an Internet issue in your neighborhood." He could not believe this was happening. The RHG had created a robot, the attack contract, to attack another robot, the DAO, and here avsa was on the phone with a robot that was telling him what he already knew about his blown Internet connection. Then the German guy's split closed. They'd missed their chance.

"I had this feeling that I'm going to be the guy to save the day," Alex said. "And then it's a shitty feeling of failing." He went out to walk his dog Sapic. It was Friday night in Rio and the DAO was still under attack.

"That was day one," he said.

● ● ●

The next morning, he woke up and went grocery shopping and did normal Saturday morning stuff. He got back in touch with the RHG but found people were busy with their kids or running errands or other stuff. It was a low point for the RHG.

"We felt like the worst hackers in history, we were foiled by bad Internet and family commitments," Alex said.

The next day, Sunday morning, Alex had to get up early. His wife Fernanda is an anesthesiologist and had to be in surgery at 5 a.m. Avsa wanted to make her breakfast before she left. With his wife off to work, he looked online and saw Griff was logged on. Luckily no second attack had begun, but they both knew that could change at any moment, so they identified several split proposals that were open and joined them all. They were finally in, and now they just had to wait for the splits to close so they could launch their attack to safeguard the remaining 70 percent of ether in the DAO.

With so much activity, and so much money still at risk, the RHG decided to get on the Mumble call that Sunday evening to coordinate. I was able to get hold of the recording of the call they made as they spoke for about an hour, which I quote from here.

There were still questions about how the actual attack would work, or if it would work, that they needed to discuss. One of the developers on the call was Fabian Vogelsteller, who'd helped Alex create the Mist wallet.

"We do need to finish this to a technical level," Fabian said to the group. "Right now the DAO is open to everybody: it's like prey in the woods with 20 wolves around it, and we're just waiting for the next one to run in and eat the prey." They were under pressure, sure, but there was still lingering doubt about the legality of what they were contemplating.

"On the other hand," Fabian said, "it might put the person who does it – in this case Alex – into a legal focus." The worst-case scenario, the one that the RHG wanted to avoid, was an endless fight with the attacker to get the money back. They didn't know if they could get into a friendly split: maybe the attacker had already joined all the available splits. If he had, that would give the attacker some control over the money that the RHG rescued. Think of the split as a lifeboat: you don't want to be in one with a maniac as you drift in the middle of the ocean. They wanted their own lifeboat. But being stuck with a maniac would be the DAO equivalent of the rescued funds being frozen and everyone losing. This potential standoff is where the name *DAO Wars* originated.

"That is a very likely scenario," Lefteris said in response to Fabian's concern about the endless fight. "I mean, that's how it's going to end." He was afraid if they left the DAO open, with its vulnerability known to the world, they'd soon be facing a thousand ether thieves, not just one.

They were also unsure if the DAO tokens they were committing to fund the RHG attack would be used up, or spent, in the attack. They had value, of course, and the group should know if spent tokens would be the price they had to pay to rescue the remaining ether. Lefteris was almost certain the DAO tokens wouldn't be used up – or burned, in code parlance – in the attack.

He laughed and said, "You guys do understand that I wrote this contract only on Friday and I haven't looked at it since then because I was also busy with other blog posts and trying to manage the community? So I don't promise anything about not losing tokens, even though we know the code says so."

Avsa said he would be okay if his DAO tokens were lost in the attack, but if they were going to risk someone's two million DAO tokens, they should be sure of what they were doing.

"Okay, so what's the consensus?" Lefteris said. "How do you guys feel?"

"Right now we have a huge open hackfest – how do you call it?" Fabian said. "Everybody can just come and take whatever he wants." They'd already seen copycat attacks, like one that day where a hacker seemed to be testing out an attack contract, but no one had yet gone so far as to steal ether.

"The bug has been talked about enough so that anyone can figure out how to re-create it," avsa said. "How would we feel if we wake up tomorrow and someone had emptied the DAO?"

"Losing everything would be devastating," Fabian said.

The RHG had created its own split contract Friday night, but that wouldn't be ready to use for seven days. They also talked about making proposals to the DAO community to create a contract to move all the ether to a safe place. Again, though, that would take two weeks, and by then they feared the DAO would be empty.

"That's the fucking problem here," Fabian said.

"I'm willing to do it if you guys want," Alex said.

"Alex, you're taking a lot of responsibility on you," Fabian said. "Will you be the one that then announces if it's successful that, 'here, look that's what we did as white hat hackers to save the tokens?'"

"Maybe I'm being dumb here, I don't know," Alex said from his apartment in Rio. "But I just feel it would be the best solution."

"You're also very far away from the Western world," Fabian said, "so you're safe there."

"I think there's police here, I've heard," avsa replied.

"Yeah, but they don't know about the Internet yet," Fabian said.

Another issue had to do with how many DAO tokens they could get their hands on to fuel their attack. The more tokens you use, the more multiplied the hack becomes. Avsa was on the phone with a big DAO token holder that evening, and Stephan Tual told the group that he was trying to speak to someone who held an enormous number of tokens.

"We have a problem," Lefteris said to the group. "You have voted with the same account in all the other splits."

"Yes," avsa said. "What's the issue?"

"We can't transfer the tokens out," Lefteris said.

"What do you mean?" avsa said.

"The transfer would fail." Alex caught on quickly. If you vote on two or more splits using the same Ethereum account, you get locked out. All the splits Alex had joined earlier that day when he found Griff online were useless. Except for one split, actually: it just happened to be the last one avsa had joined, and it closed in 33 hours. Add another blunder to the growing list. It really is a wonder, realizing what these guys pulled off despite themselves.

About 20 minutes later, Fabian spotted something none of them wanted to see.

"By the way, guys, I'm just looking at the DAO contract now," he said. "It seems like an attacker is working on here."

"Right now?" avsa said.

"We have three new transactions that are doing recursive calls," Fabian said.

Lefteris sighed and said, "This is why I said the DAO will be empty by next week."

Fabian said the transactions looked like someone was testing the hack, using small amounts of ether to pay for it and going very slowly.

Alex got to work to create the account and contract needed to launch their counterattack. But for now, they'd have to wait.

● ● ●

As avsa was on the conference call with the rest of the group, he took a minute to call a friend on a different phone. Ryan Zurrer was on the other end of the line.

Ryan met Alex after he'd posted an Ethereum meetup invitation and Alex had been the only one to show up. They thought they might be the first people in South America into Ethereum, not least of all because Argentina was full of hardcore Bitcoin followers. Back then they'd have lunch at a Peruvian restaurant and talk Ethereum. By mid-2016, Ryan knew his passion for Ethereum had overcome his will to remain as the chief executive of a Brazilian renewable energy company. He took three weeks off to go to an Ethereum developer conference in Shanghai, came back, and told his board of directors he was quitting.

"My intention was to work for the DAO," he said. He envisioned finding good investments from DAO proposals and working amid the slew of startups, just as a venture capitalist would. Except in this case, you'd be working for a bunch of automated code, not a guy in a sweater vest. Zurrer would go on to become a founder of Polychain Capital, one of the most successful early cryptocurrency investment funds. But he only did so because the DAO blew up.

On that day, when avsa reached Zurrer on his phone he found him at Rio's Praia do Pepê beach, near where Zurrer lived. He'd gone kite-surfing that day, but the conditions weren't good so he sat on the beach. His girlfriend lay next to him, having just applied coconut oil all over her body.

Avsa explained that he was working with Jordi Baylina, a Spanish Ethereum developer, on a way to secure the remaining ether in the DAO, but that they could get it out much faster if they had a ton of DAO tokens. Zurrer said "of course" and didn't think twice about pledging 500,000 DAO tokens on the spot.

"I turned over to my girlfriend, and spanked her on the bum, because you know Brazil hadn't really gone through the whole #MeToo thing.

Or it certainly hadn't at that time," Ryan said. "I said, 'come on, I've got to go home and send this Spanish guy my tokens.'" A few minutes later Zurrer had ponied up about $75,000 worth of DAO tokens to help the RHG.

Between avsa and Ryan's tokens, they now had 600,000. Then on the Sunday call with the RHG, someone offered to let them use one million DAO tokens. This was good news for the group and would let them shotgun-blast the DAO in order to save it.

• • •

On Tuesday, four days after the initial attack, a second one began. And this was no test.

Since their call on Sunday, the RHG had managed to successfully join a split. There was no block on this one, they were good to go, and the split closed with them in it. Still, they had qualms about how the rest of the Ethereum community would view their plan to steal $110 million worth of ether in order to save it. (The value of the ether inside the DAO had dropped with the fall in ether's price; on June 21, 2016, ether was valued at $13.31, with 8.25 million ether left in the DAO.) This is when avsa sent his DO NOT PANIC tweet.

Now with a second attack under way, their reticence was made moot. The RHG had no choice but to attack the DAO itself.

The Tuesday attack came from an address different from the one used for the original theft on Friday. By necessity, it used the same vulnerability to attack the DAO, yet it stole ether at a slower pace than the attack four days before had. A good omen for the RHG. One of the new attack accounts was 0x15DEF77337168d707E47E68aB9f7F6c17126b562, but we'll call it 0x15def for short. It was first funded when 2 ether were sent to it the day before by address 0x35f5 (shortened for simplicity). And 0x35f5 received its funding from 0x4fae on June 19, when 77.15 ether were sent to it from the exchange ShapeShift. This might seem confusing, but stick with me, it's an important chain of events.

When 0x15def started its attack, it only pulled in 5.8 ether per transaction. That was small potatoes compared to the attack on Friday that had topped out at pulling in 138 ether at a time. Then the attack ramped up and 0x15def was stealing 58 ether at a time. Then it went for broke and tried to take 429 ether at a time, but the attack contract had run out of gas. The thief had gotten sloppy and should have known to keep the contract loaded with gas. On Etherscan, the Ethereum blockchain explorer that keeps all the transaction records, there's a red sad-face emoji next to the explanation that the contract is out of ether. Remember: on Ethereum, no gas, no go.

Then the attacker reloaded the contract and went for broke again. This time it worked, and he was pulling in 429 ether at a time, which was worth about $5,700. But what made the DAO bug so bad was that it wasn't just one theft of 429 ether at a time. Remember the bank teller analogy: The ether thief was going down a line of bank tellers and asking each to withdraw money, but before getting the money he was moving on to the next teller. So the last teller at the end gives him the total of what he'd asked for, even though his account balance didn't cover the withdrawal.

In the attack recorded in Ethereum block 1746236, for example, on June 21, 2016, at 19:04:19 UTC, the thief pulled out 30 batches of 429 ether each, or 12,870 ether in total. That was worth $171,299 at the ether price that day. In one transaction. Six minutes later, 0x15def did it all over again. As long as he didn't let the contract run out of gas, he could do this all day.

What started slow had now become very fast, and 0x15def became a huge problem for the RHG.

● ● ●

As the good-guy hackers worked mostly in secret, the rest of the Ethereum community debated what to do about the DAO in public.

A quick review. There were two immediate responses possible for Ethereum users: they could either blacklist the addresses that were stealing ether from the DAO or change the history of the blockchain to make it as though the DAO never existed. These are both protocol changes, meaning they have to be approved by the majority of people running Ethereum on their computers. The changes are made in a software update. Users would "vote" yes for the changes by agreeing to the update. If you didn't support the change, you could "vote" no by not running the update.

But when the protocol is changed, it sends the blockchain in a new direction, which is called a "fork." A fork in the road, and blockchain communities can choose to take the path less trodden. Or not.

The option that blacklists addresses is known as a soft fork. This would freeze the ether in those accounts, basically, and isolate it so that it lost its value.

The option that changes the history of the blockchain is known as a hard fork and is one of the more contentious issues in the blockchain community. This began with Satoshi Nakamoto and the breakthrough he made with Bitcoin. Because every Bitcoin transaction is recorded and maintained by its blockchain, the problem of double spending is no longer an issue. Double spending had foiled previous e-cash projects, because if you can't prove that the digital coins you sent to me weren't already sent to someone else, those coins will have no value. Or put another way: maybe you just made those coins up and are trying to pass them off to me for a price. Bitcoin eliminated these possibilities by having its blockchain network check the history of every Bitcoin sent over its network. If the Bitcoin I'm sending to my mom can't be verified by the Bitcoin network as belonging to me based on that Bitcoin's transaction history, then my mom won't be getting any Bitcoin from me. Sorry, mom.

So the historical element of what a blockchain does is critical. Bitcoin's more fervent followers, who are derisively referred to as Bitcoin maximalists, hold fast to the idea that the blockchain history can never be changed, no matter what error or problem you are trying to fix.

It was 3:30 in the afternoon in Shanghai when the DAO attack began. Vitalik was staying at the apartment of Bo Shen, the founder of Fenbushi Capital, one of the first blockchain-only investment firms. Shen had been working with Dan Larimer's BitShares project and Vitalik had been trying to get him to come over to Ethereum instead for months. But now he had a much larger problem to deal with.

He got a Skype message that something was wrong with the DAO and he checked it to see it was draining ether. He pinged Christoph Jentzsch to ask if there was a reason for a split to be taking out so much ether, but within an hour he realized it was an attack. He organized a call with Christoph, Gavin Wood, and Jeff Wilcke to talk about how they could combat the hack. The first good news they got was that Christoph had designed the DAO to hold any money that left in a split for 27 days. So there was time to organize a response. But what response?

They spoke for an hour and a half, including a discussion about how someone needed to write a blog post on the Ethereum Foundation web site to tell everyone in the community what they were doing about the DAO. The choice seemed clear – either a soft fork or a hard fork – so Vitalik began talking to people about which method they preferred. Early on, about 80 percent of the people Vitalik spoke to supported a soft fork, with fewer wanting the hard fork. Vitalik knew a hard fork would cause the most controversy.

"A hard fork is definitely more icky," he said. It would leave a stain on Ethereum's history, but was there a better choice? "I value immutability, but I never valued it infinitely," Vitalik said.

That would be a decision the entire Ethereum community would have to make collectively. And they had a few weeks to sort it out.

● ● ●

As the race was on to drain the DAO – on one side, the attacker who struck Tuesday, June 21, on the other, the RHG – it really came down to the firepower each side possessed. Thanks to the cohesion, generosity, and unity of the Ethereum community, the DAO attacker got his ass handed to him.

By the time they were done soliciting, six million DAO tokens had been donated to help fuel the good-guy attack. That compares to less than 100,000 DAO tokens the attacker had to drain ether. But it was the scale of the withdrawals that was truly amazing. The RHG was able to pull more than 1.2 million ether from the DAO in a single transaction. At that rate the RHG emptied the DAO of its remaining ether in only a few hours. The June 21 attacker ended up stealing 268,320 ether. Assuming they are not the same person, and I don't think they are, the June 21 attack was the second-largest after the original DAO attacker got away with 3.69 million.

But just when the RHG thought they were safe, avsa and the other members discovered something terrible. The attacker was in the split where the RHG had collected all the ether in their counterattack.

Avsa compared it to the ending of the movie *Alien* when Sigourney Weaver's character has left the mother ship in an escape pod. The DAO is the mother ship, the split function the escape pod. The RHG hadn't had a choice about what split they entered to start their attack; they didn't have time to make sure there were only friendly people in it. As they looked closer, they realized they had a huge problem.

"It really looks like that's an attacker" in their split, avsa said. "We escaped the mother ship but now we're alone in space with the alien we were trying to escape," he said. The attacker had the same powers that the RHG had, in other words, since they shared the same split. "Everything we can do to safeguard that money we took out, he could do too."

That meant every time the RHG moved the money from the original split to a safe place, the attacker could follow them, and this would be repeated over and over. "The game only ends when one of these parties doesn't show up to fight," Alex said. "The DAO Wars had begun."

Twelve

As the Miami Bitcoin conference wound to a close, one of the final tasks the cofounders had set for themselves concerned how the ether they were going to create out of thin air would be distributed.

The plan, as established in the white paper, involved creating a certain amount of ether that would be distributed in two ways. The first pot of ether was simply conjured out of nothing. Known as a pre-mined cryptocurrency, this ether would be doled out to the founders and other people who helped get the project off the ground. A portion of the pre-mined ether would also be sold directly to people via a crowdsale. Ether would also be created to reward the computers that mine blockchain transactions, just as in the Bitcoin system. But unlike ether, no pre-mined

Bitcoins were ever distributed; from its origin, the only way to create new Bitcoin has been to mine it.

So there was a large pile of play money that had to be divided among a diverse group of people who had just met each other – what could go wrong?

Vitalik remembered arguments in Miami centered around this question, and around whether the cofounder's group should be expanded beyond the original five people.

"I kept trying to increase the shares of some people who had less and add other people in," Vitalik said, referring to the shares of ether to be allotted. "Charles had to fight to get Gavin and Jeff into the leadership team under the same status as the original five," he said.

That's Jeff Wilcke he's referring to, who in December had contacted Vitalik to point out what he perceived to be an error or two in the white paper, as well as to ask a few questions. Here was another developer who knew how to write code in the Go computer language. It had always been Vitalik's hope that Ethereum would be as diverse as possible. What the dev team set out to do was create what are known as clients. Clients connect to each other in a peer-to-peer system and talk directly to the servers where Ethereum data is stored. Having clients written in different computer languages is a kind of insurance policy: it avoids the possibility of a single point of failure and makes it much harder for developers to centralize around C++, for example.

This might sound super geeky, and you may wonder why anyone would need to know this, but the diversity of Ethereum clients actually prevented the entire network from going down when it was attacked on New Year's Eve in 2019. The clients that run Parity were targeted and so were taken offline, but the attack didn't work on the clients that were running Geth. That meant that Ethereum stayed alive during the 14 hours the Parity team took to release a software patch to fix the bug. The Parity attack is about as good an example as you're going to get of why decentralization is held in such high regard among the people who truly understand blockchain.

So back to 2014. Vitalik wrote the Ethereum client in the Python computer language, Gavin in C++, and Jeff in Go.

It appeared as though the group of five cofounders was about to as they prepared to leave Miami. Roles for each were becoming clear too. Vitalik, Gav, and Jeff made up the tech side of the operation. Mihai, Amir, and Anthony would help with business development. Joe and Charles would straddle both worlds: each had technical acumen to offer along with an eye for how Ethereum would stay on the good side of regulators while at the same time appealing to the wider world they'd need to ensure that the project ultimately succeeded.

Yet defining roles and job descriptions creates an environment where factions can form. And form they did. More people also meant less money per person, or at least that's how some of them saw it. Tension would soon start to surface, alliances would be tested, and the true personalities of the men building Ethereum would reveal themselves.

● ● ●

One thing is constant in the ever-changing and chaotic world of blockchain – there is always another conference. The joke that the one true use for the technology is that it enables conferences to be held whenever and wherever is only half funny.

As the cofounders left Miami this was indeed the case: there would be another conference in April in Toronto. But this was no run-of-the-mill event; this would be the first gathering Anthony Di Iorio sponsored through the group he created, the Bitcoin Alliance of Canada. There were three main jobs to accomplish now – find a permanent headquarters, try to rustle up some outside money, and start creating a working version of Ethereum. As for the working version, at this early stage all that meant was setting up a small network among a handful of nodes so that they could start sending ether to each other. The cofounders would split up to go about their tasks, then all meet back in Toronto for Bitcoin Expo 2014 in mid-April to report on their progress.

Charles had claimed the de facto title of chief executive officer by this point, never mind that not many in the rest of the group were big on titles. He traveled to Switzerland to join Mihai as the search for where to base the Ethereum Foundation began. The three candidate locations had been whittled down to Switzerland, Hong Kong, and Singapore, due to their relative ease with regulations and the fact that they were respectable locales in a Western-business sense. (Charles said that early on Amsterdam had also been considered for the headquarters.)

Switzerland soon became the front-runner for the base of operations, both because of its tax treatment and because it was closer to those who lived in North America and Europe than either location in Asia. Mihai Alisie and Roxana Sureanu settled in Zürich first, where they couch surfed and started getting the lay of the land. An important early contact they made was Herbert Sterchi, a whiz at setting up companies in the Alpine country who knew many of the Swiss regulators personally. To establish a company in Switzerland, the board of directors must include at least one Swiss citizen, and here too Herbert came in handy. The group had grown to about seven or eight Ethereum people now helping to set up shop in or around Zug, a small city on the shores of the lake of the same name. When they were in between Airbnb rentals, Herbert let Mihai, Roxanna, and the others stay at his apartment. Mihai continued to meet with lawyers and other officials necessary to establish the Ethereum Foundation as a Swiss entity.

By this point Roxana knew the group would need to rent a house. They would probably have up to a dozen people who needed a place to live and work; skipping around between Airbnb rentals wouldn't do. After a lot of looking they settled on a new house on Greinbachstrasse, what would become known as the Spaceship House for its luxury and modern architecture. An elevator shuttled people between its three levels, and there were four bedrooms, a large open kitchen, and a living room that connected to a terrace. The home is one of three identical houses on an idyllic street; a small stream runs nearby, with sloping fields giving way to towering mountains all around. On March 4, 2014, it became home to the Ethereum Foundation as the group, which now included Mihai, Roxana, Charles Hoskinson, Mathias Grønnebæk, Taylor Gerring, Richard Stark, Lorenzo Patuzzo, and a few others, moved in. Roxana organized most everything to turn the vacant house into habitable space, like buying furniture and mattresses and dishes and everything else. She now held the title of executive assistant and office manager. "I can say I was officially the first woman in Ethereum," she said.

Mathias Grønnebæk found his way to the Spaceship House in a roundabout fashion. Until he was 18, he hadn't thought much about the financial world. But the year was 2008 and Mathias watched as his grandfather, an entrepreneur and investor, started to lose money in the stock market crash. "It was quite fascinating, seeing that much wealth being wiped out," he said. He began to wonder how wealth was created and how it was destroyed. "That's when my fascination with finance really started." By 2012, he'd read the Bitcoin white paper and linked it to the financial crisis. "I wouldn't say I was a fully formed anarchist or anything like that at the time," he said. "When I saw Bitcoin, what it meant to me was – because of the context of 2008 – it was the fall of the state and the large financial institutions that are sanctioned by the state." He loved that Bitcoin took the power out of the hands of intermediaries.

But what truly captured his imagination came from a thread on BitcoinTalk where someone posted a challenge to create a stock market without a central authority involved. The New York Stock Exchange without any of the middlemen and executives and compliance officers, in other words: just a peer-to-peer market. This idea, which the person on BitcoinTalk dubbed the "Holy Grail," was being proposed in the Bitcoin-only era of mid-2013. So Bitcoin could be not just the basis for sending money from A to B – it could be used for *trade*. Mathias's eyes lit up.

"That idea was just stuck in my mind and I couldn't stop thinking about it," he said. This made him jump in completely to try to build on Bitcoin, but he didn't have the resources to create the kind of decentralized stock market of his dreams. So he traveled from his home in Aalborg, Denmark, to Copenhagen, to grow his contacts in the blockchain world. When he discovered the crowdfunding effort for Amir Taaki's and Cody Wilson's Dark Wallet project, he donated a few thousand dollars. That enabled him to attend a dinner in Milan in November 2013 where he met a bunch of big names in the Bitcoin developer world. Among them was Mihai Alisie, who had come to Milan from Calafou with Roxana.

While Vitalik had left Calafou in the summer to continue his travels, Mihai and Roxana had stayed on until November. The weather changed from being too hot all the time to being too cold. The showers only got more frigid, and they had to sleep under their clothes and towels for a time as there was no heat in their apartment. Then they made the bold move to buy a big blanket. "Oh my god, that was like the best investment ever," Roxana said.

The hardship of Calafou had left its mark on the couple. Mihai found a deepness within himself and had a new appreciation for the small things. Roxana came away knowing that material things don't mean happiness, and that she would do it all over again.

For Matias Grønnebæk's part, he now had a great connection to Ethereum in Mihai and Roxana. From Milan, Mathias went home to Denmark, shut down his business, and asked to join Ethereum. Mihai and Roxana visited him around Christmas, and soon Mathias was all in on Ethereum. It was good timing for Mathias, as he'd reached the limits of what Bitcoin could do for his dream of a decentralized stock exchange.

"Bitcoin fucking sucks for developing a financial system on top of, it's really terrible," Mathias said. When he read Vitalik's white paper and understood the idea of smart contracts, the whole world opened up to him. To put it simply, smart contracts allow for many different transactions to whiz around at the same time, much like the trading on a stock market. Some of them will fail, some will succeed. The trading paths connect dot A to dot B to F to G back to A and so forth. At the time Bitcoin couldn't handle this type of trading; it was much too frenzied. So Mathias knew he would need to use Ethereum for a decentralized stock market to become reality.

Still, that's a tall order and not something Ethereum can handle in 2020, let alone in 2014. In a basic sense, what Mathias wants to do is take the centralized authority out of the stock market equation. All exchanges use software known as a matching engine to connect buyers to sellers. Everyone on the New York Stock Exchange is known to the exchange, and it sits in the middle to facilitate trading. What Mathias wants to do is make that trading happen between two people only – the buyer and the seller – without an entity like the NYSE as the matching engine. A smart contract could bring about the peer-to-peer connection and be customized to enhance privacy between parties, for example. This is another application that illustrates the potential of Ethereum, but it isn't reality yet. Whether it ever will be is still an open question, but Mathias is a believer.

"That's why smart contracts made sense to me, and that's also why I asked to join the project," he said. Mathias also had a weird habit of reading tax regulations and financial rules for fun, and he strongly suggested Switzerland to the cofounders as the place to set up shop. Switzerland is made up of 26 federal states known as cantons. All of Europe operates under the same set of rules, but the Swiss canton system sets it apart, as Mathias knew. "You can actually go to one of the tax authorities in the canton and negotiate a tax ruling," he said. "You can't do that in the UK."

The Ethereum folks had also gotten indications that ether would not be considered a security by Switzerland. That means it would face far less stringent rules and requirements about how ether was sold, whom it was marketed to, and what kind of disclosures they would have to make. It would be a huge headache avoided. The Swiss financial regulator viewed ether "as a software product," Mathias said. "So at that point we can go and negotiate with the tax authorities, and that's when we came up with the whole utility token framework. I was part of the team that negotiated that."

The idea of a utility token would become key to how ether was eventually treated by lawyers at the SEC. In a nutshell, crypto teams want regulators to think of their new digital coins as utilities, as cogs in a bigger machine that are necessary for that machine to run. If Ethereum won't work without ether, then ether is a utility token. And that means it's not a security token, which would trigger the reporting and disclosure requirements of a company issuing new shares of a stock.

Herbert Sterchi proved pivotal in this discussion. "He was like – I don't know what you'd call it, the fixer, or whatever," Mathias said. "The guy who knows all the people in Switzerland who you need to talk to." Mihai, Herbert, and Mathias were working on the tax, regulation, and headquarter projects, with Charles joining them for the latter stages. The team shopped the idea of ether and Ethereum to many different cantons but ended up choosing Zug. "They treated it in terms of taxation as an investment vehicle, which doesn't count as being a security," Mathias said. "That means effectively the money you raise is 0 percent taxed."

This would have been music to Charles's ears. When the gang had been in Miami and Bitcoin was near $1,000, the MasterCoin project had been valued at somewhere between $50 million and $100 million. "People knew that that market was sexy, and we were thinking, 'God, we could easily get to $100 million,'" Charles said.

Yet only a few months into the project, tensions in the leadership group were beginning to show. On a call with the cofounders in February, Anthony Di Iorio and Charles Hoskinson got into a heated argument about who was in charge. Toward the end of the call, Charles blew up at Anthony and cussed him out in front of the others: just because Anthony had money didn't mean he had ideas, and Charles would lead them with his ideas. Steve Jobs, after all, wouldn't let anyone treat him this way – Charles idolized the founder of Apple and wanted to take the cofounders and whip them into shape like Jobs would. They weren't working from a garage in Cupertino, but an Airbnb in Zürich didn't feel that much different.

Anthony's point of view was that he'd brought Charles into the mix in the first place – if it hadn't been for him showing Charles the white paper, Charles would be looking at this project from the outside. Who did this kid think he was? While he acted like he was a tenured professor, Charles was only 24. Now he wanted to take the leadership role that clearly belonged to Anthony?

While Mihai, Charles, Roxana, and Mathias worked to set up the foundation's headquarters in what would come to be known as Crypto Valley, Vitalik, Gavin Wood, and Amir Chetrit headed out to another valley in search of investors.

They soon hooked up with Richard Burton, a computer programmer and designer who found himself nodding along when he heard Vitalik speak on a podcast about his idea of creating a programmable blockchain.

"It made a lot of sense to me because it's so hard to develop on top on Bitcoin," he said. Burton went to a talk given by Gavin at the Negev, the infamous shared house near San Francisco's Sixth Street known for its tech-friendly residents and fraternity-like method of inducting new tenants. Burton introduced himself and told Gav he'd like to help make Ethereum user friendly by designing things people want to use, like a wallet and a decentralized browser and a chat application. They hit it off and soon Vitalik and Gav were staying for a few nights with Burton at the Rainbow Mansion south of the city in Cupertino.

Billing itself as "an intentional community of people working to optimize the galaxy," the Rainbow Mansion is meant to bring brilliant but broke people together. It's close to Palo Alto, the mecca of venture capital, where a number of hugely successful and prominent firms are located along Sand Hill Road. After meeting with venture capitalists during the day, Vitalik and Gav would return to the mansion.

"They would come back feeling pretty despondent from Sand Hill Road. It wasn't really working out," Burton said. At the same time, a bit of rejection or indifference didn't seem to dissuade them. "They didn't really seem to give a fuck, I mean, these people just did not care," Burton said. "It was kind of like, 'fine, they don't want to buy the tokens, whatever, we can carry on.'"

No matter what they were doing, Vitalik and Gav stayed focused on the project, Burton said. They didn't go out for beers at night or veer from what they wanted to do. "Everyone was on a bit of a mission," he said. "The world computer was the idea. It was like, wouldn't it be useful if we had a global computer?" Vitalik's backpack, where he kept his precious computer and other essentials, had started to disintegrate and was full of holes, so Burton gave him his own backpack and told him, "look after that little laptop, dude, I think you're going to need it." He was also struck by the integrity Vitalik showed as a 20-year-old.

"The character of open-source movements requires some sort of thought leader or some person who really spearheads it," Burton said. "You can see it with Linux and Linus Torvalds and the way he led it with force and an iron fist. Vitalik was totally different. He was very open and very collaborative," Burton said. "I remember being in the car and he was switching from learning Mandarin to talking to me about design to discussing mechanisms with other people in the car and debating the crowdsale. His context switching is phenomenal."

While Anthony Di Iorio had stayed in Toronto to help line up lawyers and prepare for the upcoming conference in April, he did take time out to meet Gavin, Vitalik, and Amir in San Francisco for investor meetings. Among the VC firms the cofounders met with were Andreessen Horowitz and Union Square Ventures. "We were trying to see what we were going to do," Anthony said. "Seeing what options were out there." Gav and Anthony met in person with Balaji Gopinath at Kubera Venture Capital; for the Union Square Ventures meeting they used Skype, and they held an in-person meeting with Andreessen Horowitz. (Gavin didn't recall much of the meeting, just "sitting around in some VC office for an afternoon on their Wi-Fi.")

The way VC works involves a bit of a devil's bargain. For the blessing of early investment that so often means life or death for a startup, the partners at a VC fund become involved in the project and seek to direct it in ways they think will make it possible to come to market. Sometimes this is great, sometimes it's an unmitigated disaster – it just depends on the people and the ideas involved. But the business model makes sense:

for the money VCs provide they get some say in how things are done and they can make a ton of money if they're right.

Blockchain as a business was still relatively new in Silicon Valley at this time. There was already quite a bit of money backing Bitcoin ventures, like the San Francisco exchange Coinbase. Andreessen Horowitz had been early to that game. And Dan Larimer's BitShares had made the rounds on Sand Hill Road. Yet the debate over "blockchain not Bitcoin" was only just beginning: the idea that while Bitcoin is great, the underlying blockchain technology is the real breakthrough that would enable entire industries to modernize and achieve unheard-of levels of efficiency. The debate enraged many on the Bitcoin side, who bristled at the idea that Bitcoin was some secondary product. On the blockchain side of the argument stood people like Vitalik, who in the first line of his white paper and during his talk in Miami made the case. "In the last few months, there has been a great amount of interest into the area of using Bitcoin-like blockchains, the mechanism that allows for the entire world to agree on the state of a public ownership database, for more than just money," he wrote in his paper. Ethereum sprang entirely from this belief, but in February 2014 it was still too early for the moneybags in Silicon Valley to have caught on.

It wasn't a surprise that Gav and Vitalik discovered that VC wasn't the way to go. Anthony shared this view.

"We decided never to take outside capital, because we thought that would give people influence on the project we wouldn't want," Anthony said. They would keep their internal funding model, with Joe and Anthony contributing the lion's share and Vitalik and a few others making up the rest.

The most important thing that money would fund was the creation of a working version of Ethereum, and that's what Gav, Jeff Wilcke, and Vitalik set out to do. A large part of figuring out the architecture for Ethereum meant Vitalik and Gav taking time to talk things through and hash out ideas. They had a chance to get into that back-and-forth during their time together in San Francisco and Silicon Valley. Beginning in Miami, Gavin had begun to take notes on the particulars of what he and Vitalik and Jeff talked about regarding the details of how Ethereum would work.

"The white paper presented the overall concept of Ethereum in fairly broad terms," Gavin said. The job now was to begin the formal process of how, exactly, the software would be designed. After a few days in San Francisco, Anthony returned to Toronto and Gav and Vitalik had time to hash out their ideas. "The Ethereum protocol developed substantially during this time," Gav said.

● ● ●

The highs reached at the Miami Bitcoin conference were hit with a harsh dose of reality the next month, when Mt. Gox, then the world's biggest Bitcoin exchange, suspended its customers' ability to withdraw cash and coins from its market.

The exchange, which Jed McCaleb had sold to a man named Mark Karpelès in 2011, had suffered previous problems with customer funds being frozen. US authorities had also twice seized the Mt. Gox bank accounts, worth $5 million, because the exchange failed to register as a money transmitter. But the problems at Mt. Gox in 2014 were much bigger than either of those events. At first Karpelès tried to say that the issue was simply technical and that the market would update users in a few days. That sent the price of Bitcoin down 8 percent, to about $720. The problems only grew worse, and within two weeks Mt. Gox customers were offering to sell Bitcoin for $124 because of fears that their coins would never be returned, Bloomberg News reported at the time. (I wasn't yet on the blockchain beat and only have vague recollections of Mt. Gox.) At the same time, Bloomberg said, Bitcoin was trading for $566 on London-based Bitstamp and for $553 on BTC-e in Bulgaria.

Soon the full extent of the disaster at Mt. Gox was revealed. About 850,000 Bitcoin had been stolen or were missing, a loss of $450 million. Security firm WizSec would later conclude that Bitcoins had been stolen from Mt. Gox's account beginning in 2011. That means many of the people partying it up in Miami – and buying Lamborghinis on a whim – were likely being ripped off as they did.

Everyone involved with Ethereum at the time would have been paying close attention to the Mt. Gox drama. In the weeks or months to come, they were planning to sell ether in exchange for Bitcoin for the first time. Learning a lesson about dealing with Bitcoin's wicked volatility would soon become another obstacle for the cofounders to overcome.

● ● ●

As the winter of 2014 turned to spring, Anthony Di Iorio's Decentral grew into a buzzing hot spot for blockchain startups. Since leaving Miami, part of the Ethereum team had been based out of the Toronto office as the operations in Zug got up and running. There was also a cast of various characters utilizing the Decentral office as the city's blockchain scene expanded. And none of it would've happened if some Canadian Bitcoin enthusiasts had just bought more alcohol.

After organizing Toronto's first Bitcoin meetup at Pauper's Pub in late 2012, Anthony moved the meetups to a bar called the Charlotte Room. The weekly Bitcoin meetups at the Charlotte Room proved to be popular, but not everyone who came would buy a beer. They'd show up, learn about Bitcoin, and leave. This didn't sit well with the owners of the Charlotte Room, so they wanted to start charging Anthony to hold the events at their bar. But meetups are free – they are always free, no matter where in the world you attend – so Anthony knew they couldn't start asking for a few bucks at the door. This led him to realize that a dedicated place was needed for like-minded people in the world of Bitcoin and blockchain to meet, work, and collaborate. Thus, Decentral was born.

The building was tall, narrow, and deep, like a lot of housing in Toronto, and had been converted to the coworking space from a private house. The unfinished basement had cinderblock walls and a musty feel. On the upper floors whiteboards were stuck onto walls, sometimes to hide the cracks. A nice roof terrace was rarely used after the landlord said that if too many people went out there, they might all come crashing through the floor. The third story was a warren of many small rooms where people often slept on the floor in sleeping bags. It had a do-it-yourself vibe that fit the blockchain ethos at the time.

Among the first people to hang around Decentral was Gerald Cotten. He was building a Bitcoin exchange, QuadrigaCX, which would go on to be another example of the wild fraud and fantastic stories of the early Bitcoin world.

Cotten founded Quadriga in 2013 and had offices in Toronto and Vancouver, according to a 2019 story in the *Globe and Mail*. According to the newspaper story it was slow going for several years, years that included net losses far outstripping revenue and a botched attempt to take the company public on a Canadian stock exchange. Soon Cotten found himself the only one left at the company after his chief financial officer and directors resigned. Then the price of Bitcoin went on a tear in 2017, peaking at nearly $20,000, and Quadriga handled $1.2 billion worth of trades that year, the *Globe and Mail* said. By this time, Cotten was basically running Quadriga on his own, using only his laptop. Like many cryptocurrency exchanges, Quadriga couldn't obtain bank accounts for customers to deposit and withdraw money for use on the exchange. In 2018, significant delays and miscommunications began affecting Quadriga customers, who wanted to get their money off the exchange.

In December 2018, Cotten went to India, reportedly to found an orphanage. But he died there on December 12 of complications from Crohn's disease, according to a Bloomberg News story. He'd signed a will only 12 days prior to his death. After his death, Quadriga customers were told they couldn't access their money or cryptocurrencies on Quadriga because Cotten was the only person to have the private keys to the accounts where the money and crypto was stored. They were kept on his laptop, and no one besides Cotten knew how to access the private keys. About 76,000 Quadriga customers lost Bitcoin that was worth about $163 million in the fiasco, Bloomberg reported. In December 2019, lawyers for Quadriga customers asked for Cotten's body to be exhumed to address theories that he'd faked his death. The law firms asked that the process be done quickly "given decomposition concerns," Bloomberg said.

In 2018, I'd traded emails with Cotten. I was working on a story about the refusal of many banks to work with crypto exchanges. "The situation here in Canada is such that it is very difficult to obtain a bank account for cryptocurrency exchanges," Cotten wrote to me in response to questions. "All five of Canada's big-five banks (we have a bit of an oligopoly here on banking) will not permit a cryptocurrency exchange (or any business related to cryptocurrency for that matter) to have an account." That meant Quadriga had to use a series of payment-processing companies to move customer money in and out of the market. One of these was called Crypto Capital Corp., which also processed money for the controversial exchange Bitfinex and its related entity Tether.

"Companies such as Crypto Capital have proven useful in the sense that they operate as a payment processor that is able to receive transfers from clients, store funds, and then process outgoing transactions as well," Cotten wrote. "A similar comparison would be a payment company such as PayPal."

In 2019, New York's attorney general brought a civil case against Bitfinex and Tether, accusing the firms of hiding the loss of $851 million in customer money from its use of Crypto Capital Corp. Bitfinex and Tether executives have said they did nothing wrong and were victims of mismanagement at Crypto Capital Corp.

Meanwhile, in 2018 Cotten told me that the payment-processing setup had its plusses and minuses. "In general, it works well, though there are occasionally hiccups," he wrote.

One of the first tenants at Decentral was Michael Perklin, who set up the headquarters of his blockchain security consultancy there. He knew Cotten well and never would have imagined how things would end for him.

"He was a thoughtful, intelligent person who seemed to get along with everybody," Perklin said. "He was as much a fixture in that coworking space that year as Vitalik and myself." Cotten was always willing to lend a hand, be it answering questions from people who walked in off the street to sharing technical details he'd picked up as he built Quadriga. He'd involve himself in the anarcho-political debates about the benefits of Bitcoin and always had a warm and friendly personality, Perklin said. He has a hard time reconciling what happened to his friend, but after reading the exhaustive report on the history of mismanagement and fraud at Quadriga done by Ernst & Young, Perklin has a very different view of Cotten.

The "deceit and crime" detailed by the report shocked Perklin. "Why would you create these fake accounts to trade fake volume on your exchange? Why would you intermingle your exchange's funds with your users' funds?" he said. "Now I look at these facts and I say, 'okay, these seem consistent with somebody who is practicing a long con and is now trying to move the money out in a way that makes it very difficult to trace.'"

As of January 28, 2020, the fight to exhume Cotten's body was still ongoing, according to a story on CoinDesk.

• • •

The work at Decentral in early 2014 continued and Bitcoin Expo 2014 rapidly approached. The Ethereum cofounders made their way to Toronto in mid-April, having made some significant advances on the project. The headquarters in Zug was up and running, with only some paperwork needed to finalize the creation and structure of Ethereum as a Swiss entity. The tax and regulatory situation in Switzerland could hardly be better for the group as they got closer to raising money through the ether crowdsale. And they now knew firsthand that raising outside money from VC firms wasn't the way to go.

Yet there was still a lot to decide, and what can be thought of as the second official meeting of the cofounders, at Decentral, would see plenty of action.

The group decided to continue with the development of Ethereum on three different codebases: C++, Python, and Go. Gav continued working on the technical specs for Ethereum, which he was calling his yellow paper. Anthony, Joe, and Charles continued to work with lawyers on the intricacies of selling ether to US participants. They voted to make Charles Hoskinson CEO. Then there was the matter of how the group would accept and safely store the Bitcoin it received from the crowdsale. For that Charles turned to Michael Perklin, who specialized in exactly that type of blockchain architecture.

When Bitcoin users want to send the digital currency in their wallets to someone they must use a private key. Without the key, the Bitcoin doesn't move. This may seem like a small problem, but it isn't. According to a 2017 study by blockchain forensics firm Chainalysis, as reported by *Fortune* magazine, 17–23 percent of all existing Bitcoin has been lost because the owners lost their private key. That's amounts to 2.8–3.8 million Bitcoin, in other words, worth $20.1–27.4 billion in April 2020 prices.

But back to wallets. What if you have a group of people, like a company or the Ethereum cofounders, who want to manage a cryptocurrency account? You don't want to entrust all of your Bitcoin or ether or other digital currency to a single person; that's too risky. So what's needed is a way for the wallet to be controlled by a group of people. This is known as a multi-signature wallet, or multisig for short. The thing is, in April 2014 there were hardly any multisig wallets in existence. According to a story on CoinDesk, the first multisig Bitcoin wallet was created by BitGo in August 2013. The article went on to say that as of the beginning of 2014, only 0.002 percent of all Bitcoin was held in a multisig wallet.

Perklin knew that the cofounders would need to have exceptional security and that to provide that he'd have to build them a multisig wallet from scratch. His idea, though, was a sort of multisig of multisigs. The keys would be based in three cities – Toronto, London, and Berlin – and held in "footballs" – a nod to the cache of nuclear codes carried in a briefcase by a government agent who's always near the president of the United States. The Ethereum footballs would be laptops that had never been connected to the Internet and that had had all of their networking gear, like Wi-Fi and Bluetooth, ripped out. The speakers and microphones would be removed. There would be three people in each of the three cities who would have access to that city's football, and two of them would be needed to sign off on any movement of Bitcoin from the Ethereum multisig wallet.

"It was very complicated at the time," Perklin said. He had to write long and detailed instruction manuals for how to use the wallet, but in the end it all paid off. "I'm happy to say not a single satoshi went missing as a result of a failure of the wallet."

Perklin had been around the crypto world long enough to know that Vitalik and the foundation needed bulletproof security. "I wanted to make sure that people didn't take advantage of Vitalik," he said. "I strongly recommended this multi-signature setup to protect Vitalik and his vision." While there was a lot of optimism and enthusiasm around Ethereum, Perklin also saw a lot of politics already in play and that certain founders were jockeying for control.

Vitalik "had an amazing idea that had incredible potential for the world," Perklin said. "A whole lot of people who were interested in this distributed technology and understood Bitcoin under the hood – they would look at this and say, 'yes this is a great idea on its merits,'" he said. "Other people who didn't necessarily have that kind of a viewpoint looked at this and just saw dollar signs. They said, 'hey, if I can attach my name to this project somehow, some way, then I'm going to get my fair share of those millions that are going to be raised.' They didn't care about it working as much as they cared about lining their own pockets."

"A lot of people called themselves cofounders in that project," Perklin said. "In my mind, there is only one founder of Ethereum: the guy who came up with the idea – and he deserves all the credit."

Mathias Grønnebæk manned the Ethereum booth at the conference, which was front and center as you walked into the Metro Toronto Convention Centre hall.

"There were already factions," Grønnebæk said. "There was always a very deep split between the Europeans and the North Americans. Anthony is very territorial about the way that he runs a business. He viewed himself as in charge of the Canada branch and he almost viewed the North American branch as almost separate to Europe. So it was like two businesses that had to work together."

Anthony Di Iorio had always had a maverick streak in him. His father worked for IBM and the kids in his family were expected to be normal, but Anthony never wanted to be normal, he wanted to be different. "Throughout my life I never liked being told what to do," he said. "I never liked school." Working for others had never really been his thing, and he was on the older side compared to most of the other cofounders: he would turn 39 in 2014. When I first met Anthony in 2019, he struck me much more like a New Yorker than someone from the polite circles of Canada's largest city. He has a grittiness to him that had started to rub some of his cofounders the wrong way.

"Anthony's perspective was less philosophical, where he could opportunistically jump on a philosophy for his own personal interest," Joe Lubin said. "He just wanted to make sure that he was not being left out [and was able to] take advantage of whatever developments were going on. He added lots of value to the project at different points in time, certainly early and the first six of nine months. But it was pretty much all about Anthony."

An example: During the Toronto Bitcoin conference Joe went to lunch with Russell Verbeeten, a startup investor who had joined the Ethereum project in February and worked from the Decentral office. Anthony hadn't been invited, and when Russell and Joe returned

Anthony tore into Russell for having the audacity to go to lunch with another Ethereum cofounder and not include him. Michael Perklin witnessed the interaction.

"Anthony was angry that topics were discussed, decisions might have been made, with him being out of the loop. It was kind of a 'how dare you do that, don't you know that I'm in charge' kind of discussion," Perklin said. Anthony said he didn't remember this happening.

Charles Hoskinson would prove to be much more problematic for the group, however. He was described to me by the people he worked with at the time as a pathological liar, a sociopath, and as someone to not trust in the company of your girlfriend. In his early 20s in 2014, he was one of the youngest cofounders. He wore a thick beard and glasses and dressed in a way that could make you think he was much older than he was. For the first several months that Joe Lubin knew Charles he assumed that he was in his mid-30s. Charles would talk about Creedence Clearwater Revival concerts in the 1970s as though he'd been there. But it went much further than that. To convince people that he was Satoshi Nakamoto, he'd show emails that he claimed proved he'd invented Bitcoin, and a few of the people around became convinced.

He told more offbeat stories, too; like how he got his limp by mistiming a jump out of an Apache helicopter in Afghanistan. He claimed to be associated with the Central Intelligence Agency, or sometimes he hinted of his links to DARPA, the supersecret US government weapons development agency. He often kept his passport in the front pocket of his shirt.

It soon became clear to Vitalik that Charles was a liability. "I was kind of caught off guard by this, because Charles was always nice to me," Vitalik said. "But Charles seems to be one of these people that seem to be pretty common in the world, who know to be nice to their superiors, but abuse their subordinates." When Vitalik spoke to people who worked for Charles, like Mathias Grønnebæk and Taylor Gerring, he heard a litany of complaints.

Gerring found his way into the early Ethereum inner circle in a similar fashion as Mathias Grønnebæk. Taylor had also attended the Dark Wallet event in the squat in Milan in late November 2013 where he met Mihai Alisie.

Up to that point Taylor had been working on a Bitcoin wallet project, but he soon realized Ethereum was much more exciting. He hadn't known what to expect in Milan, and although he found an eclectic and inspiring gathering of hackers and coders there, he felt frustrated at the amount of actual progress being made. The squat had a glass ceiling with several broken panes that let the cold air in; they used wood-burning stoves for heat; and while there were bathrooms, there were also holes in the bathroom floors where some guys relieved themselves. When Taylor returned to Chicago he got in touch with Mihai to offer his help on the Ethereum web site. Soon he was in the mix full time, crashing at the Miami house, then going off to Switzerland. Charles first struck an odd chord with Taylor when he watched Charles being interviewed for a podcast about Ethereum at the Miami house. Taylor thought, shouldn't that be Vitalik doing the talking? "It felt weird," he said. It would soon get weirder.

"In the very early days he tried to convince us he was Satoshi Nakamoto," Taylor said. "Stories and information never seemed to line up with him." It must have been odd for many of the people surrounding Ethereum at this time to have this amazing idea before them, the chance to help Vitalik make this thing they all desperately wanted, and then to realize that the mix of people attached to the project was rather strange. In the augmented words of former secretary of defense Donald Rumsfeld, Ethereum was going to war with the army it had, not the one it might wish to have.

Joe Lubin liked Charles and wanted to help him. "I had a few conversations with him about his style of communication," Lubin said. "He got it. He could see himself and how it would affect people, but it wouldn't stick for more than a day or two." After working with Charles closely, Joe thought he "was a really bright guy." Homeschooled until early in his teens, Charles studied math and cryptography at the University of Colorado before dropping out after two years.

By April, Charles had hurt his credibility with several cofounders and people who were helping to build Ethereum. Mathias had been working closely with him in Zug on the business plan. Mathias did a lot of the plan writing, and Charles would give him feedback. As they got to know each other, Mathias developed conflicting feelings toward him: on the one hand he liked Charles, but on the other he couldn't get past his major flaw.

"The problem with Charles is that he's very manipulative," Mathias said. "He's very charming, he can spin you around his finger." Charles wasn't exactly shy about it, either. "He was telling me exactly how he was manipulating people," Mathias said.

A split was also developing between the technical side of the project and everyone else. There were far too few tech-savvy people with power within Ethereum's inner circle for Gavin Wood's taste. He didn't understand why the business development people were in line to get a share of the profits similar to that of the coders, without whom none of this would be possible. Too many hangers-on, Gav thought.

"Everyone who was involved with the project – regardless of their capacity, skill set, talent, commitment, or productivity – was treated equally, to a fault," Gav said. Referring to Lorenzo Patuzzo, one of the people staying at the Spaceship House in Zug, Gav said, "One guy who put up an interior wall in the house in Zug walked away with quite a decent drop of ether. It might be the most ever paid for a wall of its size." It grated on Gavin. "I felt quite strongly that this was a suboptimal strategy," he said.

The emotional and political stew that the cofounders were floating in had the strong flavor of rivalry by April. The trust and excitement and openness Charles and Joe and Anthony D'Onofrio had spoken of in Miami was gone, with agendas now in their place. The presence of personal drama didn't mean the group could avoid making business decisions, however. And a big one loomed. Would Ethereum be a not-for-profit or would it bow to the capitalist masters it was seeking to supplant?

The structure of a business is really one of the first things to decide upon, and yet the topic wasn't coming up in direct conversation too often among the cofounders. Perhaps everyone knew it would lead to trouble. It was in the air, is how Vitalik remembered it. Unlike when they voted to appoint Charles CEO, memories differ as to whether there was a vote to decide on Ethereum's corporate structure.

The debate was being framed as crypto-Google versus crypto-Mozilla. Google, of course, even though its early motto was "Don't be evil," had become one of the most powerful and wealthy corporations of the Internet age. Google is undoubtedly an amazing company and a key player in unleashing the power of the web; its search engine has changed the world. (And made Sergey Brin and Larry Page billionaires.)

Mozilla is perhaps a bit less well known, at least outside coding circles. It's the nonprofit foundation that maintains the open-source code for the Mozilla project. The browser is probably its best-known product, but the foundation has a set of 10 principles it operates under to help keep the Internet open and free. It's high minded all the way down.

"The biggest and most significant vote was this concept of crypto-Google versus crypto-Mozilla," Charles said. He'd helped forge the foundation strategy in Switzerland and he said that both paths were open to them at that time. "We had to make a fundamental philosophical decision about what we wanted to be. There were arguments on both sides." Even though Silicon Valley had left a bad taste in the mouth of Vitalik and Gav, advisors at the time were telling the cofounders they could raise maybe $30 million in VC funding.

"We'd already gone to the valley," Charles said. "We'd talked to everybody from Kevin Rose at Google Ventures to Naval Ravikant and others." The paths were clear in Charles's mind, and he said a decision was made.

"We took a vote, and the vote was actually eight to zero; it was unanimous," he said. "Every single person voted on the crypto-Google."

Anthony had a slightly foggier recollection of the vote. He said that the group members (minus Mihai) were all in the basement at Decentral and that a vote to appoint Charles CEO took place. "I think it was also the same time that we decided to do the for-profit," Anthony said. "It was just a majority, and everybody – I don't know if it was everybody – but it was decided to be for-profit, and that's the route we started taking after that conference."

Another idea floating around was to make it a hybrid, with a for-profit arm that would develop the Ethereum clients and then donate them to the foundation. But that didn't last.

Vitalik remembered getting some contradictory advice at the time. "The thing was originally pitched to me as, like, 'oh look, making a non-profit foundation in Switzerland is just too legally complicated, so make it simpler," Vitalik said. He favored the nonprofit route from the start, but the prospect of a long legal process eventually swayed him. "I eventually, kind of begrudgingly, went along with it," Vitalik said.

He doesn't recall an actual vote on the nonprofit question. "I remember kind of the wind blowing that way and everyone going along with it," Vitalik said. It would be possible, of course, to know exactly what happened if the notes from the cofounder meetings were available. Except no one took notes or recorded these proceedings in any way, that's just not how this group operated. So today the exact details of what took place are left to dueling memories.

Joe Lubin played long ball at this point, realizing that the scale of what Ethereum wanted to be meant that entire new computer systems would have to be built to support it. "Crypto-Google wasn't going to happen for a really, really, really long time," he said. There was a general notion that the group would still head in the for-profit direction, and Lubin wrote a detailed document that included all the things they'd need to create to support Ethereum. "Similar to the 1970s, we'd need math libraries and string manipulation libraries and that sort of thing, but I don't think any of us were under the impression that we would do commercial activities within the next two or three years."

As is Lubin's wont, he then went a bit sideways. "Crypto-Google was nothing more than two words," he said. "It's not like we decided *not* to be crypto-Google, we just kept doing what we were doing."

By April, it was becoming clear that the willy-nilly way Vitalik had assembled his cofounders was coming back to bite him. He agreed with me when I asked him about this, and about whether he wished he'd done it differently.

"The way I started the project was the first few people who reached out became cofounders, and the set of cofounders grew quickly," Vitalik said. The venture capitalists they'd visited in California had criticized them for this, which they said was usually a mark of startup failure. While that hadn't happened yet, "there was a lot of pain," Vitalik said.

Whatever the impression the various cofounders had as they left Toronto, it seemed clear they hadn't rejected the for-profit model. They were headed for profit. As lines continued to be drawn, however, the idea of monetizing Ethereum had opened a rift that would soon blow the group apart.

Part IV

The greatest trick the Devil ever pulled was convincing
the world he didn't exist.
— The Usual Suspects

Thirteen

Money had always been at the heart of Ethereum – it was Vitalik's original idea to create a programmable version of it, of course. Now several months into the project the Ethereum cofounders strained under the lack of hard currency coming in to fund development.

The crowdsale of ether had been planned for just two days after the Miami conference, but it had to be put on hold so that the legal issues around selling a security in the United States could be resolved. Then the crowdsale was put on hold again and again, and it seemed to many people working for the foundation that the payday would never come. The other obstacle they had to overcome was the security of the sale itself. Would they just open up a Bitcoin wallet and have people send them money? No, that wouldn't work. Hackers would love to get ahold of the Ethereum crowdsale Bitcoin. They needed a strong system – from the web site they'd use to the wallets where the Bitcoin they raised would be kept. All of that takes time.

"The team was really frustrated and running on fumes at that point," Joe Lubin said. While Joe and Anthony Di Iorio had footed the vast majority of costs up to that point, "there were other people who contributed quite significantly in terms of paying rent and groceries and keeping shit going," Joe said. "It was going on lots of people's credit cards and they weren't getting paid."

One of the larger expenses was the house in Zug, which Gav called "The Mansion." The monthly rent was 5,500 Swiss francs, which at the time equaled about $6,300. But the landlord of the newly built house wanted a year's worth of rent, plus a deposit, up front. That came to 82,500 Swiss francs, or just over $94,000.

"All the money was being fed to Switzerland and getting things set up there," Anthony said. "You had people there who never had money before, and they didn't do a very good job." Why did the project need a huge house with an elevator? The spending was getting out of hand, he thought.

"Back in Toronto we were trying to control things a little bit more," Anthony said. And the project's ranks were swelling on an almost daily basis, it seemed. "They're bringing in all these new people. Listen, it was a free-for-all for new people to join, which led to a lot of chaos and lack of communication." Nothing seemed to stay the same from one day to the next.

"There were a number of times where I wasn't going to keep funding the project," Anthony said. "The company was in dire need of money and it was a pretty rough time when the markets went down."

Bitcoin's value had continued in the doldrums in mid-2014 after the Mt. Gox hack was revealed in February. It traded for $400–500 for many months, off from its high of $1,000 in January, according to data on CoinMarketCap.com. It seemed that for every positive Bitcoin story there was a negative one – Yelp announced it would create a separate category for merchants that accepted Bitcoin, and then Amazon said it wouldn't be accepting the digital currency any time soon.

The repercussions of going the for-profit route were starting to become clear to the cofounders. The original idea had been to split the equity evenly among the eight, so each got 12.5 percent. Yet this didn't sit well with everyone.

"Gavin says, 'hang on a second here, I'm doing more work that this other founder,' and then this person is fighting with this person and why does Vitalik get the same as everyone else when he came up with the idea?" Charles Hoskinson said, "The even split didn't make a huge amount of sense." The egalitarian nature of this arrangement – no matter your contribution, you get an even share – had failure written all over it.

"Amir Chetrit didn't even want to be on the web site and was working on other projects, and yet his equity would have been identical to Vitalik's," Charles said. The Toronto conference had marked the point at which Amir had begun to distance himself from the others. He'd showed up to the conference wearing the T-shirt of another project he was working on instead of Ethereum's. It sounds childish, but this set people off. The T-shirt was part of the uniform, part of the team. If you don't want to be on our team, what are you doing here? Nor did he stay with the others at Decentral, many of whom slept on the floor with one towel allotted per person. Amir opted for a nearby hotel. Living up to his nickname Amir the Capitalist, he said explicitly on a conference call with the other founders that he was solely involved in Ethereum for the money.

"In reality he barely did much work," Vitalik said of Amir. "Half the time he was shilling his own colored coins thing that he was still working on. That character confuses me."

The problem the group faced if they moved away from an even equity split was that they'd have to value some founders more than others. "That creates a really toxic situation," Charles said.

By April, Ethereum had spawned 50 different meetup groups on five different continents. These are events to bring in new people and to help the already enthralled to become more so. They can be in the form of a chat at the corner pub or a meeting at the corporate headquarters of Microsoft. The Ethereum community grew at an amazing rate, and a lot of the people who were now involved felt they were helping further the project. If it's a for-profit entity, do these community members get in on some of the equity? Are they shareholders? Is there a way to reward them? Here was another issue to split the founders and add to discord.

"Anthony was very draconian about this," Charles said. "He said, 'look we need to keep it small and we need to start pushing some people out of the inner circle and basically consolidate and centralize the project or else it's going to be a management nightmare.'"

Vitalik and Mihai, who came from open-source projects, rejected this approach. They said that the very thing that set Ethereum apart was its burgeoning community; they wanted as many people to be involved as possible.

"Vitalik's kind of a Communist," Charles said. "He's not a capitalist."

It seemed as though promises were starting to be broken. Anthony had a clear vision of what he'd signed up for when he agreed to fund the early work. The project would be for profit, headquartered in Switzerland but with two offices, one there and one in Toronto, where Anthony had spent years building a blockchain community. "Nobody really wanted to be in Switzerland, but it had to be set up that way," he said.

One European convert who would soon come to play a larger role in the Ethereum story was Stephan Tual, a general software developer and marketing executive. In 2012, he was responsible for the information technology strategy of a firm called Beyond Analysis, a data analytics company that had a strategic partnership with Visa. Because of the link with the giant credit card company, a lot of Stephan's work involved the financial world of payments. But outside of his day job he'd become interested in how distributed computer power could change human behavior after participating in an online challenge to solve something called the Infinity Puzzle. The prize was $1 million, and he worked with others to digitize the puzzle and distribute the work to come up with a solution. In the end, he said, even though the puzzle was solved, no $1 million prize materialized.

Yet the idea took root in his mind, and it wasn't long until he realized that Bitcoin used the same idea of distributed work – the proof-of-work mining algorithm – to operate. He soon found himself at a Bitcoin conference, where a skinny young man named Vitalik Buterin was distributing copies of *Bitcoin Magazine*.

"He's a very shy, young paperboy, that's how he presented himself," Tual said of his first impression of Vitalik. Tual had dedicated his entire career to computer science, yet felt the power that the enormous technology firms had amassed was choking off the industry he loved.

"Like many people, I had a sense that there was something wrong with the world," he said. "I felt very disturbed by the whole system and disturbed to see centralization becoming more a part of my profession."

Soon after he met Vitalik at the Bitcoin conference, a copy of the Ethereum white paper landed in his email in-box. "When I discovered this, I told my wife, 'that's it, I'm going to quit everything, my job, quit everything, and work on this Ethereum.'" He felt Vitalik's idea could change the world, yet his wife wasn't so sure. She thought it was nonsense and that Stephan was falling for a scam, but he reassured her that Vitalik was the real deal.

"I feel like it saved my life, to be honest," Stephan said. Ethereum represented an escape from his corporate job, from the malaise that can come in the middle of a career where success can feel like complacency. He reached out to the cofounders and received an invitation to come to Zug, where he met Mathias Grønnebæk, Taylor Gerring, Mihai, Roxana, Gavin Wood, and Jeff Wilcke, among others on the project. Stephan was immediately impressed with Gav.

"Personally, I think Gavin was the driving force," he said. "Vitalik is not a developer, he's a thinker." Like a lot of people I spoke to for this book, Stephan referred to Vitalik as being otherworldly. "When you're Vitalik and you live on planet Jupiter, or Alpha Centauri in this case, I suppose, once you've thought of something you get bored of it. It's solved it's done it's finished it's no longer something that fascinates you." As for his role, Stephan knew early on that he could sell Ethereum to the masses.

"Gavin saw this and thought, 'I can do the code bit,'" Stephan said. "I saw this and thought, 'Ah, I can do the product strategy bit, I can do the marketing bit. I can do the selling to people bit.'" Stephan proved good on this, and the others on the project soon realized he had the gift of gab. Charles Hoskinson hired him on, and while he was making less than when he'd worked for Beyond Analysis, Stephan was happy. He began writing blog posts and helping to spread the word about what Ethereum was up to.

As for Anthony's contention that no one wanted to be in Switzerland: that might come as a surprise to Mihai, Roxana, Taylor Gerring, Mathias Grønnebæk, and the others at the Zug house. Progress continued there apace, with Vitalik, Joe Lubin, and Jeff Wilcke staying over between their travels to meetups and conferences around the world.

One of the most pressing issues was getting the Ethereum web site ready to handle the crowdsale of ether. Not only did the web site have to stop crashing all the time, it needed to have foolproof security to prevent an attack during the time that they would be exchanging Bitcoin for ether. Taylor Gerring worked on these issues both in Toronto and back in Zug.

One specific attack they worried about is known as a distributed denial-of-service attack, or DDoS. That's when a whole bunch of computers gang up on a web site to overload it with information in the hope of making it crash. In 2012, for example, the US government accused Iran of a series of DDoS attacks aimed at Bank of America, JPMorgan, and other banks in retaliation for sanctions, according to the *Washington Post*. Bitcoin services like exchanges were a target as well. In 2013, a DDoS attack tried to take down BTCChina, then the third largest Bitcoin exchange in the world, but the security firm Incapsula prevented the attack, according to a story in the IT publication the *Register* titled "How Mystery DDoSers Tried to Take Down Bitcoin Exchange with 100Gbps Crapflood." Crapflood, in this sense, is a technical term meaning that the attackers had an enormous amount of resources behind them, according to the *Register*. There were bad people out there, maybe even state actors, looking to take down Bitcoin-related services.

Taylor helped negotiate a deal with Incapsula to protect the crowdsale. Rather than try to pull it off using their own servers, the foundation would migrate their web services to Incapsula to prevent attacks. They'd have to pay as much as $10,000 a month for the level of security they were looking for.

"It was a very, very expensive service but we felt like we can't really do what we want to do without this," Taylor said. The foundation already knew they had a target on their back in the larger sense, so were cognizant of always trying to do things the right way. "We tried to do everything with really good optics," he said. "There were already enough people who were nay-saying the project, so we wanted to do everything in a way that seemed as clear as possible."

The work Gerring did on web-site security changed how he saw himself in relation to some cofounders. Here he was negotiating a high-level security issue on a matter of great importance to the project. Then he'd pass on the work he'd done to the higher-ups, which didn't seem quite right to him. "So what exactly is my role here, then, if I'm working on this level of stuff, making decisions, and handing that over to other people at the top?" he said. "Amir was just sitting there doing nothing."

Anthony might've liked to know that money was on everyone else's mind too. Pressure was building to get the crowdsale done. The developers wanted to go fast, they wanted to put something out to show the world their software and what this crazy Ethereum thing could do. Here again, though, the majority of the group remained cautious about walking a safe regulatory line. They were in almost daily communication with lawyers at Pryor Cashman, who were drafting a letter that stated that in their opinion ether wasn't a security and wouldn't run afoul of the SEC. The older members of the team – certainly Anthony and Joe – knew not to mess with the government, even if some of the younger members might have wanted nothing more than that.

I asked Anthony about the balance between wanting to do the crowdfund to raise millions and staying on the right side of the law and regulation. "We're not going to be doing well if we're concerned, uh, what we're doing might not be, uh, you know, might not be the, might not be a good idea," Anthony said. He almost said *illegal* there, didn't he?

Like many who found themselves able to work on Ethereum, Taylor Gerring could do so because he was living off the gains he'd made from buying Bitcoin. He was paying his mortgage in Chicago and his bills with it, allowing him to feed his passion for the project. Other people, though, had families and no savings, and the stress of no payday, and no payday really in sight, was mounting.

The social atmosphere at the Spaceship House might be described as a nerdy dinner party attended by everyone you work with that never ends. Roxana loved the smart conversation and energy. The work went late into the night with only the glow of laptops illuminating the big central room off of the kitchen. They'd jury-rigged fluorescent lights to hang from the ceiling; opposite the table they'd attached a kaleidoscope of long colored tubes to the wall that looked like light sabers. Whiteboards were filled with scribbled math equations and random thoughts. And yet while trying to remake the world they still had to do the dishes and go to the grocery store (until Roxana found out that one of the local shops in Zug delivered groceries). Late at night they might put on a Carl Sagan video and project it onto one of the whiteboards; on other nights they might watch a movie like *Fight Club*.

"I was the only girl around," Roxana said. "It was really interesting for me, like an experience, surrounded by these guys and all these ideas." But as with any group, especially a group of eight people living together, there were times when they got on each other's nerves. "The mood was not necessarily pink all the time," Roxana said.

One of the first things about Bitcoin that had appealed to her was how it could be used to send money anywhere in the world, even if you didn't have a bank. And there were lots of people in the world who didn't have bank accounts. At that time she needed to write a paper to finish her undergraduate work at the Lucian Blaga University of Sibiu in Romania. She chose to write about Bitcoin and banks and a history of money that clocked in at 40 pages. Most of her information came from *Bitcoin Magazine* articles, which she translated into Romanian. She got a perfect score on the paper, as well as a warm reception from her professors. When she presented the paper, "they didn't ask me the technical questions, but they were really intrigued by this peer-to-peer technology," she said. "I was the first student in Romania to write the bachelor's degree paper about Bitcoin in 2013 – maybe even Europe."

As work continued in Zug, Gavin Wood was immersed in writing the technical specifications for Ethereum. He took Vitalik's ideas from the white paper and formalized them in what came to be known as the yellow paper. This color coding would continue for later implementations of Ethereum as improvements were made; for example, in 2016 the mauve paper was written. Being explicit about the way Ethereum worked was important to many of the cofounders, as it would set it apart from Bitcoin. Satoshi Nakamoto's white paper had laid out his vision just as Vitalik's had, yet because from the outset Bitcoin was just a loose affiliation of people working on it in their spare time, no one took responsibility for documenting the technical specifications for the code. That's what a spec is: a guidebook for anyone who wants to come along and re-create or add to the open-source software on their own. And this is what Bitcoin lacked; Joe Lubin described the Bitcoin code as "a bowl of spaghetti." In an email from November 2008, Satoshi said that he wrote the Bitcoin code first and then created the white paper as a way of describing the code. Ethereum would be different.

Gavin set out to define a whole set of terms to be used in the code, such as logsBloom and init and gasLimit. There is enough math to made anyone's head spin. The yellow paper is not meant to be read casually; it is a detailed and complex instruction manual for only the savviest coder. Whereas Vitalik's white paper set out the vision, Gav's yellow paper gave us a bag of nuts and bolts and said, here, you can go build your own Ethereum node. He also set out to update Vitalik's vision of a generalized world computer that wore its philosophy on its sleeve.

"Dealings in this proposed system would have several attributes not often found in the real world," Gavin wrote. "The incorruptibility of judgment, often difficult to find, comes naturally from a disinterested algorithmic interpreter. Transparency, or being able to see exactly how a state or judgment came about through the transaction log and rules or instructional codes, never happens perfectly in human-based systems since natural language is necessarily vague, information is often lacking, and plain old prejudices are difficult to shake."

But if a global network of computers became judge and jury, the way humans interact with each other would radically change. That sounds crazy, doesn't it? That we'd let a global network of computers decide human conflict? For starters, it assumes the inputs will be there to come to a decision. I can imagine something like this for a very simple conflict, maybe a dispute about an insurance policy in the time of a natural disaster. The inputs are there, the details, and they could be boiled down to yes/no questions like, Did the hurricane occur? Was it covered in the policy? But I have a very hard time seeing this global network dirty its circuits with, say, a divorce. Imagine "a disinterested algorithmic interpreter" trying to navigate charges of infidelity or abuse. And yet, while this sounds ludicrous to us now, how must it have sounded in 1970 to hear about a global network of computers that sends information anywhere in the world instantly and for free? So, I don't know, maybe Gavin Wood's vision is the far reaches of what I'm trying to get across to you about Ethereum. Maybe this is the 100-year plan.

Gavin, as is his way, had no doubt about his conviction or ability to make it a reality.

"Overall, I wish to provide a system such that users can be guaranteed that no matter with which other individuals, systems, or organizations they interact, they can do so with absolute confidence in the possible outcomes and how those outcomes might come about," he wrote in the yellow paper.

The ethos was plain, but how exactly do you take those ideals and make them, you know, work? That was a main purpose of the yellow paper. A million decisions had to be made, there would be tradeoffs – for example, maybe a bit less transaction speed for better security. But here the hard work of taking Vitalik's idea and turning it into working code that could be shown to the world was being done.

One of Gavin's earliest contributions was nudging Vitalik's original idea of Ethereum as a generalized form of programmable money. While Vitalik had been explicit in the conclusion to his white paper that Ethereum would allow users to "do anything that any cryptocurrency will ever be able to do," Gavin had the broader idea of making Ethereum a generalized computing platform. They certainly fed off each other, and in many writings before Gavin became involved with Ethereum, Vitalik wrote about how he wanted the platform to be as general as possible so that users could come up with whatever application they wanted. In other words, not just money, but a system of applications all linked together to form the basis of a distributed Internet. This is where Gavin took a lead role in pushing for an even broader idea. Ethereum would handle the smart contracts. A program called Swarm would be used to store data files. Whisper was the name of the messaging system they'd create. All of them would be linked and managed by a browser, a sort of decentralized Internet Explorer. In Gavin's mind, he was laying the foundation for not just a peer-to-peer system based on Ethereum, but a peer-to-peer Internet. The vision was bold and audacious and would take years to implement, if it even worked. For now, it was all mostly ideas on paper.

● ● ●

Vitalik and Gav took the overnight train from Vienna, passing through Innsbruck and Lichtenstein, with the Alps all around them hidden in the dark. They arrived at eight in the morning at the Zug station, which is really not much more than a platform. A grocery store is across the way, past where all the buses roll in and out. Mihai had come to meet them alone; no one else knew he was there. He had to speak to Vitalik.

The tension would have been noticeable from the moment they stepped off the train. Vitalik felt it in his gut; he knew everything would come to a head today and that he'd have to be the one to make the decisions that had to be made. Too many other factions had formed to trust decisions to a vote. He'd put this random group of people together, and he'd have to suffer for it.

Only a year before Vitalik had thought of Ethereum as a side project, something he'd work on for a few months before returning to his studies at the University of Waterloo. But then it gained traction. Serious traction. It was the idea so many Bitcoin adherents had been waiting for, the *next*. The reaction he garnered from the blockchain community had sent the message that he couldn't build his project on top of another existing blockchain like Primecoin; he had to make his own. And here he was six months in, in the throes of that building, and it seemed as though it could all fall apart. While the idea had spread externally all around the world as Ethereum captured the imagination of a good number of very smart computer scientists, the kitchen council Vitalik had assembled was on the verge of dissolution. The discord could cost him the whole project if he wasn't careful. He'd now devoted years of his life to Ethereum, and he was all in. He had to save it.

The cofounders had been together at most six months, true, but that amount of time had been sufficient to let everyone see each other's personalities. They'd started as strangers, a motley crew, and now something had to change. For Mihai, the only one he didn't feel conflicted about was Vitalik, whom he counted as a friend. They'd shared ups and downs at *Bitcoin Magazine* and gotten to know each other well through the struggles as well as the fun times. But there were others who had to go.

Now on the platform at the Zug train station, Mihai asked Vitalik for some time to express his concerns, and they left the train station behind.

"We had this clandestine walk in and around Zug, and talked about things," Vitalik said. Mihai was far from the only person to pull Vitalik aside that day. The jockeying for position had started. "People started kind of taking me off and dragging me out on walks. Charles once. And Anthony once. And Taylor once. They were all coming to me with their complaints." The thing was, everyone knew something was going to happen today – had to happen – but no one knew exactly what.

People had begun arriving the day before; in all there would be 18 people at the Spaceship. It was June 3, 2014, a beautiful summer morning at Lake Zug. Like Vitalik and Gav, Charles Hoskinson and Jeff Wilcke came in the day of the meeting. Charles had pneumonia and arrived in rough shape, unable to control his sweating. Amir Chetrit made his first visit to the Zug house. Joe Lubin had come in the day before.

The ostensible reason for the meeting had to do with finalizing the for-profit structure by signing paperwork and establishing the ownership of Ethereum.

"By law we had to sign the agreements in Switzerland, so every one of the founders was meeting there to sign the document," Anthony Di Iorio said. Anthony had come to Switzerland on his own; his assistants all stayed back in Toronto. This was a day to celebrate: he was about to cement his position as one of the main backers of a for-profit juggernaut he believed would change the world and make him very rich in the bargain. The struggles over leadership roles and styles with Charles, the anxiety he'd felt at needing to be involved in every decision no matter how small, could take a backseat to this moment, when his investment and stress and hard work would all begin to pay off.

Charles would have liked to share Anthony's mood, but his eyes were open to what was happening. He knew that feelings about him – of cofounders and others involved in the project – had always been intense. Hell, he fomented a lot of the drama personally, on purpose. If he could manipulate someone to his will, he'd do it, and do it with a smile. But his angles had always been off; he misread the group, and the way he projected his need to be seen as having street cred – all the CIA talk and Afghanistan stories and the Satoshi nonsense – had always been too strong. No one fell for it for very long. And maybe his biggest gamble, his Steve Jobs moment, had been in pushing to be named CEO of a for-profit venture invented by a man Charles himself described as a communist.

There were also deeper concerns about Charles, as expressed by almost everyone involved in the project at this stage.

"I'm not convinced Charles doesn't have sociopathic tendencies," Taylor Gerring said. "Why would you give people the impression that you're Satoshi Nakamoto, that he has access to his email archive? That you've jumped out of a Blackhawk helicopter? Why?"

Anthony D'Onofrio said he had a bad feeling about Charles the moment he met him at the Miami house. "I immediately knew Charles was a sociopath, that something was wrong with him," he said. He did things to make you trust him, D'Onofrio said, that were like little tests. He'd show D'Onofrio texts from a woman Charles said he'd met in Afghanistan who he'd been having sex with ever since. But it was all bullshit, D'Onofrio believed.

Joe Lubin, in his balanced way, was more diplomatic. "Charles had said too many things not related to the truth," Lubin said. That led to the others losing trust in him. The level of emotional maturity displayed by Charles had also gotten to Lubin. "He was really about 15 years old when he was sitting at that table with us, emotionally."

In the case of Amir Chetrit, it seemed like doing nothing for forever wasn't the best plan. No one in the group knew exactly what he'd done, if anything, for Ethereum, at any time. Many of the cofounders and the other people building Ethereum early on were in it for the ideas behind Ethereum: there was passion for trying to create a better world. Among these peers, Amir's crass money grab stood out as particularly insulting.

Maybe the one thing he'd done is keep his ear to the ground. Before the meeting, Amir warned Charles that people were moving against him.

He was right. A week before, Stephan Tual and Mathias Grønnebæk had called the Spaceship from where they were staying in London. On the other end of the call, Mihai and Taylor Gerring and Richard Stott, a creative director on the project, listened as Stephan said that Gavin Wood was plotting to split the group along technical lines. Stephan and Mathias said they were joining him. Taylor remembered feeling alarm at the *Game of Thrones*–type maneuvering among this otherwise tame group of computer programmers and creative people.

"Control over the money was becoming a more and more serious issue," Taylor said. Once there was money in the bank, "people might get a little ferocious." It was May 28, and the all-hands-on-deck meeting in Zug had been called for the next week. "This was the moment, in my mind, where Stephan effectively said, 'hey, something's about to break.'"

As the cofounders gathered to start the meeting, they found the big central table in the living room cleared of the usual clutter – all the laptops and beer bottles and cables and notebooks that were normally spread all around were gone. A somber note hung in the air, and while there were several more people involved in this meeting besides the eight cofounders, anyone not directly involved – like significant others or guests – was asked to leave.

There wasn't room enough for everyone involved to sit at the table, so many people stood around it. Vitalik sat next to Mihai, with Gavin Wood and Jeff Wilcke next to them. Across from them sat Roxana; to her left was Jeremy Wood, Charles's personal assistant, and Charles. Next to Charles sat Anthony Di Iorio.

"Everyone had a chance to speak their mind," Roxana said. "It was not what you were working on," she said, "everyone knew that something had to be changed." The motion before the table was to say what you wanted, and to name names.

"Not that I think I can't trust someone," she said, "you had to say exactly who do you not trust and why, with details." Gavin and Jeff spoke passionately about their frustration with the first half year of the Ethereum project. Vitalik had come to understand the weight that Gavin now pulled within the Ethereum ecosystem. The technical prowess he'd exhibited in his work on the yellow paper coupled with his intuitive thinking on how Ethereum code should work were hugely valuable. Vitalik couldn't afford to lose Gavin, but Gav had privately given Vitalik an ultimatum. It was either him or Charles – one of them had to go.

"Gav had a long-term dislike for all the nontechnical people because he felt that they were just doing nothing and wasting their time. Kind of masquerading as biz dev and getting as much money out of Ethereum as he was," Vitalik said. In Gav's mind, people who couldn't understand the technical issues they were working through everyday had no place in leadership roles. Gav had approached Vitalik before about this; in fact, many times he'd tried to convince Vitalik that he, Gav, and Jeff should split off and do their own thing. Now he wasn't being as extreme, but Gav's position put Vitalik in a tough spot.

"I was very scared and could not imagine that Ethereum could possibly succeed without those other people," Vitalik said. Business development has a place in any venture; Vitalik knew this. And blowing up the leadership right now would jeopardize, or at least delay, the money they hoped to raise from the crowdfund that now was truly and finally only a few weeks away. That would mean going to traditional sources of money that would take more time and provide them with less capital to work with. Vitalik didn't want that either.

Now everyone had a chance to say their piece. When it came to Gav, he said he could no longer trust Charles as CEO and that one of them had to go. Jeff backed him up with the same choice. "That was the show-down," Mihai said.

Charles shot back that Ethereum didn't have to be for-profit, if that would help his standing. But he didn't realize the depths of his problems with the other cofounders. The conversation got heated. Alex Leverington, a developer who was helping build the C++ client, tried to explain his view – that there was enough Ethereum to go around for everyone. This thing is going to be huge, he told the group, everyone – developers, marketers, salespeople – they'll all be needed and can all bring valued contributions to the project. This wasn't what Gav and Jeff wanted to hear in the moment, and they told Leverington to shut it and wondered why he was even talking during such a crucial discussion.

Then Vitalik spoke. The problem with the group of people around this table was that there were actually two tables, he said: one with developers at it, and one with Charles, Amir, and Anthony. But they should all be at the same table, one team, striving for the same goal. He just wanted everyone to be at the same table.

Someone – Joe Lubin thinks it might have been him – suggested Vitalik disband the cofounders and remake the group as he wished. At that moment the skinny 20-year-old with the too-big head possessed something that no one else in that room possessed. It didn't matter if you had joined Ethereum from day one or had just arrived to help, everyone in that house knew one thing – Vitalik was the only one to trust. He'd earned it, every day, with his attention to people and interest in their ideas and ability to listen and learn from what people told him, whether negative or positive. Yeah, he was 20, but he was a leader. You can't fake that for long, not without an army behind you.

He repaired to the balcony, alone, to think it over.

The qualms raised by Gavin's ultimatum still troubled Vitalik; he knew a diverse set of people was needed to make Ethereum succeed. They needed showmen and coders and writers and thinkers and sales-women. As he paced the balcony, he struggled with the idea of whether his project could survive a leadership restructuring. Could he consider anyone in the group indispensable?

Once Vitalik returned to the meeting – the amount of time he spent pacing on the balcony was reported to be between five minutes and an hour and a half, depending on who you asked – he addressed the group.

"I made this speech that consisted of half a minute of filler," Vitalik said, "followed by the real decision, which was that Charles and Amir would be fired. They were disappointed but absolutely not surprised."

Vitalik made two additions to the leadership group, adding Stephan Tual and Taylor Gerring. The group still stood at eight.

Anthony Di Iorio couldn't believe what he was seeing. He felt blindsided. His confusion started when he arrived to a full house after only expecting to sign some papers and make his way back home. Who were all these people, when he'd left his entire support staff in Toronto? And then he'd been singled out by Vitalik as part of the group of people who were going to be fired. What the hell was going on?

"Charles was targeted because he was the CEO," Anthony said. "There was just nasty stuff made up about him." He struggled to come up with specifics when I asked him for examples but said others in the group actively searched for dirt on Charles. According to Anthony, the treachery didn't end with Charles and Amir. There was also a push to get rid of him and Joe Lubin, but Vitalik wouldn't go along.

"It wasn't just to sign the documents, it was a coup d'etat," Anthony said.

Vitalik didn't see it that way. "It was definitely an internal power struggle," he said. "Coup is when leadership is overturned. Purge is better."

●　●　●

Herbert Sterchi arrived at the Spaceship 10 minutes after the meeting had ended. He found everyone, minus Charles and Amir, out on the balcony.

"If you'd have taken a match to the air, it would have exploded," he said. "It was so tense. People were quiet." He'd gotten a call asking him to come over: the cofounders needed some advice after the leadership change. Sterchi, their fixer, had been with the Switzerland crew from the moment they'd stepped foot in the country. He'd given them tax and regulatory advice and let the advance group crash at his apartment in Lucerne for about two and a half weeks while they looked for a permanent house to rent. He was much older than anyone in the group and tried to calm the frayed nerves he found out on the balcony.

It was a change from what he'd become used to in dealing with the Switzerland-based Ethereum folks. He'd always been impressed with how close-knit they were, and how well they worked together. Maybe that came from living and working in the same place, but it set Ethereum apart from the other cryptocurrency projects Herbert had advised. Still, Sterchi knew there had always been internal conflict between the technical and the nontechnical people.

"It was Gavin's group against the others," he said. Herbert made it a point to tell Gavin that not just the coders mattered to Ethereum: the diverse skills of the entire group were needed too.

By the time Herbert arrived, tempers may have been short not only because of the unpleasant confrontation that had just gone down, but also because of the severance packages that were handed out. Charles was given 300,000 ether for his time with Ethereum. Amir received less, but it was still in the neighborhood of 150,000 ether. At the time, of course, ether had no value, but everyone around that table believed it would one day be worth something. At a $10 valuation, the payouts amounted to $3 million and $1.5 million, respectively. At its highest price to date, ether had traded at about $1,200. That would amount to $360 million for Charles and $180 million for Amir – assuming they kept it all and sold at the very top, obviously. In any case, there was a lot of gold in those parachutes.

By the time Herbert arrived Charles was down in the basement and he didn't get a chance to see him. He'd always liked Charles, but he knew that it would be better to give him space. To Charles, being fired in such an overt manner was deeply personal.

"It became a *Lord of the Flies*–style situation, where power camps were formed and whoever was most persuasive to Vitalik was the one who won," Charles said. "That's why there's some bad blood, that's why I wasn't the nicest guy on the exit. My Reddit postings weren't so happy."

I met Charles at ETHDenver in 2019 but didn't have a chance to join him at his ranch nearby as he suggested. We spoke on the phone several times over the next year until he politely, but firmly, told me he was done talking. My questions about the way people described him – sociopath, liar – had grown more pointed, and he said he was done with that part of his life and had moved on.

But in our first conversation, as Charles relayed his story to me, he described the arc of the early Ethereum days in terms of Miami being the spring and Toronto the fall. In Zug, winter arrived.

He'd begun to notice a change in the cofounders after Toronto. "It was a whisper campaign," he said. Stephan Tual and Taylor Gerring, who were both resentful that they weren't getting equity or being thought of as cofounders although they'd been around almost since the beginning, felt they were being treated unfairly. For his part, Charles said he'd been doing all of the legal work in private – you don't go emailing a huge group of people about the status of negotiations over whether ether is a security or not – so no one would have known what he was up to. (Mihai was working on this part of the project too, actually.) As far as Charles was concerned his silence fed conspiracy theories about what he was really up to.

When he told me this part of the story, he shifted into speaking about himself in the third person

"You've got this guy who's got a huge personality, kind of larger than life," Charles said. Everyone knew he was in favor of raising VC funding, his theory went, and when you don't hear from him it could be assumed that he's working behind people's backs.

"I tend to be a very charismatic, verbose guy who draws a crowd, and I tend to wear my passions on my sleeve, which is why I have so much trouble on Twitter," he said. "For me to get really private and quiet and then there's not a lot of communication occurring, it allows people to invent a narrative."

Then people who were usually mean to him began acting nice. He had a cordial, "but sometimes rough relationship" with three of the people who worked for him – Stephan, Taylor, and Mathias. "Suddenly they were all just being overly nice and at that point I figured, 'okay, there's something going on here,'" Charles said.

"I figured going into Switzerland there was going to be a big fight," he said. "I didn't anticipate how much ill will had materialized."

After the reporting for this book was done, I approached Charles to ask him for any comments he might want to make about the end of his time with Ethereum. I mentioned the stuff about the CIA, about the Blackhawk helicopters and telling people he was Satoshi. He didn't want to engage.

"I don't care what people have said about me," he said. "I've completely moved on from this."

• • •

There was still the matter of signing the paperwork. Mihai had incorporated Ethereum as a for-profit entity in Switzerland in February 2014. A main feature of this structure was that it limited the personal liability of the contributors to the Ethereum project. Yet in so doing, all the shares – 100 percent – were in Mihai's name, and he was not happy about that. What the cofounders needed to do now was agree on how to distribute the shares if Ethereum was to remain a for-profit enterprise. The cofounders continued to discuss their options as the day in Zug turned to evening. Yet Vitalik still had his doubts about going this route.

"I said, by the way, why is it that making a foundation in Switzerland is so hard that we have to give up on the foundation and do the for-profit?" he said. The lawyers were again consulted, and they came back and said, it's actually not that hard to set up a Swiss-based foundation.

"When I got this news, I was like, 'hey guys, joy, we don't have to make a profit anymore!'" Vitalik said.

This added insult to injury for Anthony, who had invested in Ethereum and spent countless hours working on it for the business opportunity it presented. He wanted to profit from it, as any businessman given that opportunity would. Yet here he was, up against a group of idealists who thought that making decisions by committee was how companies are run. He refers to the Zug meeting as "The Red Wedding," the *Game of Thrones* episode where most of the Stark family is murdered. It must have been very difficult for him to see his leadership role so diminished in the course of an afternoon. He'd thought he was coming to Zug to celebrate a great business decision. Then he could only watch as his understanding of his role within the group of cofounders completely changed. He'd fancied himself a leader, and yet none of his opinions carried weight.

If there was one cofounder who never lost faith, who was a true believer among a group of true believers, that would be Joe Lubin. Of course, Joe was also often cool and calculating, maybe reserved his enthusiasm in service to his long-term agenda. More seasoned than most of the cofounders combined, Joe knew the amazing business opportunity before him. And he wasn't the type of person to engage in personal drama. He knew what he'd come across with Ethereum was potentially world changing and he committed to the ride.

I asked him, though, if he found it interesting, or surprising, that Ethereum seemed to grow and prosper despite the fact that its leadership from the get-go was usually in some state of shambles.

"It's not surprising," he said. "Because the ideas were so powerful, the need was so big and so great." If they'd been a traditional startup from the beginning, they would've had a much different approach to putting a leadership team together. But that's not Ethereum's story.

"What this was, was a white paper that was hitting the planet at just the right time," Lubin said. "I knew it was a ragtag group of people. I also knew that we would be able to hold things together regardless of what the interpersonal challenges might be because the set of ideals were so strong and because we all did share the overarching goal of delivering the project. Even if it got heated, nobody was really inclined to say, 'fuck this stupid idea, I'm going to go build a gambling platform.'"

Everyone knew Ethereum would be transformative. "It was not just another startup," Lubin said. "It was one of the greatest ideas, opportunities, and enabling projects in human history."

●　●　●

By the time the Zug meeting ended the sun had set. It had been a long day. Roxana and Vitalik went for a run. The others fanned out across the house. Charles was in his room in the basement, making travel arrangements to return to London in the morning. He wouldn't see the group again.

Then it was time for bed, and everyone headed to their rooms in the crowded house. There were three to four people per bedroom. Upstairs, Vitalik and Gavin shared a room with Mihai and Roxana. Just before turning the light out, Gav got up. He locked the bedroom door.

Fourteen

The second time I met the ether thief was in the Chiyoda City neighborhood of Tokyo. It was January 2019 and we were on the 22nd floor of the Marunouchi Building, where Bloomberg has its Tokyo bureau. The park that surrounds the Imperial Palace could be seen from one side of the office; on the other side was the city's main train station and the Tokyo Station Hotel, a beautiful brick and granite building that looks like a palace in its own right. It was a miserable day outside, with cold rain driven by strong winds and intermittent snow flurries.

I was a half a world away from my meeting a few months earlier with the man I'd thought was the ether thief. The story had evolved since then: I had new reporting and had made a discovery on my own that had led me here to Tokyo. To explain that, we need to go back a bit to revisit why I'd thought, incorrectly, that the man in Zürich had attacked the DAO.

The first important piece of the puzzle was the encrypted message that was shared with me. That came from the 0x15def account. No one outside the RHG had ever seen the message; it was a great clue. The second puzzle piece came from a source with knowledge of the exchange world. I'd been told the identity of someone who had an account at the exchange Poloniex. The source said the person I met in Zürich had withdrawn Bitcoin from Poloniex and sent it to ShapeShift, where it was swapped for ether. That ether then shows up in the public Ethereum blockchain at the address 0x4fae.

I'd found a link between 0x15def and 0x4fae. On June 21, 2016, the 0x4fae address sent ether to address 0x15def, for a total of five ether. Why would the man in Zürich be sending ether to the account of a known DAO attacker? It was no smoking gun, but it was enough for me to get on a plane so I could meet him and ask the question.

The man in Zürich denied having anything to do with the DAO attack, though I thought it was a weak denial at best. Then I got updated information from my source and I knew I'd asked the wrong person if he'd been involved with the DAO hack. I was at home by this time; it was several weeks after I'd returned from Zürich. The news that I had the wrong person knocked me sideways. I'd thought all along that this story needed to start with the ether thief, nefariously hunched over a keyboard and waiting for just the right moment to begin his attack. I thought I had something, albeit a slender lead. And then it turned out I had nothing. It was impossible for me to write that day, even though the clock was ticking on getting my book in on time. So instead I started pouring over the blockchain records on Etherscan.

I started with 0x15def since I knew that was a bad-guy address. It had received ether from 0x4fae, but in the blockchain records I could see that these were only two transactions among dozens of others. They came in the middle of a whole lot of other activity. But I thought I should see how 0x15def began – how it had received the initial funds that were recorded on the blockchain.

The 0x15def address had received its initial funding from address 0x35f5, which had sent it two ether on June 20, 2016, at 11:29:56 UTC.

In looking at 0x35f5 I could see that it had been funded by 0x4fae on that same day at 10:56:53 UTC, only about a hour before it had sent ether to 0x15def. The accounts were all linked – the connection wasn't just a few ether transactions between 0x4fae and 0x15def. I'd found a link between the Poloniex account withdrawal and the address that'd sent the encrypted message to the RHG and that had attacked the DAO on June 21. Not only had it attacked the DAO, it was the next-largest theft after the original hack on June 17. I couldn't believe what I was seeing.

I ran to tell my wife what I'd found and took her laptop to pull up the Etherscan records to show her the linked accounts. I was elated and felt like this had been there all along for anyone to see, but not everyone had had the encrypted message and the link between the Poloniex account and address 0x4fae. Two different sources had given me pieces, and I'd put them together to make this whole.

Still, I could be wrong, I thought. It's possible that different people had sent ether to either 0x35f5 or 0x15def to fund those accounts. It didn't have to be the same person. But what if it was?

I was reassured that my theory that the accounts were linked was solid because of the initiating transactions. They provided a through line. Then there was the date and times of their creations. I thought it unlikely that there were other people sending ether to 0x15def or 0x35f5, as they were funded only 33 minutes and 3 seconds apart.

I wondered if the feds had ever made the connection I'd uncovered. Various law enforcement agencies had looked into the DAO hack back in 2016. The New York attorney general and the Boston office of the Federal Bureau of Investigation had started asking questions, according to several of the people they'd spoken to who asked not to be named. The FBI's Jeff Williams was one of the agents tasked with looking into the case, these people said. The FBI also was given the blockchain records and analysis done by Poloniex, according to an executive at a major digital asset exchange who asked not to be named. This was in October 2016, and there was frustration on the exchange side that government agents weren't more adept in understanding the information they were given. After October the trail went cold and the FBI didn't contact Poloniex again, the executive said.

When I reported in 2017 on the DAO attack for *Bloomberg Markets* magazine, I spoke to a prosecutor who had tried digital asset cases for the

Justice Department. There was a belief that many people were victims of the DAO attack, including Ethereum users in the US. But the jurisdiction would be a nightmare, I was told. It was also not an open-and-shut case: there would need to be lots of digging and subpoenas needed to get the information the government would need to try a case. Even then it would be very risky for a prosecutor to take the case due to its complexity, the former prosecutor told me. By the end of 2016, US law enforcement efforts to investigate the DAO attack had gone cold.

After I made the funding connection between 0x4fae and 0x15def I still had a problem. I'd once been given incorrect information about who owned the exchange account that withdrew the funds and sent them to 0x4fae. Forensics were much less advanced in 2016 than in 2019, so it isn't hard to believe that what looked like solid connections then might turn out not to be solid when analytics were applied three years later. The picture was much more distinct in 2019. And from what I was told, in 2016 the information the exchange had given both to me and the FBI about the owner of the Poloniex account had been the same. So at least the feds and I both got the same bad tip, I thought.

But in 2019, I still needed to know the real owner of the account. I spoke to a source again and was given a different name this time: Tomoaki Sato. I knew then that I had to make arrangements to go to Tokyo.

Fifteen

As a result of the bloodletting in Zug, Vitalik had reshaped the leadership team and succeeded in his desire to officially create a nonprofit entity – the Ethereum Foundation. The next big hurdle would be selling ether to the public to raise development funds and pay off debts.

While Vitalik was working on the crowdsale and battling the anxiety it created in him, he was still also reeling from what had happened in Zug. He'd never been in that position before and the responsibility seemed bewildering at times. The closest he'd come was when *Bitcoin Magazine* had run into trouble, although Vitalik hadn't been named in the court papers. He was simply a writer for the magazine, working mostly out of his Waterloo dorm room. Leading the Ethereum cofounders was a whole new ballgame.

"Now, I'm inside of something 10 times bigger, I'm the unambiguous primary founder, and quite often it seems like I'm the only person everyone still consistently respects," he wrote to family and friends in an email from mid-June 2014. He'd wanted to set up Ethereum so he could leave the hard decision-making to a competent group of people and be free to write code and solve difficult but fun challenges in crypto-economics. "Now it turns out that I have to be the one to keep the ship even pulled together in the first place," he wrote. "Sigh."

At best, Vitalik had been a reluctant leader of the cofounders and the Ethereum Foundation. He preferred soft power to hard and really only wanted time and space to work out the incredibly complicated problems of building Ethereum and making its business plan work. But then people entered the equation, stupid complicating people.

"One of the challenges of having power is that first of all, when people are being friends with you, you don't know if they actually like you or are sucking up to power," Vitalik said. Soon after the cofounder group had been created, Vitalik mistook the actions of some of the group; his error was in thinking that people who were being overly nice to him were actually good human beings in general. He hadn't encountered the backstabbing and whisper campaigns that marked the early months of the cofounder group when he was at Abelard or in his first year at Waterloo. Those environments were tame – filled with people who competed for grades, sure, but not for a stake in what could be a multibillion-dollar enterprise.

Vitalik doesn't limit his criticism to others: he can look at himself and see his own self-interest coming out at certain stages in his life. He knows that his own motivations might not always be pure.

"I remember for a while I fell into the trap of thinking that because I don't care about making lots of money, that means I have no selfish interests," he said. "But there are definitely other selfish interests you can have."

Still, nothing in his life up to then had prepared him for the managerial quagmire he walked into in Zug. He'd never thought of making an entry in the "Encyclopedia of Bunnies" that covered how bunnies manage groups of warring business factions. If he could have his wish, the board meeting would have been a happy reunion with the eight cofounders of Ethereum. "In reality, I walked into organizational hell," he wrote in the email. People had split into factions and were at each other's throats. Vitalik alluded to Dan Larimer in the email without naming him, and to Larimer's past with Charles Hoskinson. Larimer and Hoskinson were among the founders of BitShares, which Charles had left under a cloud of suspicion. "Words that I had thought to be vicious lies from the CEO of one of our semi-competitors about one of our employees turned out to be essentially true," Vitalik wrote. "Some people were uncomfortable sleeping at night because of what was going on."

The waves made at the Zug meeting didn't subside for a while. Vitalik found himself having to play peacemaker over and over again. It exhausted him.

"I just want everyone to work together and am spending hours every day trying to pull people together and then seeing glimmers of success, but then hear five hours later that they are arguing again," he wrote. Vitalik seemed to be growing up and realized there might not be a solution to the infighting amid the cofounders.

"There are massive ideological and financial divides that seem in the short term very deep and difficult to reconcile," he wrote. The financial aspect of what he'd done in making Ethereum a nonprofit wasn't lost on him. That decision "knocked my estimated theoretical net worth, as well as that of seven other people, down by something like three million dollars (i.e., back to almost nothing)," he wrote.

The stress of past events was compounded by his ongoing worries about the crowdsale. He felt anxious and in limbo as they waited for their lawyers to give them the okay to sell ether to the public. If they had to delay the ether sale for another year due to legal and regulatory reasons, Vitalik didn't know how many on his team could weather that.

Then, after months of legal analysis and thousands in fees, the Ethereum Foundation was given the green light to sell ether, including to people in the US.

While in private Vitalik was enduring some of the toughest weeks of his life, in public he put on an air of happy optimism as he announced the crowdsale in a blog post on the Ethereum Foundation website on July 22, 2014. He began by thanking the people working to build Ethereum "who in many cases abandoned their jobs to dedicate their time to it" and said "we have been promising that the sale would arise in two weeks for six months, and many team members have endured substantial hardships because of expectations that we set regarding when we would be able to provide funding."

He took the opportunity to update people on the progress they were making. They now had four clients in various stages of production. In addition to the C++, Python, and Go clients, one was being built in Java by Roman Mandeleil. Vitalik had always felt it important to have Ethereum written in as many computer languages as possible, if for no other reason than it would be impossible for one group – say Java developers – to dominate the project. It was also to address a security concern: if one or two clients were disabled in a malicious attack, the network could continue to run on the unaffected clients.

Vitalik also listed certain technical changes that had improved Ethereum's performance as it was going through proof-of-concept versions. One such improvement was reducing the time it took to confirm a block on the Ethereum blockchain to 10–20 seconds, down from 60 seconds. This was in comparison to an average of 10 minutes at the time for a block on the Bitcoin blockchain and 2.5 minutes for a Litecoin block to be confirmed by their respective network of miners.

Mihai Alisie was at the Spaceship in Zug the day that Vitalik had the breakthrough that reduced the block time.

"Vitalik was sitting off to one side of the table, and usually, you know, he's typing like 'rat-tat-tat-tat,'" Mihai said. "And then at some point he paused, and did one of those, 'hmm,' like he's thinking. That got my attention." Vitalik took a piece of paper and began drawing squares and lines, trying to show Mihai what he'd discovered. "It was a big breakthrough for the time," he said. "That was epic."

The Ethereum Foundation would sell ether for Bitcoin at prices that would vary over the course of the crowdsale, which would last for 42 days, from July 22 to September 2, 2014. Early birds would receive 2,000 ether for every Bitcoin; 14 days later the ratio would drop to 1,337 ether per Bitcoin. On July 22, 2014, Bitcoin traded for $621, meaning ether bought that day would be priced at 31 cents each.

Vitalik also made sure to include an unambiguous statement in the blog post, complete with bold typeface: "Ether is a product," he wrote, "**NOT a security or investment offering**." He continued, "Ether is simply a token useful for paying transaction fees or building or purchasing decentralized application services on the Ethereum platform; it does not give you voting rights over anything, and we make no guarantees of its future value."

What the Ethereum Foundation should have been more concerned about at the time was not the future value of ether, but that of Bitcoin.

●　●　●

What the Ethereum Foundation was attempting to do would later be known as an initial coin offering, or ICO. But in July 2014 that term didn't exist. Only a few other projects, most notably MasterCoin in 2013, had raised funds from the public in the same way that Ethereum planned to.

It shouldn't be overlooked that cryptocurrencies enabled an entirely new funding model for startups. An ICO allows direct fundraising from users or investors or speculators, without the need to go to VC firms for seed money or banks to undertake the long and complicated road to an initial public offering. This was decentralized finance in its purest form, and as the world would see in just a few years, staggering amounts of money would be raised – and lost – by crypto firms via the ICO market. The scams and charlatans were everywhere: you were lucky to get a white paper to explain some projects. Some white papers brazenly plagiarized existing ones. The funds raised through an ICO were meant to fund development of that particular project, of course. Yet that happened only very infrequently at best. Most of the money raised was dumb money looking for the next big rising star. The ICO market also gave rise to a host of shady cryptocurrencies that traded on shady exchanges that did no due diligence checks on their users, meaning price manipulation was rampant. Scammers brazenly organized pump-and-dump schemes on chat boards, and to call this period of crypto the Wild West does a disservice to frontiersman. There were laws in the 1800s, of course; they simply ignored them. The ICO market was a law-free zone.

Yet none of that changes the fact that ICOs now opened up a path to capital like none that had existed before. Never before had a type of value – of money – been created at such a low cost. Of course, calculating a value for that digital currency wasn't easy; many ICO projects lost their entire value after failing to deliver on their promises. But it was the very nature of digital money that was new. Money until then had been held by bankers or rich investors. Gatekeepers, in other words. And whether you think the advent of cryptocurrencies is a revolution or an unmitigated disaster that will one day crash and burn to the ground, there is no denying that for the first time, access to value could be had entirely outside the realm of the traditional financial world. It democratized seed investing and gave power back to the little guys and gals who wanted to make something cool. A well-run, legitimate project could tap directly into its potential future user base in a revolutionary new way.

Ethereum arguably initiated the first ICO, given that it went on to have such an important role in the ICO craze that hit in 2017. That is, all of those new coins that were created were hosted on the Ethereum blockchain and known as ERC-20 tokens. MasterCoin had come and gone by then. Ethereum was the new kid in town.

At the end of the 42-day sale, 60,102,216 ether had been sold to the public. In return, the Ethereum Foundation got a stash of 31,529 Bitcoin, which was worth about $18 million.

Now the cofounders had to address the matter of how the pre-mined ether would be distributed to the core group and others who helped bring Ethereum to life. This debate had been ongoing since Miami; it always seemed to lurk in the background those first six months of the project. After so much back and forth, the cofounders created a simple solution to allocate pre-mined ether based on the amount of blood, sweat, and tears each person had contributed.

"For every month we would allot the ether proportionately to how much time everyone contributed, with slightly more ether allocated to earlier months," Vitalik said. The cofounders agreed to set aside 9.9 percent of the total ether sold to the public to be split among themselves. That came to 5.95 million ether. Vitalik received the single largest chunk: 9 percent of that, or roughly 535,000 ether. Other cofounders received 5 percent, or just under 300,000 ether. In all, 86 people received pre-mined ether for their work, from Gavin Wood who was leading the code development to Lorenzo Pattuzo who built a wall in the Spaceship House.

Vitalik could finally relax, a bit, now that the crowdsale had been pulled off without a hitch. "This first big milestone was finally finished," he said. "We could breathe one sigh of relief." With more than 30,000

Bitcoin burning a hole in their digital wallet, however, they also had to pay some bills. First up were the loans made to the development team by Anthony Di Iorio and Joe Lubin.

Anthony's original loan terms said that for every Bitcoin he lent he'd be repaid with 3,000 ether. In the end, though, this didn't come to pass for several reasons. Anthony had entered the loan deal thinking he'd gotten better terms than what would be offered in the crowdsale, meaning he'd gotten the best ether buying opportunity of anyone on the planet.

"A lot of things didn't happen as they were supposed to. Our motto was, 'things change,'" Anthony said. "Contracts were meaningless. We were supposed to be for-profit, that's why I put my money in. Then we weren't."

The terms of Anthony's repayment had been changed ahead of the crowdsale, in part because the foundation didn't know if they'd get enough ether to pay everyone back in ether. That could have led to even more tension among the group, something no one wanted.

"The intention was that the ether distribution was kept pure in the sense that there weren't claims on the actual genesis ether," Vitalik said. Instead, they'd repay their debts with the Bitcoin raised in the crowdsale. For every Bitcoin Joe Lubin or Anthony had loaned the development effort, they'd get back between 1.25 and 1.5 Bitcoins.

Before you rush to defend the loan terms of Joe Lubin and Anthony Di Iorio as sacred – immutable, even – know this. They are both billionaires because of their early investment in Ethereum. Anthony now owns the largest condominium in Canada, which encompasses the entire top floor of the St. Regis hotel building. It's so high up you have to take one elevator, get out, and get on a second elevator to reach it. He lives there and uses part of it as an event space, utilizing the amazing wraparound views of the city and Lake Ontario.

Joe Lubin has always been more cagey about his wealth, but when lists of the rich were published in 2017 and 2018 as Bitcoin, ether, and other cryptocurrencies were hitting their peak values, Joe was always listed as being among the most wealthy. In 2018, *Forbes* magazine estimated his net worth at between $1 billion and $5 billion.

Part of the proceeds from the crowdsale were also reserved for the Ethereum Foundation. It would receive about 6 million ether, or 10 percent of what was sold to the public. This would allow the foundation to be self-sustaining, award grants, and have some money in the bank if needed.

And the old argument about the developers doing more work than others associated with the foundation also came to bear on the crowd-sale, as a developer purchase program was created. The devs felt the pre-mine allocation unfairly favored people who had been around in the early days but who wouldn't be around in the coming months when the really hard work of getting Ethereum to go live would be done.

"Realistically, they were completely right because we really under-estimated the timeline and we expected Ethereum to be launched by the end of the year," Vitalik said.

The purchase program was meant as an incentive to keep the devs happy. It allowed the 50 or so developers who were building Ethereum to buy ether to a max of 20 percent of their salaries at the same price offered in the crowdsale: so, 2,000 ether per Bitcoin, or roughly 31 cents per ether.

From Vitalik's point of view, the developer team he spearheaded with Gavin and Jeff as equal partners was an island of calm in the still-tumultuous sea of the broader Ethereum Foundation community. The Berlin operations, which Gav and Jeff named EthDev, were purposely walled off from the political debates at the foundation so the coding work could continue without distraction.

Along with the foundation drama, what also continued as the foun-dation sold ether for Bitcoin was a worrying drop in the value of Bitcoin. During the crowdsale itself, from July 22 to September 2, Bitcoin had dropped 23 percent. As September drew to a close, Bitcoin continued to crash and fell 38 percent to $383, its value on October 1. The foundation had first accepted Bitcoin for ether in July, when it traded for $621. Surely someone at the foundation had sold the Bitcoin the crowdsale had brought in for cash to protect against such a drop, which of course would cut into the money the Ethereum Foundation had to fund its operations? Not exactly.

"The reason why the Bitcoin never got hedged is basically I had entrusted Joe with the task of selling it," Vitalik said. "He was selling it at these very slow, trickle-y rates." Joe was optimistic that Bitcoin would rally again, and he managed the foundation's money with that view in mind. But there was another, more contentious reason Vitalik thought Joe didn't want to sell the foundation's Bitcoin even as it crashed.

"If the Bitcoin had turned into fiat [currency], that fiat would be available to Gavin, and Joe distrusted Gavin," Vitalik said.

Vitalik stepped in and accelerated the sale of the Bitcoin, but the damage had been done. While the Ethereum Foundation started September with $18 million, it now had seen its funds cut in half to $9 million, thanks to the drop in Bitcoin value.

I asked Joe Lubin about this, if his belief in Bitcoin had clouded his judgement about hedging the foundation's stash. He said there was an elaborate system for selling the Bitcoin – the one Michael Perklin had created, where several people in three locations around the world had to agree to sell. But he didn't seem like he regretted it too much.

"I wish we knew the future at all times," Joe said. "I remain a true believer."

● ● ●

Anyone who thought the removal of Amir Chetrit and Charles Hoskinson from the Ethereum project would settle nerves and lead to a period of stability would have been sorely mistaken. The rancor seemed to grow among the group after the successful crowdsale, as simmering personal feuds, which may have taken a backseat to other leadership drama, now came to the surface. The factions that had developed among the cofounders seemed to provide the space needed for combustion, similar to how the logs in a bonfire must be spread to give the flames the air they need.

Maybe the most prominent of these feuds was the long-held beef between Joe Lubin and Gavin Wood. They had already clashed over leadership issues, but now with Gav ensconced at EthDev in Berlin, the fight for control intensified.

Speaking of Gavin, Joe said, "control is a theme in his life. Tension is also a theme in his life, and he wasn't really happy with how things were going with respect to control." Gav had pushed for the ouster of Charles and Amir, but Joe thought his desires went further. A few times, Joe said, Gavin "attempted to divide and conquer the project."

Gavin said that Joe was wrong. "There is no truth to this accusation," he said when I asked him about Joe's comments. "Joe does not know me nearly well enough to comment on the 'themes in my life.'" EthDev got under Joe's skin because it seemed to be separate from the rest of the foundation operations, and Joe didn't want their budget running out of control with little or no oversight.

Vitalik stood in the middle. "Joe was very distrustful of EthDev," Vitalik said. "He wanted to give them money on a shoestring budget." That made Gav and Jeff Wilcke extremely uncomfortable because they felt they deserved more trust and not knowing whether the money to pay developers was going to be there in six months made hiring them a challenge.

"Gavin was interested in essentially moving most of the assets in the project, and control of the Ethereum project, from the Ethereum Foundation to EthDev," Joe said. The stakes couldn't be higher. "I wasn't comfortable with that. I wanted to see some checks and balances." EthDev could, of course, do its job and create the software, but Lubin didn't want to see other people's money put under EthDev control. They tried to hammer out agreements about a payment schedule of sorts, but Joe and Gavin and Jeff couldn't agree to the terms.

"I don't think there was any slowing of the work – ever – for lack of funds," Joe said.

Gavin said the financial concern Joe expressed was misplaced, as EthDev had provided a detailed budget to the foundation so that future spending could be monitored. Also, how could Anthony or Mihai or Stephan provide oversight on EthDev when they didn't have the technical know-how to understand the work?

"In reality, I believe Joe was upset that he would lose his ability to oversee the project's development and exert influence and control where desired," Gavin said. "He fancied himself as Vitalik's mentor and disliked the fact that I had, to some degree, fulfilled or made redundant that role."

Richard Burton worked for Gavin while he was helping with the design aspects of Ethereum. "I'm one of those people [Gavin] was very kind to," Burton said. "Which is quite rare." Gavin was very open to people who wanted to help him accomplish what he set out to do. "Gav is a master of finding people who will basically work for nothing and follow him into battle. He really looks for missionaries," Richard said. Wood can also be very difficult to work with and has a cutting eye – and comment – for anyone who debates him on issues related to coding. "You should see some of the things he's written on GitHub," Burton said. "It's just tirades."

Joe seemed to epitomize Gavin's distaste for the non-coders involved in early Ethereum. Upon first seeing Lubin at the Miami house, Gavin said he "couldn't work out what Joe was doing there." Then there was Joe's relationship with Vitalik, and the fact that Gavin bristles at anyone who doesn't give him credit for the long hard hours of work he put in to build Ethereum. Joe told Vitalik at the time that Gavin's prominence in the project was problematic.

"I vehemently disagree with that notion," Gavin said. "I could imagine that I was problematic for his designs. Joe has spent a lot of effort trying to convince the world of the 'boy-genius-creates Ethereum' genesis narrative. My being around, and not being willing to take a backseat, takes away from this myth."

When I spoke to Joe in 2019, the feud seemed to have cooled to a degree. "I think Gavin is quite brilliant," he said. "I feel like Gavin and I could hang out and enjoy talking to one another over a beer. But I do believe that he dislikes me."

Mihai Alisie walking up the stairs to the hack lab at the compound at Calafou.

Graffiti inside the hack lab.

Remnants of the destruction from the fire that burned when the factory at Calafou was struck by lightning.

Vitalik Buterin is mobbed by people asking questions after giving his Ethereum presentation at the Miami Bitcoin conference. Joe Lubin and Antony Di Iorio are to his left.

Source: Taylor Gerring.

The Ethereum booth at the Miami Bitcoin conference, January 2014.
Staffing the booth are Paul Paschos (left) and Stephan Tual (right).

A group of early Ethereum supporters at the Miami house rented by Anthony Di Iorio for the 2014 Miami Bitcoin conference. Top (left to right): Dino Mark, Yanislav Malahov, Charles Hoskinson, Anthony D'Onofrio, Steve Dakh, Wendell Davis, Jonathan Mohan, Joseph Lubin, Louis Parker. Bottom (left to right): Gavin Wood, Vitalik Buterin, Anthony Di Iorio, Taylor Gerring, Jason Colby (above), Kyle Kurbegovich (below).

Stephan Tual (left) and Mathias Grønnebæk (right) (on the laptop screen) during a video call with Mihai Alisie (left) and Richard Stott (right) at the Spaceship House. This is the call where Tual warned the Ethereum crew in Switzerland that Gavin Wood was making moves against them.

Gavin Wood, Mihai Alisie, and Vitalik Buterin (left to right) along the shore of Lake Zug. A moment of serenity before the early cofounders group imploded, waiting for Jeff Wilcke to arrive by train.

Christoph Jentzsch in Brooklyn with a slock before the DAO hack had occurred.

Sixteen

One of the most talented coders to find his way into the RHG was Jordi Baylina.

A Spanish computer scientist, Jordi proved instrumental in the RHG counterattack. Just like so many others who'd gravitated to Ethereum, Jordi had found the possibilities for expanding on top of Bitcoin very limited and frustrating. But once he understood the power of a smart contract in a blockchain system he was hooked. And the biggest smart contract of them all, the DAO, hooked him even further.

"The DAO was not only about the technical side, it was about the social side," he said. He loved getting involved with other developers and helping them fashion proposals for the DAO. He spent hours on the

DAO's Slack channel, answering questions and giving other developers feedback on what they were designing. "You could see how powerful this technology could be, even if it was very difficult and very technical."

This period – when the DAO glimmered with possibility and no one had yet exposed its vulnerability – may have been short, but for Jordi it was a powerful time that left a lasting impression. "For me, I would say life changing, when you really see the power of a community," he said.

On the morning of the first attack, Jordi woke up in Barcelona to his phone going crazy with messages. He tried to get on the DAO Slack channel, but there was too much going on for him to make sense of it. It seemed that everyone he'd been helping was reaching out to him to ask if he knew what was going on and what they could do to help save the DAO. Jordi knew about the DAO bugs that had been pointed out by Peter Vessenes, Emin Gün Sirer, Christian Reitwiessner, and others; he'd poked around in the DAO code a bit before the attack as well. He knew he could probably figure out the exploit used and help the community that he'd grown so fond of.

Jordi had long been involved with the Catalan independence movement in Spain, where he'd helped to keep technology infrastructure like local government web sites up and running when the Spanish government was trying to shut them down. Keeping the public informed about voting locations through local web sites became a vital tool of the independence movement. Jordi knew how to fight, and he'd bring that to help protect his beloved DAO.

The first thing he did was replicate the DAO attack on a test net – a sort-of practice version of Ethereum where developers can see if their code works or if it's full of bugs without risking any live executions of the code. Once he had the attack figured out, he contacted people at slock.it, who told him they were already on to the problem. From there, he got in touch with Griff Green and others in the RHG.

They were lucky to have Jordi, who's one of the most natural hackers Ryan Zurrer has ever encountered. Zurrer had lent his DAO tokens to the RHG in an instant when he heard Jordi was helping them. Along with Alex Van de Sande, whom he trusted implicitly, Zurrer considered Baylina to possess one of the best minds he'd encountered among the Ethereum developers.

"He spun up the same attack, not by looking at the code from the other attacker, but by going through the same process himself," Zurrer said. "The fact that this guy can look at a smart contract and hack it, basically, at will – I keep thinking, imagine if he went black hat tomorrow. I bet he could totally take down the system." That's not Baylina's style, though, and soon he was working in concert with the rest of the RHG.

After the RHG attack had been underway for about five or six hours, the RHG had managed to collect $96 million worth of ether from the DAO. But there was a small bit left, about $4 million, that was harder to get out for various reasons. This is where Jordi entered the picture.

"I told them, 'hey, I've got my smart contract and I didn't test it yet in the main net, but maybe it works," Jordi said. "It's a small piece, but $4 million is a lot of money." He was surprised at the number of DAO tokens the group sent him to launch his attack, and after a few tries he was able to pull out the remaining $4 million in half an hour. Then he kind of freaked out. He'd never really done much with cryptocurrencies, and now he owned a DAO contract with $4 million that didn't even belong to him.

"From a personal perspective, it's kind of crazy," Jordi said. He knew he had to be extremely careful regarding the security of the contract, that he had to ensure the private key was safe and a lot of other things that he didn't usually have to deal with as a code writer.

The DAO was now consuming his life. After three months of neglecting his job as chief technology officer at a small software firm, he was let go. Maybe even fired; he's not quite sure. But he didn't care: the DAO needed his full attention. It also had an effect on his relationships with friends and family. At dinner he couldn't concentrate on the conversation; his mind was elsewhere. "I had no life," he said. He'd been obsessed with things before where the outside world faded away and all he could focus on was the problem he was trying to solve in his head. That could last a few days. The DAO saga stretched out over several months.

He also came to respect what the DAO attacker had accomplished from a technical point of view. The attacker was the first to find the vulnerability in the DAO, string two contracts together to execute the attack, and pull it off.

"From the technical perspective, hats off," Jordi said. "From the ethical perspective, that's another story." Looking back on that time, Jordi is still amazed at what he went through. "This is the story of your life," he said. "It's like you're in a movie and you cannot believe this is happening to you."

● ● ●

Yet for all the technical prowess the RHG had at its disposal, they couldn't escape the DAO code – the code that allowed others to join in the splits that the RHG needed to get the remaining ether out of the DAO safely. That code had allowed the attacker to join the split where the RHG had stashed the reclaimed ether, and it suddenly seemed as though all their work had been for nothing. People were getting tired and frustrated. It had been weeks that they'd been at this and the stress was building.

Adding to the bad mood was the fact that the RHG was on unequal footing in fighting the attack. Whereas they had vastly outgunned the attacker with the amount of DAO tokens at their disposal, now the RHG had to win every fight going forward to be successful in moving the money out of the split they were in. If they slipped up just once, the attacker could make off with the money. RHG members weren't being paid for what they were doing to protect the DAO; it was an all-volunteer effort. Given the possibly endless nature of the battle they faced, many of them began supporting the hard fork option as a way to solve the problem once and for all.

"They were realizing it was going to be a huge amount of unpaid work, and they didn't want to do that," Alex Van de Sande said.

Another option was to temporarily freeze the attacker's stolen ether by updating the Ethereum software. That's the soft fork approach. The software update written in the Go language, called "DAO Wars," was released on June 29, 2016. According to the notes accompanying the software release: "If the community decides to freeze the funds, only a few white-listed accounts can retrieve the blocked funds and return them to previous owners." It also warned, however, that the software update would block all DAOs from being able to release ether held inside them and not just the DAOs the community considered to be under attack.

A flaw in the way the soft fork would operate, though, ultimately killed this approach. The next Go version update, called "The network strikes back," came out the same day as DAO Wars. Its notes said that DAO Wars had been recalled because of the way it exposed "the entire Ethereum network to resource abuse by malicious users."

The hard fork remained the only option left to the Ethereum community, but it would take a lot of convincing to get people on board. Changing the history of a blockchain to reverse a hack had never been done before. It wasn't as if the problem was in the Ethereum code; it wasn't. The bug was in the DAO, an application that ran on top of the Ethereum codebase.

"All those discussions became very political," avsa said. "That's how we got into a huge fight." Alex initially stood against the hard fork; he thought it wasn't the correct choice. But he came around when he realized that his opposition came from his political beliefs related to blockchain governance.

Griff Green, for all his efforts with the RHG to secure the vulnerable ether left in the DAO, supported the hard fork. He'd worked tirelessly to make sure the Ethereum community would have at least 70 percent of what they invested in the DAO. But then it became nearly impossible to guarantee they could return that money, since the attacker was in the split with them.

"The only good outcome is where we hack the hacker and steal the money back," Griff said. "The only way we do that was a hard fork."

As June turned to July, the Ethereum community – and the blockchain ecosystem in general – carried out a vigorous and sometimes pointed debate about the merits of changing Ethereum's history to erase the DAO fiasco. Peter Todd, a well-known if contentious Bitcoin developer, wrote on his blog, "This fork is a very bad idea, and I'm not alone in thinking that." He cited a tweet from the time (which seems to have since been deleted) from a user named Ryan Lackey, who describes himself in his Twitter bio as a cypherpunk. Here's what Lackey wrote, typos and all: "I'm impressed how Ethereum managed to take a compromise of DAO into an opportunity do destroy all of ETH by killing fungibility/ect."

Peter Todd, who incidentally had attended the first Bitcoin meetup in Toronto at Pauper's Pub, spelled out his wishes for how the hard fork decision should be made. A clean vote of token holders was essential, he said.

"Soft or hard forking as a response to the DAO attack isn't technical minutia: not only are there tens of millions of dollars at stake, but many (most?) of the core Ethereum developers also have significant financial interests at stake," he said. "Put it up for a vote, one coin, one vote, and get cryptographic proof that you've actually got the support of the people who have invested their funds in Ethereum."

The web site Quartz framed the fork debate as "existential" for Ethereum. "One of its underlying tenets is that it's a decentralized platform, meaning the power lies almost exclusively with all of its users," the story said. "By stepping in to fix this problem, it would completely undermine that objective. This has led to a heated debate between those who want to return the funds and the 'code is king' purists who say that the power of smart contracts lies in their immutability."

Others in the community who were closer to the DAO appeared to be a bit more aggressive in their tactics. Peter Todd quoted a tweet from Stephan Tual, one of slock.it's founders, about efforts to vote against the hard fork. "I'd be VERY interested to know the identify [sic] of anyone coordinating an effort to oppose a hard fork," Tual wrote from the slock. it Twitter account. Todd commented, "There's also been significant pressure on the community to support a fork, even going as far as what appear to be veiled threats against those opposing the fork." Tual could've meant, of course, that an organized campaign against the hard fork would be a huge benefit to the ether thief and that knowing who was behind such a movement could be a clue to his identity.

As debate continued, the number of days available to do something grew smaller. That's because the DAO code Christoph Jentzsch had written included lock-up periods for moving money out. But they didn't last forever. The DAO attacker would be free to withdraw the stolen ether 34 days after the hack. That meant if the Ethereum community didn't want to watch their money disappear forever, they had until Thursday, July 21, 2016, to do something about it.

Seventeen

The first version of Ethereum came to life on Gavin Wood's laptop at midnight on January 30, 2014. A few days before, while still in Miami, Gav had completed the first-ever trade of ether when he sent a test transaction to Charles Hoskinson. Even though it was in its infancy, Gavin had now built a full working version, which he called the alpha client. It would go through nine revisions, known as proof-of-concepts, before being released publicly in 2015.

For the blockchain to be effective it needs applications running on top of it. And for that you need a programming language for smart contracts. Gav wrote the first one, dubbed LLL. Vitalik and Jeff Wilcke followed his lead when they created their own languages, Mutan and Serpent. Gavin started writing smart contracts, kicking the tires as it all advanced. His first was for a name registry to link people with their test net accounts. Another one he wrote was for a decentralized exchange, where buyers and sellers find each other directly with no party in the middle of the transaction.

This particular part of the Ethereum network, the applications that will run on its blockchain, held a special fascination for Joe Lubin – but maybe not for the reason you might think for the founder of ConsenSys, one of the largest application incubators in Ethereum. Joe actually loves the protocol layer. That's the guts of the blockchain, the code and the clients and how it all interacts. Being an expert in this part of the infrastructure allowed Lubin to instruct and help people who wanted to build decentralized companies.

"The really fun stuff for me is the foundational protocol layer," Lubin said. "It's where the fundamentally new is being built."

As Joe battled with Gavin over the balance of power, he also incorporated ConsenSys in November of 2014. Lubin still had crypto-Google on his mind, even if he knew it was years in the future. His belief that it will arrive one day has never wavered; he simply upped the ante by creating a for-profit developer studio. Of course, EthDev continued to hum along in Berlin, and the stakes became a bit more long-term for Joe and Gavin. They were no longer just trying to wrest control of Ethereum for short-term control over how it would be built; their antagonism extended to commercial competition for the applications and industries that would want to use the Ethereum network.

While these issues began to expand in the background, Joe continued to work full time on Ethereum during the fall of 2014 on things like helping to fix a bug that had affected a small number of people buying ether in the crowdsale.

After the Zug meeting, Vitalik headed to San Francisco for a summit of the Thiel Fellowship. He'd been named a fellow in 2014 and had been awarded $100,000 to fund the continuation of Ethereum. Overall he'd been a bit disappointed in the summit; he'd hoped to meet Peter Thiel, a successful venture capitalist and founder of Palantir Technologies, the enormous and secretive data mining and analytics firm that features in the nightmares of privacy advocates the world over (an April 2018 *Bloomberg Businessweek* story carried the headline "Palantir Knows Everything about You"). While some of the sessions were boring, Vitalik did meet Nick Szabo at the event, whom he described as "one of the major pre-Satoshi pioneers of cryptocurrency." It turns out Szabo was putting a substantial amount of work into Ethereum, Vitalik wrote home in an email.

But soon, the newest crisis within the Ethereum leadership team would again remake how the foundation was run.

The new makeup of the Ethereum Foundation hadn't helped relieve any of the tension that had come out in the open in June 2014. Gavin recalled many instances after the Zug gathering where Anthony, Mihai, and Stephan Tual engaged in various fights.

"Vitalik attempted to avoid taking sides," Gav said. "This generally resulted in indecision," and even small details were taking hours of bickering to resolve. "No individual person was to blame for the bickering, though I think Vitalik could have stepped in if he wanted."

The crowdsale had changed the calculus for Gavin. The foundation now held public money; they had shareholders in a sense. While owning ether wasn't as clear-cut as owning shares of IBM in terms of shareholder rights, Gavin felt he had a duty to deliver Ethereum in a professional, responsible manner. Put another way, *not* the way the cofounders were behaving on any given day.

"I came to the realization that the project would be endangered if this ineffectiveness continued," Gavin said. A developer named Aeron Buchanan, a friend of Gavin's, had joined the project in February, and by the fall of 2014 was helping Gavin run operations in Berlin. The team of developers wanted Ethereum to go live in the winter, and the work seemed to never end.

Vitalik spent the entirety of November in Berlin, hacking away with Gav and Jeff to get their respective clients ready to go live. In February they traveled to Seattle for a security audit. But by March 2015, the next identity crisis was about to erupt. A mandatory meeting of the cofounders was called, again in Zug.

"At that meeting Gav, Jeff, and Aeron took me aside and convinced me that the other half of the leadership was counterproductive," Vitalik said. "That they're parasites, essentially." The old divide between the technical and nontechnical sides had never been resolved, it had only grown worse as time went on. Now Vitalik had been convinced that major changes were needed.

Gavin had never fully trusted most of the other cofounders. When he locked the bedroom door in the Zug house after Charles and Amir were fired, he did so because the house was full of tension. Part of that tension came from his insistence that if some of the cofounders weren't let go he would leave the project. His desire to reshape the leadership team was about to be realized.

Anthony Di Iorio had spent the months since the Zug meeting shifting his responsibilities to others. He had to dissolve the for-profit Ethereum entities he'd created and he went back to working on his own projects, like KryptoKit.

"I needed to start planning my exit," he said. The meeting in March took care of that. Anthony was the main power player pushed out of Ethereum this time around. Joe was already on his way out, with ConsenSys taking up more and more of his time. Taylor Gerring and Stephan Tual were stripped of their leadership roles but continued to work for the foundation (Gerring continued to serve on the foundation board with Mihai and Vitalik, as the rules required that it have three members). Anthony though, was out, and he was not happy with how it came about.

Gavin had persuaded Vitalik that with real money in the bank now they had a responsibility to use it effectively, and they needed a professionally run management team.

Gavin and Jeff were of the opinion that "the foundation needed leadership," Vitalik said. "And we can come up with more competent leadership than this existing set of bozos."

Vitalik, Jeff, Gavin, and Aeron decided to hold an open call to hire board members and an executive director. In a blog post announcing the new positions, Vitalik said the expanded size and scope of the Ethereum Foundation required it to make changes in how it was run "to more closely resemble a mature organization." Among the qualifications he noted: "Lack of prior unethical or illegal behavior, particularly in the areas of embezzlement, insider trading or fraud." They received about 80 applications.

The resumes were narrowed down to a group of 3 people for the executive director position and 10 for the board seats. They rented a hotel room in Zürich for interviews, and it became clear that Gavin, Jeff, and Aeron wanted executives who had significant work experience. Vitalik wanted something different.

"I cared less about that," he said. "I cared more about whether the people had a soul, if that makes sense." The candidates for executive director were Ming Chan, André Laperrière, and Denis Flad. Flad didn't get too far in impressing the foundation members, but Laperrière had an impressive resume, including work for the International Criminal Court, the World Health Organization, and UNICEF. He came with a steep price tag, however, with a starting salary requirement of $230,000.

"This was cash-crunch time, so that was very crazy," Vitalik said.

For Vitalik, Ming Chan made the biggest impression. "I remember being very impressed with Ming because she was the kind of person I could have a three-hour conversation with and enjoy it," he said. Gav and Jeff, however, weren't on board with Ming and found her unimpressive.

"To them, a person who can laugh and cry is a disadvantage," Vitalik said. "To me, it's an advantage." Vitalik, Jeff, Gav, and Aeron decided to give the executive director position to André Laperrière. As the negotiations were being finalized, Laperrière came in with additional compensation requirements, like moving expenses and severance; his total comp was ballooning.

"When we hired André instead of Ming, we made an agreement that if André's salary demands go really crazy, if they go over $300,000, let's go with Ming," Vitalik said. Ming had asked for a salary of $150,000. With all the extras André asked for, his annualized salary would have been $320,000. In July 2015, the Ethereum Foundation hired Ming Chan as its first executive director.

● ● ●

Testing on the Ethereum network continued to home in on more problems as the leadership questions were being settled. Vitalik, Gavin, and Jeff all met in Berlin for three days in March after the Zug meeting. They undertook a hackathon to ensure that the three clients – Go, C++, and Python – all interpreted blocks on the Ethereum blockchain in exactly the same way. If there were different interpretations of the information a block contains on Go and C++, the chain would fork, and the transaction history would be in doubt. Over the three days they succeeded in getting all three clients in perfect synchronization. Now they were ready to release Olympic, the final test net version of Ethereum before the public release of the software. The name came from the fact that everyone involved in Ethereum was trying to crash the software on the test net. It was a competition to find a bug or to overwhelm it with a smart contract that sent 20,000 transactions to 20,000 individual users. The foundation had a bug bounty program, where it paid anyone who discovered a problem in the code. This was one really big, long stress test on the network.

With the development coming along nicely, Vitalik went to China toward the end of April. He stayed for about two months with his friend Bo Shen, who had helped organize his visit to the country the year before. Vitalik had been trying to get Shen's company ZAFED to move its operations onto Ethereum from BitShares. He now understood that not many people in China had bought ether in the crowdsale, and Vitalik wanted to raise its profile in the country. He took meetings in Hong Kong and Singapore, and then flew back to Switzerland to handle the selection process for executive director and board member positions.

Out of the 10 candidates for board members they chose 3. Lars Klawitter was a computer scientist and had founded a startup in the late 1990s. He'd worked for many years at Rolls-Royce, first as manager in its IT department and then as head of the bespoke unit of the company, which created custom cars for customers around the world.

Wayne Hennessy-Barrett was the founder and CEO of 4G Capital, a Kenya-based mobile money and financial technology company. Hennessy-Barrett had served in the British military for 16 years, including a stint as an assistant to the chief of staff at the British Permanent Joint Headquarters.

Vadim Levitin was a physician who'd worked on technology issues for the United Nations and ran a business development firm in Eastern Europe. Vitalik held the fourth board seat, and with Ming as executive director the Ethereum Foundation was set to release its blockchain to the world.

To do that, they set a kind of timer. When the test net processed a certain block, when it was said to reach a predetermined "height," it would switch to the live Ethereum blockchain. They set that block as 1028201, which Vitalik proudly described to me as "a palindromic prime." He'd flown to Berlin from Switzerland on July 28, and they spent a few days checking the code for any last-minute issues. On the evening of July 30, Vitalik, Jeff, Gav, and other developers like Vlad Zamfir were waiting for the countdown.

"And then the network launched," Vitalik said. The countdown was being shown on a TV screen and it switched over to broadcast the first live transactions on Ethereum. Unfortunately for history's sake, there were no fireworks here, no "hello, world" moment. For the first five days of its existence, no transactions could be sent on Ethereum; they'd been disabled. Mining of empty blocks was the only activity on Ethereum for those five days.

Vitalik stayed up until midnight watching the network grow. But there were no crazy celebrations. After years of hard work, management struggles, money pressure, and the simple but stressful constant worry that maybe what they were doing wouldn't work after all, it did work. They'd brought Vitalik's invention to life after toiling collectively for thousands of hours.

In a photo posted by Lefteris of that day, the group with Gavin and Jeff and Christoph Jentzsch and Aeron Buchanan had all gathered in front of the TV monitor. Vitalik is standing behind Liana Husikyan and is barely visible. A few people appear to have small glasses of wine. Vlad Zamfir might be holding a shot of something, it's hard to tell. They didn't go out to dinner that night but ate in the EthDev office.

"We just didn't know how to celebrate," Vitalik said.

● ● ●

Once the network was live the cryptocurrency ether could now trade publicly on exchanges, replacing the paper value of the ether held by Ethereum developers with a real-life value. That fall, ether bounced around between $1 and $2, then dipped to 50 cents. It rose back up to about 80 cents for a while. The crazy thing here about cryptocurrencies like ether is that Vitalik, Gav, Charles, Joe, and anyone else who'd received an allotment in the pre-mine were only ever looking at how much profit they'd made. Losses weren't possible with the pre-mined ether each of the cofounders received. I can't think of another area of finance where this is the case. A line from *The Usual*

Suspects comes to mind: the devil's greatest trick is convincing the world he doesn't exist. The ether trick did the opposite, convincing people that Ethereum would exist, that there would be a product. In the beginning, though, the price of ether suggested that people agreed with its potential but also agreed that there was nothing there yet to push its value higher.

Eighteen

After Ethereum went live on July 30, 2015, Vitalik flew to Asia. He visited Korea and then China again before heading back to Switzerland for a meeting to introduce the new board members and Ming Chan to each other. Even before the meeting, though, there was trouble among the newest additions to the Ethereum Foundation.

Ming had been in touch with Vitalik when he was in Asia to tell him that she and Wayne Hennessey-Barrett weren't getting along. He'd yelled at her for two hours, she told Vitalik.

"She was very unhappy with how they treated her," Vitalik said. Then things took a turn for the worse after Ming sent a text message to the wrong person.

"The consternation was in the open because at one point, Ming made this mistake where she was complaining about the board, and was talking to her sister – well, she thought she was talking to her sister about the possibility of finding a different board,"Vitalik said. "Instead of sending some text messages to her sister, she sent them to one of the board members."

With that setup, the new Ethereum Foundation board members and executive director were about to meet in person for the first time. Ming arrived a day early and Vitalik tried to talk her through how to get past what had already happened. Board members Lars Klawitter and Vadim Levitin had made the trip to Zug for the meeting, but after getting in a row with Ming, Wayne Hennessy-Barrett didn't show up. He participated by video conference.

Ming wore a suit for the meeting and ran it very professionally with timed topics – 5 minutes on this issue, 15 minutes on that issue – all in the hopes of avoiding any discussion of how everyone already hated each other.

Her tactic worked. But then Lars and Vadim left and immediately went back to their hotels. This didn't sit well with Vitalik. On the one hand it showed him how uncomfortable the members of the new management team were around each other. And it also showed him that there wasn't much passion for Ethereum in this new group.

"They weren't really that deeply interested in us or Ethereum," Vitalik said. "They just saw it as a job."

The meeting spanned two days, and on the second day Vitalik held a private meeting with the three board members. "The board members were, like, 'hey, dude, we've got to get rid of Ming.'"Vitalik agreed, and not even a month into her tenure, Ming was told she wouldn't be continuing as executive director.

The next meeting that day was taking place at the offices of MME, the foundation's lawyers, where they were going to discuss Swiss regulatory issues. Ming cried as she walked there with Vitalik, Lars, and Vadim. "Ming wasn't invited to the lawyer meetings we were going to because she was now not going to be executive director,"Vitalik said.

Yet while he was in the meetings with the lawyers, Vitalik again got the impression that Lars, Wayne, and Vadim just weren't really that into them.

"I remember during the meeting, looking at the other board members' reaction, the way that they were interpreting the information," Vitalik said. "I expected that I would feel warm and safe because there were these high-powered, professional people with lots of experience helping us now. But their body language and mood was like *ugh, huh, okay okay*. They were just so clearly not into it. That's when I realized I was not comfortable with them being the board."

After months of searching and a public call for submissions for the board and executive director positions, after in-person interviews and negotiations, the Ethereum Foundation professional board – the one that would take the group to the next polished level – had been blown apart in less than two days. This wasn't another bump in the Ethereum road. This *was* the road.

A week later, Vitalik was in Toronto. Ming had stayed in touch even though she'd been told her services were no longer required. But Vitalik grew to appreciate her dogged interest in the foundation. This was the sort of passion and dedication to Ethereum and the foundation Vitalik wanted to see.

They began working together in Toronto on foundation issues, like an upcoming financial audit. None of the other board members knew Ming was still in the picture, and certainly not that she was now in Toronto working daily with Vitalik. On September 1, 2015, Vitalik sent an email to the board members updating them on his thinking about the foundation management.

He emphasized that he didn't want to do anything rash, but that big decisions needed to be made. "I feel that I, perhaps, in a lot of ways, have been too hasty in agreeing to things both there and many times previously in my career," he wrote. He said any decisions would be postponed until September 10, after he'd sought advice from others about what to do.

Ming, he noted, had been doing good work on the upcoming audit. "I got quite scared when seeing just how much work there is to be done and realizing that we don't have any dedicated staff to do it," he wrote. "She would be extremely hard to replace if she were to stop working tomorrow, and the current ongoing audits are a critical matter that would severely impact the foundations' situation if we were to miss deadlines."

Even though she had been told that she'd been let go, Ming was on a contract as the executive director of the foundation, and the board members had been pushing Vitalik to finalize her removal. But he put that off. When he shared the September 1 email with me, he described it as "when I was bullshitting to procrastinate for a week about firing Ming."

A week later, he sent an email to the three board members and the foundation's lawyers, saying he wanted the board to step down. They agreed. Ming now held the executive director position, as well as a board seat, and would come to exert great control over the foundation in the months to come.

A graduate of MIT, where she'd studied computer science and media arts and sciences, Ming had been born in Switzerland to Chinese parents. Her family moved to Michigan, and Ming had worked for the University of Michigan from 2007 to 2015, where she helped the school maintain web content dedicated to Chinese art, history, and culture. Her first task as head of the Ethereum Foundation staff was to cut costs, which were out of control.

In 2015, the peak monthly outlay for the foundation was over 400,000 euros. That covered the cost of developing Ethereum on the Go and C++ clients, and included money spent on hosting web sites, maintaining existing servers, and covering other information technology expenses. One of the larger chunks went to paying executive and staff salaries. They were bleeding money and weren't helped at all by the fact that half of the capital they raised in the crowdsale – $9 million – had been wiped out when the foundation didn't hedge its exposure to Bitcoin in late 2014.

"Ming turned all her attention to cost cutting," Vitalik said. "At the time, we were basically completely out of Bitcoin and completely out of fiat [currency]. All that we had was our three million ether. We had to start selling huge amounts of ether to survive." The three million ether the foundation had left was down from the six million it had been allotted from the crowdsale because three million had been allocated to the developer purchase program and all of it had been bought up by devs. At the time of the Ethereum launch in July 2015, the foundation had $1 million in cash. By mid-September all that was gone.

Vitalik loves precise numbers, and as we spoke about the financial straits the foundation found itself in in late 2015, he said he was able to arrange a private ether sale to raise funds. How much ether? "I managed to sell 416,667 ether for $500,000," he said. The buyer was a firm working with Bo Shen, whom Vitalik had been courting in China for many years. "So, we were happy."

The lack of funds had repercussions in the world outside the Ethereum Foundation, as their 2015 annual developer conference, DevCon 1, was set to take place in a few weeks in London. Yet the money wasn't there to put on the show, and the foundation considered canceling the event. When Joe Lubin got wind of this – Joe Lubin, who had now hired staff at his Ethereum application incubator ConsenSys – he said no way.

"Then Joe stepped in and said, basically, 'no, we're doing DevCon 1 and if not, ConsenSys will organize a conference,'" Vitalik said.

None of these negotiations were known to the outside world. If all you had for your information about Ethereum was the blog on their web site, you would have been hard pressed to know what was going on. A post on September 2, 2015, announced that DevCon 1 – set to begin in a month – had been postponed until further notice. The foundation claimed the postponement was due to not being able to secure the London location they wanted on the dates they had scheduled. Behind the scenes, the situation was far more tenuous, and Joe Lubin and the people he'd hired to build the for-profit ConsenSys were about to run headlong into Ming Chan's new and improved nonprofit Ethereum Foundation.

●　●　●

The first Ethereum meetup in New York City took place two weeks before the ether crowdsale in the summer of 2014 at the Cardozo law school, spitting distance from Union Square. Hosted by Aaron Wright, an associate clinical professor of law who specialized in Internet and new technology issues, one attendee at the meeting had come from the world of medical database companies, the firms that process insurance claims electronically. His name was Andrew Keys and he would become one of the first employees at ConsenSys.

Through the business of his company, MedAZ, Andrew had come to understand everything that was wrong with databases and with payments. Nothing connected to anything else, and it took days or weeks to process some claims. Errors were rampant. He wanted a way to bring payments and database entry together in one holistic system. Bitcoin had done that to a degree, but Andrew soon realized its limited capacity to handle complicated transactions. Then he discovered Ethereum.

"I followed the blockchain ecosystem but didn't get professionally involved until I started seeing the promise of smart contracts," Keys said. Once he'd seen the light, Keys saw the notice about the Ethereum meetup at the Cardozo law school and went with the intention of meeting Joe Lubin.

"I remember Joe being so confident that this would change how society works, I just fell in love with that notion," Andrew said. "Once I started to understand the implications, I couldn't stop thinking about it. I still can't stop thinking about it."

An Ethereum blockchain application that really drove it home for him was the update on what could be done with double-entry bookkeeping. That's the system – developed by a monk in 1494 – where one party to a transaction puts into their books that they were paid 10 dollars and the other party to that transactions puts in their books that they paid 10 dollars. But what prevents the side being paid from claiming they received 5 dollars and the side doing the paying that they forked over 15 dollars? They could pocket the difference. With Ethereum, a new type of accounting – triple-entry bookkeeping – became possible.

"There was nothing that basically watermarked that transaction, there was no handshake," Keys said. With an unchangeable ledger in the middle of that transaction on Ethereum, there would now be a receipt. "That basically automates auditing," he said. "KPMG, Ernst & Young, Deloitte, PWC, how they work, will be radically transformed."

He was willing to put his money where his mouth was and offered to work for Joe at ConsenSys for free, which he did for six months between March and September of 2015. Lubin had never let go of the idea of Ethereum as a for-profit enterprise, even as the cofounders voted against it in the Zug meeting in June 2014. Now Joe had his own for-profit design studio, and he was pushing everyone involved with ConsenSys to make sure the commercial side of the Ethereum project had all the funding, advice, and support it needed to create the applications that would make or break the underlying blockchain ecosystem he wanted to create.

That meant, in the bigger picture, that as the Ethereum Foundation was running out of money in the fall of 2015 and telling its community that DevCon 1 was on hold, it was all systems go for ConsenSys to seize the opportunity to start driving the conversation in the direction it wanted. Throwing in a bit of cash and lining up big name sponsors wasn't a bad way to accomplish that goal.

"I did loan the Ethereum Foundation something like $100,000 to put on DevCon 1," Andrew Keys said. He then sent an email out of the blue to an executive at Microsoft who happened to be playing around with Ethereum. His name was Marley Gray, and Andrew decided to reach out to him based only on the fact that Gray had the word *block-chain* in his LinkedIn bio. They soon hit it off. Andrew is nothing if not persuasive and can talk the balls off a rhinoceros. Andrew and Marley began collaborating on a partnership. Andrew also pitched the idea to Marley that Microsoft should be a lead sponsor of DevCon 1. Whether the event would be a ConsenSys undertaking or whether the Ethereum Foundation would get its act together in time to put it back on was still up in the air.

For Joe, the stakes were too high to not have a developer conference. "I felt like we needed an event to catalyze the ecosystem," Joe said. "I suggested we create it and if the foundation will put its name on it, we'd call it the Ethereum Foundation DevCon."

Then in late September, Vitalik announced that DevCon 1 was back and would take place at Gibson Hall in London, on November 9–13. In October, the foundation said that Nick Szabo, the inventor of the term *smart contracts* and the idea behind them, would be the keynote speaker. The Ethereum Foundation branding was starting to take shape as well. In that October release, Szabo was quoted as saying that Bitcoin was like a pocket calculator while Ethereum was like a general-purpose computer. I'd first heard this comparison made by Joe Lubin, though a bit later in 2016. Szabo's initial work with smart contracts was an attempt to allow contract law to be embedded into the programming languages that make the Internet possible. At the end of the release, the foundation tried out a bold new marketing ploy: "Ethereum is how the Internet was supposed to work."

The collaboration between Andrew Keys and Marley Gray paid off in November, when Microsoft announced it was adding Ethereum to the applications available to its customers through its cloud services unit, Azure. They called it Ethereum Blockchain as a Service, because this was a version of the blockchain meant to be used by banks or companies that wanted to experiment with it to see if it could streamline their operations. This enterprise version of Ethereum had many of the public features of the blockchain removed; for example, there were no miners needed to verify transactions and the participants in a private network would all be known to each other.

Marley Gray was a big fan of Ethereum from early on. In the announcement about the deal with ConsenSys he wrote, "Ethereum provides the flexibility and extensibility many of our customers were looking for. With the Frontier release last summer, Ethereum is real and has a vibrant community of developers, enthusiasts and businesses participating."

The partnership, importantly, was between Microsoft and ConsenSys, not Microsoft and the Ethereum Foundation. This was also announced on the first day of DevCon 1. It may have been the first shot across the bow of the Ethereum Foundation ship, which Ming Chan was now steering.

Andrew Keys said that ConsenSys at the time was the only outfit in the Ethereum world building anything for the blockchain's application layer. This led to ConsenSys dominating many of the DevCon 1 talks, "And that really pissed Ming off," he said.

Joe Lubin said that initially he and Ming got along well, but that their relationship soon soured.

"She demonized a lot of people and she demonized me the most because we were an evil commercial force in her pure, nonprofit world," Joe said. "Ming is a complicated individual. Very capable in many ways, but prone to extreme emotional situations which many, many people witnessed many times."

I tried to get Ming to talk to me over the course of several months in 2019 and 2020, but she refused. From what I've been told by others, Ming felt as strongly about Joe as he said she did about him. There was no love lost between her and ConsenSys.

Andrew Keys didn't see eye to eye with Ming, and said she made several business decisions that hurt early Ethereum adoption. A big one involved IBM, which was considering using an altered version of Ethereum for its blockchain research and development. The deal would be enormous for the fledgling foundation. "IBM has a tremendously powerful distribution arm," Keys said. "I didn't appreciate until ConsenSys how embedded IBM is into *Earth* – all the central banks, all the banks, all the supply chains." Keys said Ming wouldn't take calls from IBM executives Jerry Cuomo, vice president of blockchain technologies, and John Wolpert, a global product executive for blockchain. IBM ended up creating its own blockchain, Fabric, for its R&D.

The loss of the IBM deal created a huge schism amid the broader community, Keys said. "You could have had everybody working on a private Ethereum," he said. Ming wasn't the only one in charge at the foundation, of course, but Keys still thinks she bears a lot of the blame. "I lay a lot of it on her doorstep," Keys said.

Another business decision that came to hurt Ethereum had to do with how it went about choosing its open-source code licensing. This may have been an extension of Vitalik and many other early founders' allegiance to being nonprofit and ensuring that all of its code was open source, or available to the public for free. That's all fine for the main version of Ethereum that went live in July 2015. But if a corporation wants to use a private version of Ethereum to build applications for its business, it wants to be able to keep the proprietary rights to the code it created. Two of the main types of licensing are GPL (GNU General Public License) and Apache 2 (Apache License 2.0).

GPL doesn't allow for the code that's written atop its system to be commercialized; its rights are only granted if the derivative product is also made free to the public. Apache 2 licensing is looser in this regard and allows commercial use by the application's creators. All of the clients built by Ethereum teams – Go, C++, Python, and others – had been built using GPL.

"Enterprises are allergic to GPL," Keys said. "Any attorney for any company, when they see it's Apache 2, they'll say yes to the software, if it's GPL they'll say no."

To those inside of ConsenSys, the Ethereum Foundation wasn't quite ready for prime time. But it was still so early in Ethereum's development that there was no comparable force like the foundation. In time, not doing anything about this would turn out to be something Ethereum could no longer afford to do.

● ● ●

When Marley Gray began tinkering with Ethereum in August of 2015 at Microsoft's innovation lab in Manhattan, no one around him had any idea what he was up to.

What he really wanted to do was to get nodes on a private Ethereum network to talk to each other, but he was having a devil of a time getting it to work. He didn't know how to write code in Go, the client he was experimenting with, and there was no one at Microsoft he could go to for help. Then Andrew Keys reached out and Marley was amazed that ConsenSys was just over the East River in Brooklyn. He went to their offices in that graffiti-covered building in the Bushwick neighborhood, when the furnishings consisted of picnic tables and there were 10 people there, tops.

"Joe would sit in the corner, and we just pulled up chairs and I told him what I was doing," Gray said. He'd spent an entire weekend with very little sleep trying to get two Ethereum nodes to talk to each other, with no luck. He knew businesses and banks wouldn't have that sort of patience, so if Ethereum wanted to appeal to them, they'd have to make the tools available much easier to use to set up a test Ethereum environment.

ConsenSys wrote some code for use with Linux and Marley handled the cloud computing side and soon they had the Ethereum Blockchain as a Service product ready. Marley specialized in financial services innovation for Microsoft, so he knew that Morgan Stanley and Goldman Sachs wanted to experiment with private blockchains. The demand was there.

The time was right at Microsoft to be taking gambles on innovations like Ethereum. Satya Nadella was CEO at the time, and he'd sent word out to every Microsoft employee about his desire for them to explore new ideas and have what he termed "a growth mind-set."

"I said this is a growth area, I guarantee you," Marley said. After some haggling and a positive story in the *Wall Street Journal* about Microsoft's work with Ethereum, Marley got the okay from his bosses to be a lead sponsor of DevCon 1 and to also send him there to give a presentation.

Gray and Microsoft got a frosty reception from the Ethereum developers in London. "It was a lot of, 'what are you doing here?'" he said. "It was not very welcoming." In his presentation he'd tried to emphasize that Microsoft was now in the cloud computing business and that they didn't want to create their own blockchain. Microsoft wanted to make it easier to use Ethereum by providing cloud-based tools to Ethereum developers. He thought his talk went over well and waited to see how the press portrayed it.

By the next day, he hadn't seen a single story about Microsoft's interest in Ethereum or about anything he'd said. Two friends had joined him in London, and they were eating lunch at the restaurant at Level39, a tech incubator and shared working space in the heart of Canary Wharf. Marley was frustrated that he hadn't made an impact and that he couldn't seem to get his message across. He decided to write an email to Microsoft's CEO Satya to tell him that he was sorry, that he'd tried, but for whatever reason he couldn't get people to see the big picture. His lunch companions told him not to do it, but he kept writing.

"Then an email comes in, 'ding,'" Marley said. "I look down and two threads below is Satya; he'd read a *Reuters* article and sent it to his direct reports, the entire leadership team." The news agency had put out a story earlier that day with the headline "Microsoft Launches Cloud-Based Blockchain Platform with Brooklyn Start-Up." Marley hadn't seen it.

"This is the perfect example of growth mind-set," Satya had written to his deputies in the email. "And I was like, okay, we're here," Marley said. "That's was how everything else all got started."

Ethereum was now attracting significant interest from some of the largest and most powerful corporations in the computing industry. Banks were sniffing around the edges, growing more confident that Ethereum was a different beast, not tainted with the aura of scandal and money laundering like Bitcoin. What the project needed now was to prove what it could do. It needed applications, and it needed to keep growing the number of people who fell in love with its promise of a whole new world.

Nineteen

Another company to give a presentation at DevCon 1 was a little startup called slock.it, which had a big idea for a newfangled thing called a DAO. Its effect on the price of ether would mint millionaires among the cofounders and many others.

For all the business developments at DevCon 1, the price of ether didn't move during or after the conference. It hit a high of $1.31 on October 29, the day after the *Wall Street Journal* story about the partnership between Microsoft and ConsenSys was published. Then it fell into the 90-cent range, where it stayed until January.

Then it began to rise, and no one could really put a finger on any catalyzing event. In February 2016, it hit $2, then $3 then $6. In March, the Ethereum Foundation released the next software update after

Frontier, the version of Ethereum that had been released in July 2015. Called Homestead, the newest version drew a lot of attention to ether and the price rose to an all-time high of $15 on March 13, the day before the Homestead launch. A cryptocurrency market report on CoinDesk noted the huge jump in ether's price and compared its price to where Bitcoin was trading.

"Because of Ethereum's success in drawing attention, some members of the digital currency trading community believe that ether is starting to serve as an attractive hedge for the uncertainty surrounding Bitcoin," the site said.

There were very few applications that were actually using Ethereum at this point. That's why the DAO carried such weight. It was in one sense the only game in town, and it was getting closer to April 30, when DAO tokens would go on sale. Ether fell from its March high of $15 to down around $11 as the DAO token sale approached. On April 30, the first day you could buy DAO tokens with ether, it traded at $9.33.

Quartz noted the skyrocketing price of ether in a May 20, 2016, story with the headline "The price of Ether, a bitcoin rival, is soaring because of a radical, $150 million experiment." The story went on to say, "The DAO has proved so popular among holders of ether, that the DAO now accounts for almost 14 percent of the value of all ether in circulation."

By May 28, the last day of the sale, ether was up at $12.03. But it wasn't until June that the DAO drove ether to new all-time highs. The rise in Bitcoin's price to a two-year high of around $700 did help to buoy ether. But there wasn't much else in the news at the time to justify ether's incredible gains – besides the DAO, that is.

A day before the DAO attack, ether was trading for $21.02. At the crowdsale's starting price of 31 cents, that was an astounding 6,680 percent increase.

The DAO-driven demand for ether had made every one of the Ethereum cofounders incredibly rich. The people close to the project who had gotten pre-mined ether were now incredibly rich too – although, as Andrew Keys noted, many of those people had sold their pre-mined ether when it hit $1 or $2.

Assuming Vitalik kept the entire allotment of 535,000 ether he'd received in the pre-mine, his share was worth $11.2 million a day before the DAO attack. He, of course, had made some private sales, though it's not known if these were from his own ether stash. The DAO had made many a millionaire in the Ethereum community – albeit for a brief time. Doing whatever it took to protect that gain, ensuring that what they had all worked so hard to build wouldn't fall apart, would be a priority. There was too much to lose to allow the DAO to take them all down.

● ● ●

As the date to implement the hard fork that would reverse the theft of ether from the DAO approached, debate grew heated. On July 7, or 14 days before the ether thief would be able to move his money out of the DAO, Vlad Zamfir wrote a passionate plea to the Ethereum community to support the hard fork.

Vlad had been involved with Ethereum almost from the beginning, though he was never one to be part of its leadership group: Vlad is more of a lone wolf. But in his blog post he implored the rest of the Ethereum community to think of the community first and consider the consequences of not acting in its best interest. "Ethereum is based on a social contract that is constantly evolving," he wrote. While implementing a hard fork to improve security or the performance of Ethereum wasn't controversial, applying a hard fork to fix the damage done by an application like the DAO hadn't yet been attempted. He warned that it would be a mistake to make rules about when a hard fork could to be used, as that would take away from needed flexibility and "places the Ethereum community in a position where it can be compelled to make bad choices, to be unable to make good choices, and more generally puts the platform at risk of being gamed by motivated parties."

Vlad knew there were hardened opinions about hard forks. Even Vitalik had called them "icky." It would hurt Ethereum in the long run, however, if those opinions trumped the welfare of the ecosystem.

"If we place community cohesion above all of our other values, however, then in the long run it will be impossible to prevent a majority from controlling the protocol in a way that runs against our core values," he wrote. He concluded by saying they didn't have much time to reach agreement.

"In any case, we will be making cryptocurrency history," he wrote.

● ● ●

In late July, several Ethereum developers and cofounders traveled to Ithaca, New York, to attend a boot camp being sponsored by Cornell University's computer science department. Emin Gün Sirer was running the show, with Vitalik, Alex Van de Sande, and Vlad Zamfir in attendance. The time for talking about the hard fork was over: as July 20 dawned cool and clear in Ithaca, the Ethereum community was about to decide to rewrite the past.

The newest version of the Go Ethereum client completed the DAO Wars trilogy, in terms of its name, anyway. It followed the aborted DAO Wars (v 1.4.8) and The Network Strikes Back (v 1.4.9). Called "Return of the ETH," it was created to do one thing: if you had sent ether to the DAO to buy tokens, you could now get your money back. All that was needed now was for the majority of computers running Ethereum to update and install Return of the ETH.

One way the community had kept track of sentiment around the hard fork was through an online "voting" system called Carbon Vote. It allowed Ethereum holders to use their ether to signal whether they supported or opposed the hard fork. The vote was nonbinding, but it did serve as a way for people like Vitalik to gauge where the support lay. As of July 16, 87 percent of the ether holders had voted in favor of the hard fork.

Alex Van De Sande was in a café in Ithaca around 9 a.m. on the morning that the boot-camp classes began. Everyone was anxiously watching the blockchain for block 1,920,000. This block held the DAO rewrite.

"Two blocks left, one block left, then no blocks, and we forked," avsa said. The network upgraded and history had been undone.

This fail-safe in the DAO code was thanks to Christoph Jentzsch. Many in the Ethereum community blamed him and slock.it for the problems with the DAO, which seemed justified. Yet it was also his code that allowed the community to get its stolen ether back. Even though someone had effectively robbed a bank, they had to wait 34 days before crossing the street to make their getaway. While they waited, the money was stolen back. A month after the original heist, the ether thief had nothing to show for his caper.

The only part of the Ethereum blockchain that was changed by the hard fork was the operation of the DAO. After the fork was implemented, the DAO contract only existed so it could return the ether it held. While not altering any information stored in the network besides the DAO, the hard fork still changed the Ethereum blockchain's structure. Imagine a hard fork is a branch of a tree that grows in a particular direction at the end of the main limb. The end of that limb is supposed to wither after a hard fork is applied, and a new branch – the blockchain – grows in another direction. This is important and often gets overlooked: the hard fork didn't change anything else that had happened on the Ethereum platform in the weeks between the DAO attack and the application of the fork. All the other transactions that took place on Ethereum were intact.

Back on the Cornell campus, the Ethereum folks celebrated the successful hard fork.

"It felt like the battle had been won at the time, so we opened up the champagne," Gün said. He'd printed labels for the bottles that said, "Congratulations on the fork," complete with a picture of the contentious utensil.

"It was shit champagne," Alex said. They took pictures and posted them to Twitter, which caused an immediate backlash. People online, many of them probably not fans of Ethereum to begin with, said look at these rich jerks with their champagne after they've desecrated the idea of blockchain immutability.

"I didn't think of the optics at the moment," avsa said.

Then one of the strangest things in this story that is absolutely bursting with strange things happened. The main limb of the Ethereum blockchain, the one that was supposed to wither after the fork, continued to grow. That is to say, miners continued to validate transactions on the chain that held the DAO attack. No one had seen that coming.

Vitalik, avsa, and Vlad all kept an eye on Ethereum on the day of the fork to see how it was behaving. At first it seemed as though the old chain was dead. Then they saw a very small number of miners in the Ethereum world still processing blocks on the old chain. Nobody knew what they were doing.

"There was this nagging 1 percent that wouldn't go away, and we had no idea what was going on," avsa said. It turned out to be the work of f2pool, a Chinese cryptocurrency mining operation.

"What f2pool basically did is they forgot to install the code to run on the fork," Vitalik said. "To this day I have no idea if that was just them being stupid or whether that was a deliberate strategy on their part." The thing that's weird about this is that for the first several blocks on a forked blockchain, the economics are terrible for miners. The blocks are very difficult to process and have little or no reward to offer a computer that puts in the work. This is why people expected the old chain of Ethereum to die off: it just didn't make economic sense for anyone to keep it alive.

"If there is no one person to sacrifice themselves and take the hit mining those first few blocks," Vitalik said, "then the chain would not be viable."

Problem was, f2pool took the hit, and as the Ethereum community watched a new version of their blockchain was born. Or, to be precise, their old blockchain wouldn't die. It came to be known as Ethereum Classic, or ETC.

"There is this possibility that f2pool was pretending to be stupid but really they were trying to help the ETC chain along," Vitalik said.

While this is all very technical, the real-world consequence of ETC being kept alive is that it now had its own cryptocurrency, an ether twin. That's because anyone who had an ether balance on the old chain – on the Ethereum blockchain that still contained the DAO attack – now had the same amount of ether classic. So let's say you're the ether thief and you stole 3.69 million ether from the DAO. Then you had that ether ripped from your sweaty little paws and returned to its rightful owners thanks to the hard fork. Now you had 3.69 million ether classic instead. Neat trick, right?

If ether classic began to have a value – if it approached anywhere near what ether traded for – then the ether thief would have his booty back.

Two days after the hard fork, Vitalik and Gün and about 10 other people were in a room in Gates Hall during the Cornell boot camp. They were playing a game called Hive, which is like chess, when Vitalik got an email with the subject line "An offer to purchase ETHC."

It read, "Greetings. Ethereum Classic chain looks like a fun test net-work. I'll pay you 0.2 BTC for 500,000 ETHC. If that isn't enough, please make a counteroffer."

The email was from Greg Maxwell, a Bitcoin Core developer and diehard supporter of Bitcoin in its purest form. He'd already publicly and harshly criticized Ethereum as going in the wrong direction and was known to be no fan of Vitalik or the Ethereum Foundation.

In fact, on the day of the DAO attack, June 17, 2016, Maxwell sent Vitalik another email. The subject line read, "Don't be a greedy idiot," and in the message Maxwell implored Vitalik not to go along with the hard fork.

"Beyond the personal risk you might take on by demonstrating con-trol of the system, it would risk bringing more uncertainty on the cryp-tocurrency ecosystem," Maxwell wrote to Vitalik. "Other developers might be pushed to try to do the same things by authorities. It's a bad road."

But now here he was offering to buy Vitalik's ETHC. Bitcoin traded that day at around $650, so Maxwell was offering to pay $130 for 500,000 of Vitalik's ether classic coins, or 0.00026 cent apiece.

Vitalik looked up and said to the others, huh, that's weird; Greg Maxwell wants to buy my ether classic.

Gün had a horrible feeling. "Do not respond to that email, that is a hostile email," he said to Vitalik. Gün was thinking along the lines of, why would Greg Maxwell suddenly want to buy ether classic, unless there was an effort underway to start trading it to give it value? In fact, that's what was happening. The day after Maxwell's email to Vitalik, Poloniex – a US-based cryptocurrency exchange that had one of the largest markets for ether in the world – said it would list ether classic. According to a July 24 story in CoinDesk, ether classic was now trading for about 66 cents on Poloniex and had traded as high as $6.

Maxwell said he had no knowledge before he made his offer to Vitalik that ETHC would be listed on cryptocurrency markets. He said he'd seen Vitalik posting messages online that the old chain of Ethereum would be worthless, and his offer was meant to test Vitalik's resolve.

"If Vitalik actually believed what he was telling others he should have taken my offer – or at least a better one like it from someone else," Maxwell said. "A high counteroffer would have allowed me to establish that he was being dishonest about his opinions and aided me in arguing some sense into other people (and potentially saved some people from losses)."

In any event, ETHC now had value. At 66 cents, the ether thief now held $2.4 million in ETHC. The second attack, on June 21, would have been valued at $177,000 at that price.

Alex Van de Sande couldn't believe what he was seeing. He got in touch with the RHG guys, and they all realized that ether classic was going to have value. They also realized almost immediately that the RHG also had a huge stash of ETHC now. On the ether classic blockchain, remember, the fork had never happened, so the RHG still had 70 percent of the ether it had rescued from the DAO. Now that had become ETHC.

They'd worked tirelessly to protect ether in the DAO and thought the hard fork had solved the problem. While it did solve the original DAO problem, the hard fork had now created a new one. Were they going to have to fight the attacker all over again for the ether classic?

"We did everything to avoid this, but now we're being dragged back into this fight," avsa said. "Did we just fork for no reason?"

● ● ●

So we've arrived at the point in our heist story where the thief has lost all his money but then receives a duplicate bundle of cash in the mail, courtesy of the people he stole from. Totally normal; this is fine.

This doesn't happen in traditional finance. If something happens with a publicly traded company like Ford, you don't suddenly have a clone of Ford to deal with.

I'm tempted to say there's nothing traditional about crypto, but that's not exactly true. There are people involved, so of course there will be human frailties we can recognize in this story. One that comes to mind is that the Ethereum community is sometimes too nice for its own good. This plainly comes from Vitalik and how he manages people. Kindness and patience are of course good qualities, but it's usually necessary to have a bite as well if you're going to succeed in American-style capitalism.

Think about this in terms of how they prepared for the hard fork. Vitalik and everyone else should have realized that of course everyone *could* update to the new software, but what if not everyone did? What would that mean? They don't seem to have prepared for this possibility; they were too nice to gear up for what should have been seen as a battle. It was their chain, they'd spent years struggling and fighting about how Ethereum should be made, they needed to protect it. But when the time came, they didn't.

It's hard to refer to the DAO as an unforeseen consequence. The code was put through a security audit, and its author, Christoph Jentzsch, was a respected authority on finding bugs in the Solidity language. People like Gün and Peter Vessenes had exposed several problems in its code, and everyone was fully aware that the DAO was a gamble. It had all the smartest people as curators of the DAO project; how could it go wrong? Yet in reality, it was destined to go down in flames.

The creation of ether classic is different – I think this one is an unforeseen consequence. It has to be, as no one seemed prepared for it or had planned on what to do if the hard fork wasn't unanimous. While the hard fork had the support of basically the entire Ethereum community, the result played right into the hands of the thieves it was meant to thwart. Was anyone really in control as Ethereum lurched from one disaster to the next?

There certainly was no road map for navigating the problems created by the DAO and hard fork. For the most part, these were kids or very young adults making decisions about what to do next. Their business naivete revealed itself many times over. Yet I can totally identify with what Vitalik and Gavin and Griff and Christoph and Roxana and everyone else must have been feeling during this era. This was history writing itself in hyperdrive. They were tapped into a worldwide audience that had money at stake, people who had bought into the Ethereum story. Everything moved at twice the speed and small decisions seemed to have huge consequences, like in a hash function when changing one character – an *a* to a *b* – gives an entirely new output. There is an all-consuming beauty to living your life even briefly in such tumult. You can still see it when you get someone like Griff Green talking about Friday, June 17, 2016. Or when Alex Van De Sande describes pushing the button to launch the RHG counterattack. Their voices get louder, they cuss more, the words spill from them. The live-wire passion is still there in many of the people who lived through those times. Not only that, but they all got really rich in the bargain.

That leaves the question of whether the ether thieves cashed in the ether classic they now owned. I have little doubt they made off with real money at the end of their exploits by selling ether classic. But it's hard to say for sure, unfortunately. The tools to track transactions on the ETC blockchain were not nearly as developed as Ethereum's in 2016.

One person chasing the ether thieves on the ETC blockchain was BokkyPooBah, an Australian developer and self-proclaimed "Ethereum fanatic." One of the more interesting details he shared with me was that the original ether thief, the one who attacked on Friday, June 17, had used a vanity address to move his ether classic. The attacker used an address with 11 *a*'s in a row in it, Bokky said. Because addresses are created randomly, the attacker would have had to run 17 billion *billion* transactions to get that address, he said. Let's write that out. That's a probability that comes out to 1 in 17,592,186,044,416, he said.

He was able to trace the ether classic in the DAO attacker's address to ShapeShift, but when he told ShapeShift what was happening "they told me to go away," Bokky said. The trail has grown cold now, Bokky told me. Like years cold.

"It was an expensive learning exercise," Bokky said, speaking of the DAO. "It was a lesson the Ethereum community had to have."

There's another twist to the creation of ether classic. Everyone who had an ether balance on the Ethereum blockchain at the time of the hard fork would now have an equal number of ether classic on that blockchain. Ether classic wasn't worth as much as ether, yet it still represented free money to anyone who held ether prior to July 16, 2016. That means that when all was said and done, the people who believed in the DAO, who sent their ether in exchange for DAO tokens, not only got their ether back but got a bonus account of ether classic for their troubles as well. Again, this is totally normal; everything is fine.

It's worth noting that some people who pushed ether classic at the beginning have a dark history. The RHG had changed; it had lost some of its founders, like Alex Van de Sande, and added new people. They now referred to themselves as the White Hat Group, and early interactions between the WHG and ether classic owners got nasty. I've spoken to several WHG members who asked me not to write about this part of the story; it's still traumatizing to them. Threats were made, and some in the WHG fell into depression and had suicidal thoughts, I was told. Some of the ETC supporters were bad people. But I never planned to write about this part of the story anyway. From the outset, I wanted to stop after the hard fork. There is another whole story to tell, another book, I'm sure, about what occurred behind the scenes in the early months of ether classic coming on to the scene. But I am not including that story here.

It seems fitting that one of the strangest thefts in modern history ended as strangely as it began.

Twenty

When I met Tomoaki Sato in Tokyo in January 2020, he wore a black overcoat buttoned to the top. Over the course of the more than an hour that we spent together, he never once loosened his coat; the button stayed fastened. Quiet to begin with, he got quieter when I started to ask him about the DAO attack.

Born in Tokyo in 1993, Tomoaki had attended one of the city's best high schools but dropped out of university. Once he discovered Bitcoin in 2013 he started reading pieces by a writer named Vitalik Buterin. He was too young then to buy Bitcoin. Years later, he heard about Ethereum and was able to buy a little ether in the crowdsale. In November 2015, he went to DevCon 1 in London, where he met Vitalik, Gav Wood, and others. It was an exciting time. While not many people knew about blockchain in Japan at first, that soon changed, and Tomoaki created Smart Contract Japan in 2015. He wrote code and hired engineers to help with blockchain projects as demand rose. One of his previous jobs had been helping people recover passwords to their Bitcoin wallet, which is no easy feat. He also made fixes to the Ethereum Go client, according to his GitHub page.

In 2016, he started a new venture called Starbase. The ICO craze was gathering steam, and he wanted to help startups that were funding themselves by selling a cryptocurrency. So far, Starbase has helped about five or six companies do an ICO, Tomoaki said.

I wasn't meeting with him in Tokyo to talk about Starbase, though. I was as nervous as I had been in Zürich, but in a more focused way. I had much better information now and a trail to follow. It was my job to talk to Tomoaki, to show him the evidence I had, and to ask him for his side of the story.

After some small talk I told Tomoaki I wanted to ask him some questions about the DAO attack. I explained I had a trail of transactions that started at Poloniex and then moved to ShapeShift, the exchange that allows users to change one cryptocurrency into another cryptocurrency with no way to track user identity. There were two Bitcoin withdrawals from Poloniex: the first had changed Bitcoin into ether and the second had changed Bitcoin into DAO tokens. I showed him how the ShapeShift outputs had landed in the same Ethereum address: 0x4fae.

Here's the sequence again: 0x4fae was used to fund address 0x35f5, meaning the 0x4fae transaction is the first that shows up under the 0x35f5 address. Thirty minutes later, 0x35f5 funded account 0x15def. I showed Tomoaki that 0x15def had created the attack contract that stole over 200,000 ether from the DAO beginning on Tuesday, June 21, 2016.

I said I had been told by someone familiar with the matter that the account at Poloniex was the starting point of the attack. Both Bitcoin withdrawals from the same Poloniex account were sent to ShapeShift and then to the Ethereum blockchain. I'd been told the Poloniex account belonged to Tomoaki.

He said he didn't remember any of the Ethereum addresses I showed him. That seemed fair; it had been years and who can remember alphanumeric gobbledygook like blockchain addresses?

But this wasn't the only evidence I had. The encrypted message to the RHG had been sent from 0x15def, the one that complained about the soft fork. A part of me felt ridiculous, to be honest, showing Tomoaki this odd little missive. Encrypted messages! On the blockchain! From one hacker to another! The stilted English is a bit cliché, don't you think?

Anyway, I'd found a direct link between 0x15def and Tomoaki's Poloniex account. I showed him a copy of the encrypted message and asked if he wrote it.

"No," he said, and laughed.

To stall a bit as I decided what to do next, I backtracked and again went over the details of the attack where huge batches of ether had been drained from the DAO. I told him I thought this was a copycat of the original DAO attack that'd happened on Friday June 17.

"I don't think I sent this kind of message," Tomoaki said.

We went back and forth on this for a bit, and again I was stalling. I didn't know how this was going to go, of course, but a flat denial hadn't quite made the list. Why hadn't I thought this out a bit more? (And who am I to criticize the Ethereum cofounders about the hard-fork repercussions?)

After a few minutes, I remembered the theory that the original DAO attack on Friday was the work of a group of people. I asked him if he had anyone else who worked with him who could have done this.

He said he was using his Poloniex account to invest other people's money on the exchange. He was acting as a broker for people who didn't know how to buy or sell cryptocurrencies but wanted someone like Tomoaki to do it for them.

Again, we ran through the links between 0x4fae and 0x35f5 and 0x15def. And ran through them again, all the way to the encrypted message, which he strongly denied writing. I asked him once more if anyone else besides him had access to his Poloniex account.

"I supported some other person at the time because this other person cannot manage a local account," he said. He gave the person access to the Poloniex account – the private key needed to move the crypto – because it wasn't Tomoaki's money. Imagine having a Charles Schwab account but not having instant access to your money. No one would ever do that, and it could be the same case here.

I asked whether it was possible that the person he'd shared his Poloniex account with could have sent the message.

"Yeah, that's possible," he said. He hadn't spoken to this person in years, he said, and he didn't want to tell me who they were. "I don't want to communicate with them," he said.

I was floundering here, to be honest. His answers were so tentative. I asked direct questions to get direct answers and was failing miserably. Interviews are living things, and they can be really weird. Why wasn't Tomoaki outright denying having anything to do with the DAO attack? Like I said about the man in Zürich, if someone accused me of stealing $55 million and I hadn't done it, I'd get really angry at a certain point. I'd tell them to fuck off. That wasn't happening in the small conference room in Tokyo, though. I needed him to either spill his guts or deny everything, I was really confused by this strange middle ground we occupied. I went straight for it.

"Did you have any idea they could have been doing this?" I asked.

The 17-second pause before he answered my question – I've listened to it many times on my recording of our on-the-record interview – is a very interesting pause, and the longest time he took while we spoke to choose his words.

"Maybe, maybe. Yeah," he said. "Some of the persons know engineers."

He then asked a fair question of me: Why would someone at Poloniex tell me that his account was the one that had made the withdrawals that were sent to ShapeShift? The standard answer is that sources always have an agenda, just as reporters do. I told him I had faith in my sources and that I wouldn't be asking him these questions if I thought he had nothing to do with the DAO attack. Then I pleaded for the story: I said I just want to tell this story and I need the details from the Dark DAO side of the attack.

Then it got more confusing. I reiterated that I was just trying to understand that there were other people who had access to his Poloniex account. He said no, not access, because he had Google two-factor authentication set up on the account, and he didn't share that security measure with anyone.

"I want to make sure I'm clear on this," I said. "Did your Poloniex account – where you could send Bitcoin, ether, DAO tokens – were you the only one who had control over that account? Or could other people log on to that account and do things on their own but under your account?"

"I think sometimes they can, yeah, because sometimes I had other people's money." We were back to the brokerage idea and the Charles Schwab analogy. He said he still has a Poloniex account, though he doesn't use it often.

"So then, it's possible," I said, "that this was done by somebody in your account that wasn't you?"

"Yeah, that's possible," Tomoaki said. The people Tomoaki said he was working for as a broker wanted to send ether to other people, but couldn't, so they needed him to do it through his Poloniex account.

"They want to keep their funds safe, but they don't know how to keep them safe," he said. "So I kept them safe instead of them. One way is the Poloniex account."

During our interview he asked twice about what the authorities thought of the DAO attack, if it was still something someone could get in trouble for. He mentioned Griff Green and asked if the US government was still interested in the theft. I said no, that I thought this was all in the past from law enforcement's point of view.

We talked for a while longer and went through the attack in more detail. I was running out of questions but had saved a good one for the end. Were the people who had access to his Poloniex account really good at Ethereum?

"The person's friend is good at it," he said, "but not the person himself." So, this friend could have done the attack? "Yeah," he said. Then he added, "Actually this attack is not so very difficult."

● ● ●

I have mixed feelings about my use of the term "the ether thief" in this book.

On the one hand, it's catchy and I like it as shorthand when describing the DAO attack. And of course, the ether thief exists – as we know there were probably several ether thieves – so it's not something I made up. But I don't know who the ether thief is. I did my best to track down every lead I got. So why did I refer to the man in Zürich in the sweater vest as the ether thief? Good question.

I told this part of the story as I experienced it. In the fall of 2019, I believed the man in Zürich had played a role in the DAO attack. He was the closest I had come to finding the ether thief at that point, so I wrote it as I lived it. Of course, I was wrong about the Swiss man, and the story went on to detail that.

I do feel good about setting the record straight about our friend in the sweater vest. The few people who know who I'm talking about can stop mentioning this part of the tale.

After more reporting and a bit of luck on the blockchain, I came to suspect Tomoaki. In January 2020, I thought he was the ether thief, so I wrote it that way. I want to be clear, however. I'm not accusing Tomoaki of being the ether thief. I can't make that claim; I don't have any direct evidence for it, just a link from a source I'm not naming and Tomoaki's own words when we spoke.

Tomoaki's story is plausible. If someone else had the ability to withdraw Bitcoin from his Poloniex account, as he claimed, once that Bitcoin was sent to ShapeShift it was gone. Only the person who had sent it to ShapeShift had control of it now. If Tomoaki hadn't sent it, he would have no idea how that Bitcoin was being used.

But it felt like a dog-ate-my-homework excuse too. If he wouldn't tell me who he was brokering cryptocurrency transactions for, I had hit a dead end.

Once back in the US from my visit to Tokyo, I sent Tomoaki a series of emails asking him to back up the story he'd told me. I was hoping he could send me proof that someone else had access to his Poloniex account. I'd been told he could take screenshots of his account log-on history that would show the IP address for anyone who'd logged on. He could also have shown me his withdrawal activity at the time in question, when the Bitcoin allegedly moved from the Poloniex account to ShapeShift. If there was none, that would exonerate him.

Eventually, Tomoaki wrote back to say he checked and discovered he closed his Poloniex account in 2018, so he couldn't provide screenshots from 2016. As for ShapeShift, he said the exchange didn't keep records of customers' transactions in 2016.

I'd also reiterated in my follow-up email what I planned to report in this book, giving him one last chance to say if anything I was reporting was inaccurate. He didn't reply to that.

Twenty-one

As the summer of 2016 turned to fall, the DAO fiasco and the hard-fork drama receded, albeit slowly and not without controversy, into the background. Ethereum's annual developer conference approached, and this time it would be held in Shanghai.

Corporate support for blockchain as a platform, which had started a year before with Microsoft coming aboard as a lead sponsor of DevCon 1 in London, only grew at DevCon 2. The likes of IBM and R3, a consortium of all the world's largest banks that were now experimenting with blockchain, were major presences in Shanghai. The problem was, they were slagging off Ethereum, saying it couldn't be trusted for commercial applications.

Corporations and the financial world were now fully in hype mode about the benefits of blockchain to their businesses. The longstanding refusal of regulated companies to have anything to do with Bitcoin had passed now that *blockchain* was a buzzword. If a supply chain–dependent business like a car manufacturer could get all its subsidiaries and suppliers on the same network, on the same blockchain, it could save them millions of dollars a year. Imagine being able to pinpoint a breakdown in the supply chain with a blockchain, being able to reroute orders and supplies instantly. That kind of real-time analysis and communication was incredibly difficult to do with a disparate network of firms that communicated over different time zones with various people in charge of keeping the assembly line moving. Similarly, bankers were intrigued by the potential of creating a private network for all the participants in a market like credit derivatives. That could cut the time it took to settle trades from days to minutes and save the banks millions of dollars in the bargain.

To form these private networks, banks and corporations didn't need to use the public blockchain systems that had made Bitcoin and Ethereum successful. There was no need for JPMorgan and Bank of America to use a proof-of-work system to mine blockchain transactions because they already knew each other. A proof-of-work system is only needed when strangers are interacting. It injects trust into a transaction where the parties don't trust each other. JPMorgan and Bank of America, on the other hand, already trade billions of dollars' worth of financial products between themselves every day, both for the bank's own account and on behalf of their customers. People began applying the term *distributed ledger* instead of blockchain to this kind of transaction system.

Distributed ledger projects were being created by IBM and R3 in the fall of 2016, and their executives had come to Shanghai to pitch them. Jeremy Millar had been involved with ConsenSys since April of 2016, and he became convinced that Ethereum needed a commercial enterprise arm to complement the foundation.

John Wolpert from IBM and Richard Gendal Brown from R3 presented at DevCon 2, "both of which had slides in it that basically said companies can't trust Ethereum, it's a fringe open-source project that can't be trusted for commercial work," Millar said.

Microsoft's Marley Gray was in Shanghai and remembered the IBM and R3 presentations. "IBM was particularly heavy on the FUD," he said, referring to the acronym for "fear, uncertainty, and doubt" that crypto people use as shorthand for anyone criticizing their work. "I still give Jerry some grief about that," he said, referring to Jerry Cuomo, IBM's VP of blockchain technologies.

It was clear in Shanghai that Ethereum needed to create its own commercial development arm aimed directly at banks and corporations, or someone else would steal that market right from under them.

Joe Lubin, Vitalik, Jeremy Millar, Marley Gray, Alex Batlin, and Andrew Keys were among the people in Shanghai who had the first conversations about what would become the Enterprise Ethereum Alliance. About 10–12 people initially joined the group, which Joe bankrolled until membership dues were enough to pay the bills. Marley Gray offered the Microsoft offices near Times Square for EEA meetings.

As always when Ethereum is involved there were political minefields to navigate, and the early enterprise team discovered one right away. The first name it came up with for itself was the Enterprise Ethereum Foundation, which went over like a ton of bricks with Ethereum Foundation leadership. There was already bad blood between Ming Chan and Joe Lubin, and here Lubin was backing a commercial project that seemed to be trying to take the very name of the Ethereum Foundation for itself.

The Ethereum codebase would need some work as well if it was going to appeal to businesses. This was the early advantage IBM's Hyperledger project and R3's Corda blockchain had over Ethereum.

Marley Gray said Ethereum was under pressure from other enterprise blockchains like Hyperledger that had better privacy controls and performance. "Corda was starting to make some noise. We felt like if we didn't do something. . .," Gray said.

An organization that was doing something was JPMorgan. Its Quorum enterprise blockchain project was in its infancy, but to Marley and others, the fact that JPMorgan was willing to throw its lot in with Ethereum only strengthened their belief that the EEA would receive broad support.

One of the earliest JPMorgan employees to work on Quorum (back before it was called Quorum) was Amber Baldet. She'd always liked to build things, to create: Back when she was a kid she'd watch and sometimes help as her dad worked on their car engine or replaced their roof with the help of Amber's brother. She spent a lot of time in the garage with power tools and made jewelry out of spent bullet casings. The home improvement network HGTV used to show *This Old House* and Amber couldn't get enough of it. "I learned how to install a lot of plumbing," she said.

Her love of technology goes back to when she was 13 and persuaded her parents to let her use a 9600-baud modem left behind by a deceased relative. The experience was life changing. Baldet connected to university message boards, whose members didn't know they were interacting with a wee teenager. The respect she was able to garner from them was a huge confidence boost.

Baldet first encountered finance while working at a small arbitrage brokerage in her home state of Florida. She'd started to code when she was 10 years old and rewrote part of the brokerage's middle-office software to let the salespeople and research people know what was working for their clients. She thought a career as a secret agent, like in the CIA, was in the cards, but it didn't seem to be a good fit. What she really wanted to do was move to New York City and work on Wall Street.

She found her way to JPMorgan after working at a consulting gig and being hired by Vikram Pandit's hedge fund, Old Lane, in 2008, just as the financial world was about to implode. In 2009, she discovered Bitcoin, so a few years later when the banking world was starting to talk about blockchain she felt she had a good background to help JPMorgan sort through this new technology.

The team Baldet joined was known at first as Gemini, which oversaw several avenues the bank was pursuing. One area was strategic partnerships, like the investments JPM had made in startups Digital Asset Holdings and Axoni. Another was the issue of using public blockchains for business, which is problematic because public blockchains reveal too much information for businesses to feel comfortable using them. To address the latter issue JPM could try to use Ethereum – if Ethereum could be tweaked to be more private – or go with R3 and its Corda blockchain or build its own internal blockchain from scratch.

Since no one at JPM knew what the best path to take was, the company decided both to build its own blockchain version, known as Juno, and to tinker with Ethereum to see if it could be made suitable for the regulated banking world. "We had an internal bake-off," Amber said.

The problem that Baldet had to solve to appease her bosses was that Ethereum, like Bitcoin, is public. Every transaction is viewable on a blockchain explorer like Etherscan, and banks can't have that level of transparency because it could expose their customers' private information. There had to be a way to get the benefit of a network like Ethereum but to also shield the details of those customers' transactions.

Christine Moy was Amber's first hire in the blockchain unit, and she helped during the bake-off. Patrick Nielsen came in to help the team with a crucial idea about how to get the needed level of privacy. "He and Amber and a couple others on the team architected this private contract store node that would sit in parallel with the Geth node," Christine said. The private node would store all the private transactions, which would be encrypted and then hashed so they could be uploaded to the public version of the bank's blockchain.

This was huge and solved the privacy issue. In essence, all you could see was an event log. It would show that something had taken place, but unless you had the private keys to that transaction you couldn't access any more detail. The name Gemini came from the twin servers, one private, one public; JPM eventually changed the name and introduced the project to the world as Quorum.

Baldet and her team worked with Jeff Wilcke and some other Ethereum Foundation members to get Quorum up and running. Whereas support from Microsoft had helped establish Ethereum as a serious player, JPMorgan basing its entire blockchain model on it was a vote of confidence at a whole new level. The financial world was beginning to pay serious attention to Ethereum and what smart contracts could do for business.

Alex Batlin played an important role in the early adoption of Ethereum by the financial world through his position running UBS Labs, a fintech-focused unit at the Swiss bank. His first foray into Ethereum involved creating a "smart bond," where a token on the blockchain represents corporate debt. Batlin named the blockchain project at UBS "Pathfinder," because in the early days they had no idea where this would lead.

"The public Ethereum blockchain absolutely makes a lot of sense, but if you're going to be trading security tokens between regulated banks then you didn't need to have the burden of proof-of-work," Alex said. As each member of the bank-trading network would be known to each other, UBS used a system called proof-of-authority, which doesn't require an ungodly amount of electricity to maintain.

There were three big areas where Ethereum, or some version of it, could specifically help the financial world, Batlin believed. The first was in doing away with what's called issuer risk – in this case, let's use the case of the issuer of government-backed currency. In the China-US trade relationship, for example, most debt is held by China in the form of US dollars. "They're now not just subject to credit risk, i.e., the US going bankrupt, they also have an issuer risk," Batlin said. "If the US were to suddenly print a huge amount of new money, effectively they would devalue any loans a third party has against them which hold them in dollars."

He brought up the fact that gold has been used as a substitute for fiat currency when there is a lack of trust in the government issuing the currency. But on a practical level gold is hard to deal with, and you might not get it back from the US government if it happens to be holding it for you. "Where do you sell the gold?" Alex said. Cryptocurrency sidesteps both of these concerns.

"A zero physical-settlement risk currency, with no issuer risk, that's a pretty good idea," Batlin said. "It's more applicable in international settings rather than national."

A second point is that cryptocurrency provides a way to pay people more directly and to incentivize them. The incentive can build on itself if a certain blockchain network rewards its users and developers. That way the cohesion grows and the network effect can be multiplied.

Lastly, there is the thorny problem of national interests in securities markets. For understandable reasons, perhaps, most countries have centralized control over their own domestic stock markets and the associated back-office settlement procedures that are arguably more important. That makes it difficult to sell shares across the world because business in London has to be reconciled with US-based business, and Asian share purchases have to be reconciled with sales of shares in the Middle East. You get the idea.

"A distributed ledger technology, or blockchain, is perfect because it's both local and global, so you no longer need to reconcile between nations," Batlin said.

"My view is this is a natural evolution," he said. Paper money worked well when most trade was regional – within the Eastern Seaboard of the US, for example. When trade went global, however, paper money slowed down transaction times.

Or, as the EEA's Jeremy Millar put it, "Global business needs global networks."

JPMorgan took this idea seriously and soon realized that just sticking a blockchain into an existing financial market only adds another layer of complexity, often without improving efficiency. "But what if we built a new debt instrument from scratch on a blockchain?" Christine Moy said. "That's where the cash token was born, or JPMCoin was born."

This was the banks' way of moving money around its global locations: from Frankfurt to Auckland in less than a second, using a digital representation of the bank's deposits. While cash has been electronic for a long time, what's different here is that all the recipients of JPM's money are on the same network. In the traditional model, my bank sends another bank money electronically, yet this has to be recorded in each set of books at the bank. This takes time, up to three days in many markets right now, and can be error prone. In a digital system, the sender and receiver are connected via the same payment rail, so the debit and credit are instant on each set of books. This is not only faster, it saves the banks money as they are required to set aside some of their funds for the duration of a trade in case it fails. The syndicated loan market can take more than 15 days to settle. The money to be saved there is immense, and only one small example.

Christine Moy had an already varied and probably exciting career for a banker under her belt when she joined the bank's blockchain effort. During the financial crisis of 2008 she'd helped to renew credit lines for the big three US automakers so they wouldn't go bankrupt. She traded commodities under Blythe Masters, helping North American mining companies hedge their risk. Then she went to JPMorgan's private bank, where the idea of digitization was beginning to take hold. She'd been told that the bank's loss given default calculator, which is used to assess loans given to private bank clients, couldn't be automated. So she automated it.

"At that time, it felt like I'd done all the things at JPMorgan," she said. Then she saw the job posting Amber Baldet put out where she asked for a Twitter handle, and Christine knew this was not just any other position within JPM. "It was the most mysterious job post," Moy said.

The focus on blockchain was all happening at the bank because of Sanoke Viswanathan, who was then JPMorgan's chief administrative officer of the corporate and investment bank. Moy referred to him as the blockchain godfather at JPMorgan. He set the permissive tone needed to experiment with emerging technology at the staid and bureaucratic enterprise that is JPMorgan. "It was really important because you need the culture to change to be open to new technologies," Moy said. We were in a conference room in the bank's headquarters on Park Avenue, and as I took notes Moy realized I was having trouble with the spelling of Sanoke's last name. She grabbed my notebook and wrote it out for me. I remembered Vitalik looking over my notes once, too, and helping me correct the spelling of Mihai Alisie's name. But he'd just spelled it out for me; Christine took matters into her own hands. That's Wall Street, baby.

And even though this was the first time I'd met Christine Moy, our paths had kind of crossed before. She mentioned a 2015 cover story in *Bloomberg Markets* titled "Blythe Masters Tells Banks the Blockchain Changes Everything." That story had a big effect on the street and helped change the philosophy of banks on blockchain, Moy said. I'd written that story with my colleague Edward Robinson. It was one of those small, neat times like in *When Harry Met Sally* when a writer can tell someone, I wrote that!

JPMorgan is thinking about this paradigm shift in a 5- to 10-year time frame. After I spoke to Christine in the JPMorgan headquarters in Manhattan, I noticed something in the lobby of their building. The Starbucks there no longer accepts cash.

• • •

In late February of 2017, about 200 executives, coders, and developers gathered in the downtown Brooklyn office of JPMorgan. This was the official launch of the EEA and it was to be an all-day affair. The founding members of the group showed the breadth that had been achieved in just a few months from the initial idea for the EEA in Shanghai. Tech giants Microsoft and Intel were among the founding members, as was CME Group, the world's largest futures exchange; BNY

Mellon, Banco Santander, Credit Suisse, UBS, and JPMorgan repre-sented the financial sector, with accounting firm Accenture among the founders as well. Oil behemoth BP was in the mix, as was Thomson Reuters.

I attended this event for Bloomberg News and remember a glitch at the beginning that seemed a perfect metaphor for Ethereum at the time. Vitalik wasn't in Brooklyn that day but had recorded a video message that the EEA wanted to play to kick the meeting off. Except they couldn't get it to work: the computer hosting the message had crashed. A frozen image of Vitalik's face hung on the screen in the conference room, then disappeared. As people tried to get the video to play, Amber Baldet stood up and took control of the room. She was funny and force-ful in a way that quieted everyone immediately. After about 30 minutes they got the video to play.

As the world was waking up to Ethereum, it still had a long way to go. It was slow, first of all, in a performance sense. Then too it had to convince regulators that it was safe and capable of replacing critical infrastructure in the corporate and financial worlds. These were big hur-dles, but there were also signs that once stuffy and staid corporations were willing to give this a shot.

One example of this was how Baldet and her team convinced the JPMorgan higher-ups to allow Quorum to be open source. JPMorgan had never done an open-source project before: Why would a bank work hard to create a software product and then give it away to the rest of the world? It was about as antithetical to banking as publicly declaring your customers' positions in the middle of Broad Street.

"The good thing about approaching this with a blockchain project was, it's not an argument, it's an easier narrative to build that we're giving away the operating system, but charging for the apps," Amber said. "We'll be able to introduce a number of products to market that are monetized that sit on top of it. So that resonated and made sense to people."

It also led to interactions like the Central Bank of Brazil getting in touch with Amber to let her know it had downloaded Quorum and was experimenting with it for the bank's real-time gross settlement processes.

In a larger sense, though, while the EEA was helping establish Ethereum as fit for business, Amber and a lot of other people involved with the group wanted enterprise blockchains to lead to a better public blockchain system. The hope was that, like in the early days of the Internet, private intranets would one day merge with the public Internet. If in business or on the public chain, many in the Ethereum community wanted to move the ball in the same direction.

I asked Amber about these ambitions at the EEA launch in Brooklyn.

"I don't want to build AOL," she said. "I want to build the world wide web."

Twenty-two

The camp Griff runs is called Decentral; in 2019, you could find it at E and 6:37. That's Burning Man–speak for the schematic used to map out the gyroscope that is Black Rock City. He's been doing this for years, trying to expose the Burning Man community to the decentralized-economy community, and he was back at it again.

This is the playa, an insanely flat, big space in the Nevada desert that's transformed for a week every year by over 70,000 people who come to basically do whatever they please. It is breathtaking in the way that the Grand Canyon is; you have to see it with your own eyes to get it. At night on the playa, looking out across the vast space, on your left and your right you can see the multitude of parties and people going by, not to mention the art cars: it's a carnival every night. And then you shift your focus, and out in the distance, across the dark middle ground, you'll see they're doing exactly the same thing half a mile away. It's a lot to take in.

I'd come to see Griff on his mission to spread the blockchain gospel. On Tuesday, I went to the first presentation I could at the Decentral camp. They had a few different spaces: one a large tent that could probably hold 150 people or so, and then some smaller spaces for more detailed discussions. I'd ridden my bike across the playa dust, eye goggles and mask on, battling the wind. It was so bright and hot I constantly thought of water. I stepped in the tent and took my shoes off, my eyes adjusting.

There was a man with curly hair and a microphone giving a talk. He had orange sunglasses stuck in his hair and referred to his phone from time to time, where he had a copy of his presentation. He couldn't have put his phone away in his pocket because he wasn't wearing any pants. No shirt either – he was fully nude. A woman in a bikini slept behind him in a big chair behind a table. There were about two other people sitting on the floor. To be fair, it was hot as hell out – at 2 p.m., it was right in the middle of the day.

The naked guy took a question from a shirtless guy wearing white Ray-Bans, who asks about incentives and how people can be trusted to do the right thing in a decentralized setting. This is the aim of Griff and the others behind Decentral: the chance to answer questions, explain the technology in simple terms. To get your eyes to widen when you finally got it.

Still, it felt dead, and not what I had expected. A lot of people had lost personal fortunes when the cryptocurrency bubble popped in 2018. Bitcoin had briefly topped $20,000, and it seemed that every mom and pop had gotten in right around that top. I wondered how many of them were here at Burning Man. The event itself is too big to sum up from one perspective – like people mostly being here to party. That's somewhat true, but not even close to the full story of who attends Burning Man.

It is still true, though, that the price of cryptocurrencies like Bitcoin was by far the most salient thing that the average person understood about blockchain or distributed systems. People always ask me if they should buy Bitcoin. That's one thing, at least, that Decentral wanted to change.

After helping the RHG secure the vulnerable ether in the DAO, Griff Green had moved on to be part of a similar but different Ethereum group that called itself the White Hat Group. This group included some of the RHG people but many new people too. They were involved in efforts to secure the ether classic that resulted from the Ethereum hard fork. That in itself was a long and vicious battle that is worthy of an entire book, and which I won't be dealing with here. Afterwards, the WHG helped to resolve two hacks on Parity, the blockchain project started by Gavin Wood and others after they left the Ethereum Foundation.

More recently, Griff had founded Giveth, a way to bring decentralized ideals to the nonprofit and charitable-giving communities, like cutting out middlemen and increasing transparency in how funds are raised and spent. He wants people to start thinking about incentives and how they are aligned or misaligned and to create projects that align users and creators and everyone else within a system.

On the playa at Burning Man Griff is known as Santa. This is one of the tenets of Burning Man for many people: taking on playa names and/or identities for the week in Black Rock City. For Griff, it's Santa, and he wore a Santa cap, a long red Santa robe, and a wicked pair of Santa shorts that had a black belt and buckle printed on them. His Santa robe was mostly open, showing his hairy and well-tanned chest. He wore a necklace that read "Own Your Data."

He paid for everything at the Decentral camp using Bitcoin. As I learned, running a Burning Man camp is a huge endeavor. You have to feed and care for people: the sign of a good camp is one that's gone to the trouble of providing private portable bathrooms so that the public Port-O-Potties can be avoided, and it's even better if it has a shower stall rigged up in some fashion. Griff put this all together with the help of many others associated with Decentral, all with the goal of cross-pollinating between the blockchain and the Burners.

At the second Decentral talk I attended on Tuesday, this point was driven home. It was called "Blockchain for Beginners" and had more people in the tent than the previous discussion had, but not many more. The man running the show (who was clothed) compared a decentralized blockchain to Black Rock City.

The 70,000 people in Black Rock City had come together to make a community they would support for a week, and many had come early to build the camps and other infrastructure needed. Yet no one was in charge. Or, *you* were in charge. In other words, everyone was in charge and to make the thing work everyone in Black Rock City had to do their part to ensure their little piece of it worked.

A blockchain community is much the same, Chris, the discussion leader, said. No one is in charge and yet everyone is in charge. It is made piece by piece by individuals doing what is, hopefully, best for the wider community.

I asked Chris about how blockchains can deal with the inconvenience factor. That is, when you are in charge you have to be willing to take on the responsibility of mediating disputes and solving disagreements. In centralized systems all this is done for you, and in a trade-off for that convenience we all lose things like privacy and run the risk of identity theft and having our habits be commodified at every turn. In a decentralized system, I asked, are people really going to be willing to take on the burden of solving disputes that might not even involve themselves? It seemed like a big hurdle to overcome.

Chris said that not everyone had to be involved, only enough people who were willing to mediate or organize votes about changes to the underlying software. The community has to be diverse enough to have these types of people in the mix, he said. That's why they were here at Burning Man, in fact, to spread the word to non-technologists.

As he was speaking, sometimes he'd almost get drowned out by the electronic dance music being blasted from the tent across the way. Then he was entirely silenced as a remix of Men at Work's "Down Under" overtook him.

● ● ●

I went to Burning Man to check in on the future of Ethereum. It made sense to me that Griff and his cohorts would try to find new adherents here in the Nevada desert. The people who attend Burning Man are adventurous yet resourceful. This is no dance party; the playa is unforgiving and if you don't come prepared you can get into real trouble. So it seemed like a great pool of people to draw from.

I didn't realize it at the time, but it also provided a window into how people who knew nothing about blockchain, or who knew a just a bit about Bitcoin, thought about these things. I would be able to watch the Decentral folks try to win converts in real time.

At the smaller venue Decentral used, called the Fishbowl, I overheard a comment outside the yurt-like tent: someone said that understanding this technology deeply isn't necessary, that it's all about bringing all sorts of varied people into the mix of blockchain and decentralized markets. Griff was in full Santa regalia that day and spoke with a group of people who were a mix of novices and people like Jonathan Levi, who helped create the Linux Foundation's Hyperledger Fabric, an opensource blockchain system used by tech giants IBM and Cisco. Once I realized who he was, I wanted to tell the people in the tent how lucky they were to be asking him questions in such an intimate setting, but that's not exactly Burner culture.

Griff made the point several times that decentralized markets have the ability to align incentives between users and producers in ways that don't often happen with centralized systems. He used CureCoin as an example, which is a way for people to rent out their unused computer processing power to Stanford University's Folding@home project. The project describes itself this way on its website: "a distributed computing project for disease research that simulates protein folding, computational drug design, and other types of molecular dynamics. As of today, the project is using the idle resources of personal computers owned by volunteers from all over the world. Thousands of people contribute to the success of this project."

CureCoin was created to reward people who donate their computer power to the project. Its cryptocurrency, Cure, is issued to people who support the work of Folding@home. In February of 2020, Cure traded for three cents, according to CoinMarketCap.com.

While Cure may seem nearly worthless at that price, it still has a value, which incentivizes people to donate their spare CPU power, collect Cure, and then cash it in. To Griff Green, this alignment of incentives is far superior to a system where someone donates money to a charity that researches cancer cures, for example. In that situation, your money is gone except for the tax benefit you receive. In a system where something of value like Cure is in the mix, you own a financial asset that can increase in value in return for your donation to the effort to fight disease.

It was fascinating to watch this argument seep into people in the Fishbowl. There was plenty of skepticism. How could something like Cure have a value, Griff was asked. He answered that it's possible to trade Cure for Bitcoin at many exchanges around the world. That means plenty of people believe it has a value, and therefore it has a value. All money operates on this principle. It's a type of magic, really, to assign a piece of paper a nonarbitrary value.

As I listened, I couldn't help but think that the Folding@home market was like any other financial market that I knew. Since I used to cover energy trading for Bloomberg, I thought first of the oil market. How was the CureCoin economic model any different from the oil market? On one side you have the producers: the people who donate computer time to earn Cure coins. In the oil market the producers are the energy companies that drill for crude all over the world. Then you have the speculators; in the Folding@home market they're the folks who are willing to buy Cure on an exchange because they think it will rise in value. In the oil market, speculators are a vital part of the oil futures market, where they buy or sell derivative contracts in the hope of making money by crude's price rising or falling. Without speculators, no market can be healthy or survive.

Griff was trying to impart to his audience that these types of microeconomies are alternatives to the way things are done today. The combination of decentralization, cryptocurrencies, and a new way of aligning incentives all made it possible to fundamentally change how local markets work now. He doesn't want a global cryptocurrency; that would just be co-opted by already huge and powerful governments and corporations. No, he wants a thousand microcurrencies to allow for a different way forward.

He boiled his pitch down to the bare bones as he told the small group in the Fishbowl: "We have the tools now to change the story of money."

● ● ●

Griff's message has been heard loud and clear by some of the world's largest financial institutions and corporations. It has also won favor with regulators, notably the SEC.

In October 2019, the SEC granted Paxos Trust Company, a block-chain company that caters to financial institutions, the green light to settle stock trades in near real time. This wasn't a pilot program or a proof-of-concept, as Wall Street has been so fond of doing for years. It's real stocks trading in US equity markets. The move was seen as a direct threat to the Depository Trust & Clearing Corporation, the industry-created body of banks and brokerages that works to settle trades in a centralized fashion, and it marked a turning point in the DTCC's half century of dominance in the equity market.

The approval allowed for a small-scale program where Credit Suisse and Société Générale were allowed to use a private version of Ethereum to transfer shares and money once trades are complete.

"This is really a completely different way for the securities to be set-tled," Paxos chief executive officer Charles Cascarilla said to me in an interview for a Bloomberg News story I wrote. "This process is a really big deal because I don't think you've had any good examples of real assets using blockchain," he said.

The DTCC isn't letting its business be taken away that easily, though. In a different area of what it does it's using distributed ledger technology, or DLT, to help improve how credit default swaps are managed. CDS trades became notorious during the 2008 financial crisis, of course, and efforts to regulate them included requirements that completed trades be collected and maintained in a common location. That gave rise to the DTCC creating its Trade Information Warehouse. While such trade repositories have always been centralized in the past, DTCC is close to implementing a distributed ledger that would allow the banks and inves-tors that trade CDSs to all be on one private network. That network is based on Ethereum.

In April 2019, Société Générale, one of France's largest commercial banks, issued a bond worth 100 million euros on the Ethereum block-chain. "This live transaction explores a more efficient process for bond issuance," the bank said in a statement at the time. Société Générale said it expected to benefit in many ways by switching to using a tokenized method to issue debt, including better transparency and quicker settle-ment times.

Then there is the Bank of France, which has completely replaced a component of one of its key payments systems with Ethereum. The

Single Euro Payments Area, or SEPA, allows merchants in the 34-nation EU to collect payments from their customers. "The central bank identified an opportunity where DLT could be valuable to automate and digitize a manual and time-intensive process that requires coordination and information sharing with multiple banks," according to a 2109 World Economic Forum white paper on how central banks are adopting blockchain technology. Smart contracts in an Ethereum-based system have rewritten how the process works. "The Bank of France considers the implementation a success," the WEF said. "In addition to greater time efficiency, it cites benefits such as process auditability and disaster recovery, along with greater accountability for commercial banks within the process."

Other central banks that are far along in their experimentation with blockchain include the Bank of England, the Bank of Canada, and the Monetary Authority of Singapore, the WEF said. When you hear about projects in the commercial or financial world that work with blockchain, it nearly always means some form of Ethereum is being used.

JPMorgan has continued to broaden its Quorum offering and started the Interbank Information Network, or IIN, in 2017. As of early 2020, it counted 397 banks around the world as members of IIN, including large competitors Toronto-Dominion Bank, Deutsche Bank, Santander, Lloyds, Crédit Agricole, Mizuho, and many others. IIN was built to speed up payments in the correspondent banking system, which can sometimes take weeks to move money around the world while charging high fees. IIN allows multiple parties to a payment to be aware of its status in real time, and it's all based on Quorum – Ethereum's younger brother who went to business school.

The move to implement smart contracts into the existing financial world appears to be best suited, as of early 2020, to smaller markets. One example is equity derivatives, which are used by investors and banks to do customized deals using an underlying stock like IBM. The bank and investor then trade payments based on whether the stock rises or falls in value. It's a private market, only for sophisticated investors, and it trades off exchange. That gives rise to operational problems, as these contracts can last for years. Both sides to the transactions have to maintain their own books and records and disagreements can muck up the process. With all this in mind, Axoni, a blockchain firm using a smart contract–enabled blockchain system, partnered with banks and investors to put all the participants in the equity swaps market on a blockchain.

In February 2020, Axoni reported that data from the first live trade was processed, using smart contracts between Citigroup and Goldman Sachs.

"This is a significant milestone, which reinforces our commitment to embracing technology to solve real challenges faced by the industry," Puneet Singhvi, Citigroup's head of financial market infrastructure and lead for blockchain, DLT, and digital assets, said in a statement at the time. "The platform, using smart contracts, will enable significant efficiencies while mitigating risks in post-trade processing of equity swaps."

The outlook in 2020 is that adoption of blockchain by the financial world finally seems to be gaining steam. It has been years of thinking about projects and testing ideas, and many applications have been thrown by the wayside. There's been a lot of skepticism, and rightfully so in many cases. The hype about blockchain and Ethereum and smart contracts was thick and ever present in 2016 and 2017. Yet it appears that for all the missteps banks have kept building, and real projects have started to emerge that have changed how people buy and sell financial products everyday around the world.

It's an open question as to whether these blockchain advances in the corporate and financial worlds will continue. If it's a big corporate interest that first makes a breakthrough with DLT – say an insurance company or a global supply chain – I'm not sure we'll even notice that something has changed. The mechanics of how actuarial tables and trade routes work play out behind the scenes, and there's no reason to think big efficiency gains would make for compelling news. Any blockchain breakout – if it happens – would more likely be noticed on the consumer front. It's likely that some form of crypto will be required to interact with a blockchain app. That could be ether, or it could be a stable coin (which is still digital but isn't supposed to fluctuate in value because it's collateralized in some fashion to tie it to a real-world asset like the US dollar). It would need to be easy to buy that crypto and easy to use the app. Then you could see real threats to companies like Uber, Airbnb, and eBay – and basically any company that sits in the middle of a transaction and takes a fee for the privilege.

The thing is, as of now, there are no real, solid examples of decentralized products or services that you can easily buy or use. We don't know
how Airbnb and Uber would react to decentralized versions of their
services because they don't exist. Ethereum is still in its promise phase,
where it has been for many years now. There is impatience from some in
the community at the slow pace of adoption, yet this ties right back to
the lack of products. If there's nothing to adopt. . .

And as can be seen from its history, Ethereum has always gone much
slower than people said it would go. It's like the crowdsale that was
always two weeks away. It can feel like the entire Ethereum ecosystem
lives in that wait-and-see moment. The challenges are on many fronts
too, and not just related to how to get people to use Ethereum-based
products. The challenges are technical as well. For what it wants to be,
Ethereum needs serious improvement in its performance stats. Visa
claims its payment network can handle more than 24,000 retail transactions per second. Ethereum is a fast blockchain that does 15 per second.
(Though it should be pointed out, you could potentially be sending an
enormous amount of money, say $50 million, over the Ethereum block-
chain. Try that on your Visa card.) In late 2019, Vitalik said on Twitter
that an optimistic view would see Ethereum increase to 3,000 transactions per second with the improvements it was making, which shows
you how very far it has to go.

Bringing along regulators is another hurdle Ethereum has to clear.
Episodes like the DAO attack should, on the one hand, terrify regulators
due to the "unstoppable" nature of an application running with a software bug that can't be fixed. On the other hand, the Ethereum community voted to fix the problem, and regulators like flexibility (even if
blockchain purists abhor it). When it comes to critical business systems
of the type regulated under the systemically important financial market
utility framework, US officials are going to be extremely cautious about
allowing a network of banks and investors to reshape the bond market,
as just one example. The SEC has been criticized repeatedly for not
spelling out its views on cryptocurrencies in a formal fashion. People
have been left guessing in a lot of cases until the feds came in with an
enforcement action.

An exception to this approach was the SEC report released in July
2017 on whether the DAO, slock.it executives, and others violated US

law by selling unregistered securities. The SEC decided that DAO tokens were in fact securities, but stopped there. "The Commission has determined not to pursue an enforcement action in this matter based on the conduct and activities known to the Commission at this time," the SEC said.

So no one at slock.it or the DAO were charged with any offense. The SEC instead used the matter as an opportunity to remind people in the decentralized world that just because they had a shiny new toy didn't mean they could ignore the law.

"The automation of certain functions through this technology, 'smart contracts,' or computer code, does not remove conduct from the purview of the US federal securities laws," the SEC wrote. "This Report also serves to stress the obligation to comply with the registration provisions of the federal securities laws with respect to products and platforms involving emerging technologies and new investor interfaces."

The test the SEC uses to determine if a financial product is a security is known as the Howey Test and dates to a case in 1946 involving a Florida company that owned orange groves. Based on this test, federal regulators asked three questions to determine if ether is a security: (1) is there an investment of money in a common enterprise with (2) the expectation of profit that (3) comes from the efforts of a third party?

The SEC declared DAO tokens met all these criteria, yet still declined to bring an enforcement action.

An interesting side note is a section of the SEC report that looks a bit different to me now that I've spoken to so many people involved with slock.it and the DAO. SEC lawyers wrote that one characteristic that made the DAO seem like a security was that DAO token holders didn't have control over how decisions were made.

"Although DAO token holders were afforded voting rights, these voting rights were limited," the SEC wrote. "DAO token holders were substantially reliant on the managerial efforts of slock.it, its cofounders, and the curators." Reading that again years later, I recalled how Christoph Jentzsch told me that the slock.it team planned to apply to the DAO for jobs. They were going to create a proposal to be put to a vote by DAO token holders asking to work for the thing they had created. Then there was the name. The DAO never got beyond that boring acronym because a name change wasn't able to be voted on before the hack. If the DAO had lived, I think we would have seen much more voting activity and interesting outcomes, as well as voting rights, secured by token owners.

As of mid 2020, the Ethereum community was in the midst of its biggest upgrade since going live in July 2015. They're calling it ETH 2.0.

The changes being worked on boil down to making Ethereum process transactions faster so it can grow into the type of network needed for a global reach. The first change is doing away with the proof-of-work system that's used by Ethereum miners to confirm the latest transactions on the blockchain. The computer power needed uses an enormous amount of energy, and Vitalik and others in the Ethereum community have long wanted to get away from this environmental black mark.

While Bitcoin is known to use a larger amount of electricity for its proof-of-work than Ethereum, Ethereum is estimated to gobble a quarter to half as much, according to *IEEE Spectrum*, the magazine of the world's largest group of engineers and applied scientists. That means Ethereum's proof-of-work uses the same amount of electricity as Iceland on any given day, *IEEE Spectrum* said. Put another way, one Ethereum transaction consumes more electricity than the average US household uses in a day, the magazine said.

The proof-of-work system also requires every computer on the network to hold the entire history of the blockchain on its hard drive. Then all of the computers have to be in synch and update with new transactions as they occur throughout the day. That makes for great security, but the trade-off is that the network can only run so many transactions per second. It's safe, but slow.

The way Ethereum wants to change that is by switching to a confirmation process known as proof-of-stake. Proof-of-stake requires users who want to be rewarded for validating transactions to deposit ether for a set amount of time. The more ether they set aside, the bigger the reward for verifying the network. In a proof-of-work system, the winning miner who first validates a block of transactions is rewarded with an amount of Bitcoin or ether. In proof-of-stake, there are no miners. There are now validators, and they make bets on which block is next to come up for verification. If they are right, they get rewarded with a percent of ether proportional to how much ether they have committed to the proof-of-stake system.

There will also be a feature that causes people who do things deemed to be harmful, like trying to take the network over or passing off a block they know to be invalid, to lose their ether in a lockup. If that occurs in proof-of-stake, that validator's ether could be taken from them (what's known as slashing).

Anyway, proof-of-stake would get rid of miners, so electricity usage would be cut dramatically. ETH 2.0 also moves to a system known as sharding to get away from the requirement that every hard drive on the network has to hold the complete blockchain in its memory. Sharding in effect splits the blockchain into regions, or shards, that work on a sort of regional basis. So the validators on a particular shard would only hold the transactions occurring on that shard, meaning they would be able to process things much more quickly than in a proof-of-work scenario. The various shards – in early 2020 the number being considered was 64 – all link to a main chain called the Beacon Chain.

Vitalik has said that he wants these upgrades to Ethereum to improve its transactions per second from 15 to 100,000. That seems a bit on the optimistic side (I recall that in an interview with me in 2017 he said he expected Ethereum to switch to proof-of-stake by the end of that year). As of this writing, the first of three phases to move to ETH 2.0 is expected to begin by mid-2020.

The challenge here, above all else, is that Ethereum is a living network right now. There are people using it as you read this. And Vitalik and everyone else who want to upgrade it don't have the option of taking it offline for a few months to do the work. As I've heard from many people over the years, upgrading Ethereum in real time is like fixing a 747 in midair.

● ● ●

The last time I saw Griff Green at Burning Man we sat down to talk in the canteen area of the Decentral camp. It was quite an affair they had built in the desert, a full kitchen and pantry with cooking shifts worked out on a whiteboard. On a different whiteboard they'd written out the schedule of talks they'd give over the week. It was impressive how many discussions they'd committed to and the wide range of topics they'd cover. I got excited when I saw that Brock Pierce was scheduled to give a presentation. Pierce has a long – and some would say tortured – tenure in crypto, yet he's mesmerizing to watch as he spreads the good word about Bitcoin or the EOS platform or the alternative future these touch upon. I'd seen him speak in Santa Monica, where he was very good, so I couldn't imagine how being on the playa would infuse his presentation. But then he didn't show.

I thought it would be particularly good to ask Griff about the future of Ethereum. He's been in it for years now, has seen ether go from being created to trading at over $1,200 to crashing back at somewhere around a couple hundred dollars.

He was optimistic about ETH 2.0 and how it would change the Ethereum ecosystem. "Getting rid of the whole miner thing is what I'm really excited about," he said. Was he dressed as Santa? Yes, he was. Had I taken him up on his offer to do our interview in the steam bath, naked? No, I had not, mostly because of the difficulty of taking notes in such an environment.

Griff knew it was still early days for Ethereum and decentralized finance in general. It had been early days since I'd started covering block-chain in 2015. This was mid-2019. You could have filled the playa with the number of times I've heard the term *early innings* over those years.

"Ethereum is great, but it's not the point," Griff said. He meant the possibilities unleashed by Ethereum were the point, but the future didn't necessarily depend on Ethereum's success. It could fail and other projects would continue to build on what it had started, just as Ethereum built upon the ideas of Bitcoin. He doesn't think of his efforts with Giveth and The Commons Stack as a confrontation with traditional finance or nonprofits. He wants to create a parallel system.

"Let's play the game," he said. "You're creating all this value for your-selves. Why not create some value for ourselves?" The money part of it is inescapable, "the oil of our machine," as he put it. Decentralized pro-jects have to be able to finance development so they have room to grow. "If you can't have independence there, you can't have innovation," Griff said.

It was clear to me that a big part of the excitement Griff had for this world was the real-time nature of the economic experiment they were engaged in. He got how it all worked, the world back beyond the Burning Man boundary fence. He wanted a lot of the same benefits that system produced, just on his own terms. This fit perfectly with his love of Burning Man, where people simply give everything away. It's a giving economy; the only things for sale are coffee and ice. You will be given everything else for free – from margaritas to street tacos to vegan muffins to cold keg beer.

"Burning Man is a magical economic experiment," he said. "It's re-created the natural economy you're born into."

The parallels between Burning Man and blockchain kept springing to mind, like the one that had been brought up a few days ago: no one's in charge, meaning everyone is in charge. A second parallel had occurred to me as I thought about the police presence in Black Rock City. I'd talked to people about the changes to the festival over the years, like how before there was personal lighting wear (like LED) the playa had been almost totally dark at night. But the one that stuck with me was the number of police and Bureau of Land Management officers on patrol. I knew from talking to some old-timers that there hadn't been cops at Burning Man in the beginning. I thought about regulators and how they'd been caught many years behind the curve when distributed systems and cryptocurrencies burst onto the scene. They were all sniffing around now, asking if this stuff was even legal.

One night, the people in the camp I was staying in took their amazing art car, the Pyrobar, out on the playa. We served free drinks and one of the guys in the camp played DJ. I tended bar that night and had to ask people for their IDs before I was able to serve them. It seemed ridiculous, but camps and art cars were being ticketed and harassed if they were found serving minors.

But the officers on horseback on the playa have a role to play, just as regulators in the financial world do. The amount of money at stake in a system like Ethereum has built is enormous. Anyone can buy crypto or participate in an ICO with no oversight. Lots of money has been lost – amounts in the billions, and growing.

The last time I spoke to Vitalik was over the phone. I asked him how his vision of Ethereum, the one he crafted on his European travels, was working out.

"It's definitely slower than I expected," he said. "But it's happening." Back several years ago he became excited about stable coins. Now there was Dai, a stable coin collateralized with ether that's in wide use. He'd also wanted to see a decentralized naming system for the Internet. Now a lot of people use a service called EthDNS, where you can buy domain names that end in .eth. According to CoinDesk, foundation.eth sold for $27,000 and exchange.eth went for $609,000 in 2017. He's also excited about decentralized storage systems, which aren't quite here yet but are close.

He was seeing the ecosystem he'd envisioned being built. There was no killer app yet, however. No Netscape browser or AOL to open up whole new worlds for people. But every day he's working toward the time when that no longer will be the case.

Griff Green is patient about the work of educating folks too. He'll keep coming to Burning Man to tell people about a different way of structuring human organizations until it finally sticks.

"I don't think we need to tear anything down," he said. What he's become a part of is the long game, a piece-by-piece amalgam of the new and alternate world he wants so badly to live in.

"I'm a big fan of evolution over revolution," Griff said. "Revolutions fail all the time. Evolution can't be stopped."

● ● ●

The Man Burn is preceded by fireworks. And then the giant wooden statue, created anew each year, is engulfed in flames. This is the highlight of the week, and I was in awe of the number of people and frenzy about the entire place. My brother, who had been to Burning Man a few times before I went, put it well. He said the most beautiful natural phenomenon he'd ever seen was Yosemite Valley, and the most beautiful man-made one was Burning Man.

The man burned for far longer than I thought it could without crashing down. And then as it fell, it only fell halfway, as though it was genuflecting. The pause was magical, and as it stayed in that position, I realized that Burning Man is about renewal. It's not about burning something to the ground. It will arise again next year, and many of these people will be back to do it all over again. It is about re-creating the world in the image you want it to be. Here, out on the playa of dust and nothingness, the future is not broken. It seems limitless.

Sources

The vast majority of reporting in this book came from interviews conducted by me with primary sources. I conducted more than 70 interviews, most on the record and some with unnamed sources, to piece this story together. When a quote or thought is from an interview, I tried my very best to always use "said" in the text. If a statement came from someone's writing or a news article, I used "wrote" or "according to" to try to keep the distinction clear. Not all of the interviews I conducted made it into the book; for those of you I left out, please know you helped me shape and understand this story and I appreciate every minute of your time. The notes section that follows includes a list of citations for third-party sources, divided by chapter and listed by page number.

Prologue

x   McLuhan, Marshall, and Fiore, Quentin. *The Medium Is the Message* (Berkeley, CA: Gingko Press, 1967).

Zero

4   Etherscan blockchain records. https://etherscan.io/txs?a=0x969837498944ae1dc0dcac2d0c65634c88729b2d&p=6

9   Robinson, Edward, and Leising, Matthew. "Blythe Masters tells banks the blockchain changes everything." *Bloomberg Markets* (August 31, 2015). https://www.bloomberg.com/news/features/2015-09-01/blythe-masters-tells-banks-the-blockchain-changes-everything

11   Dubner, Stephen J. "The silver thief." *New Yorker* (May 17, 2004). https://www.newyorker.com/magazine/2004/05/17/the-silver-thief

12   Etherscan blockchain records. https://etherscan.io/txs?a=0x969837498944ae1dc0dcac2d0c65634c88729b2d&p=6

12   ETH Zürich digital library. "Einstein's studies at the Polytechnic Institute in Zuürich (1896–1900)." https://www.library.ethz.ch/en/Resources/Digital-library/Einstein-Online/Einstein-s-Studies-at-the-Polytechnic-Institute-in-Zurich-1896-1900; "Professor at the ETH Zürich (1912–1914)." https://www.library.ethz.ch/en/Resources/Digital-library/Einstein-Online/Professor-at-the-ETH-Zurich-1912-1914

14   Network Working Group. "Request for comments: 2068, Category: Standards track" (January 1997), p. 60. https://www.rfc-editor.org/rfc/pdfrfc/rfc2068.txt.pdf

17   Nguyen, Chuong. "Reddit beats out Facebook to become the third-most popular site on the web." Digital Trends (May 30, 2018). https://www.digitaltrends.com/computing/reddit-more-popular-than-facebook-in-2018/

17   Tsanajev, Magomet. "What are Reddit's blockchain-based community points?" Medium (April 10, 2020). https://medium.com/@MagoTsan/what-are-reddits-blockchain-based-community-points-363117e53733

17 ConsenSys blog. "Ethereum has 4x more developers than any other crypto ecosystem" (August 20, 2019). https://consensys.net/blog/blockchain-development/ethereum-has-4x-more-developers-than-any-other-crypto-ecosystem/

22 Jentzsch, Christoph. "slock.it DAO demo at DevCon 1: IoT + blockchain" (London, November 13, 2015), YouTube video. https://www.youtube.com/watch?v=49wHQoJxYPo

23 Pfeffer, Johannes. "The rise of the Dark DAO." Medium (June 17, 2017). https://medium.com/@oaeee/the-rise-of-the-dark-dao-72b21a2212e3

25 Van de Sande, Alex (@avsa). Twitter post (June 21, 2016). https://twitter.com/avsa/status/745313647514226688?lang=en

25 Etherescan blockchain records. https://etherscan.io/tx/0xda43911686119545 9372666568f10a5d3a70803a11290e69e5537dfe5a42db3e   [To   see   the encrypted message, expand the transaction by using the Click to See More option, then click View Input As to change the view mode on Input Data from Default View to UTF-8. That's as far as I can take you; I wasn't given the private key, only the unencrypted message the private key unlocks.]

Two

42 Harney, Alexandra, and Stecklow, Steve. "Twice-burned – how Mt. Gox's customers could lose again." Reuters (November 16, 2017). https://www.reuters.com/investigates/special-report/bitcoin-gox/

42 Vessenes, Peter. "Ethereum contracts are going to be candy for hackers." Peter Vessenes blog (May 18, 2016). https://vessenes.com/ethereum-contracts-are-going-to-be-candy-for-hackers/

42 Vessenes, Peter. "More Ethereum attacks: Race to empty is the real deal." Peter Vessenes blog (June 9, 2016). https://vessenes.com/more-ethereum-attacks-race-to-empty-is-the-real-deal/

43 Dwork, Cynthia, and Naor, Noni. "Pricing via processing or combatting junk mail. In: Advances in Cryptology – CRYPTO '92 (ed. Brickell, E.F.) Lecture Notes in Computer Science, vol. 740 (Springer, 1993, pp. 139–147) via Cook, John. "What is proof-of-work?" John Cook blog (November 11, 2018). https://www.johndcook.com/blog/2018/11/11/proof-of-work/

44 Mark, Dino, Zamfir, Vlad, and Sirer, Emin Gün. "A call for a temporary moratorium on the DAO." Hacking, Distributed (May 27, 2016). https://hackingdistributed.com/2016/05/27/dao-call-for-moratorium/

46 eththrowa. "Bug discovered in MKR token contract also affects the DAO – would allow users to steal rewards from the DAO by calling recursively." DAOHub forum (June 12, 2016) via the WayBack Machine [original web page no longer exists]. http://web.archive.org/web/20160702202124/https://forum.daohub.org/t/bug-discovered-in-mkr-token-contract-also-affects-thedao-would-allow-users-to-steal-rewards-from-thedao-by-calling-recursively/4947

Three

47 Gibson, Steve, and Merritt, Tom. "Bitcoin cryptocurrency." *Security Now* podcast (February 11, 2011). https://twit.tv/shows/security-now/episodes/287

50 Buterin, Vitalik. About.me web hosting service (n.d.). https://about.me/vitalik_buterin

53 Buterin, Vitalik. "Bitcoin adoption opportunity: teenagers." *Bitcoin Magazine* (February 28, 2012). https://bitcoinmagazine.com/articles/bitcoin-adoption-opportunity-teenager-1330407280

57 Buterin, Vitalik. [A catalogue of the stories written by Vitalik Buterin]. *Bitcoin Magazine* (n.d.). https://bitcoinmagazine.com/authors/vitalik-buterin/1

57 Buterin, Vitalik. "Bitcoin 2013: Day 1." *Bitcoin Magazine* (May 18, 2013). https://bitcoinmagazine.com/articles/bitcoin-2013-day-1-1368906536

Four

69 Falls, Arthur. "The Third Web #14: Dawn of an ecosystem: Substrate and polkadot" Arthur Falls podcast (n.d.) via SoundCloud. https://soundcloud.com/arthurfalls/the-third-web-14-dawn-of-an-ecosystem-substrate-polkadot

69 Select Committee on Intelligence, US Senate, 116th Congress. *Russian Active Measures, Campaigns, and Interference in the 2016 US Election,* vol. 2. Report 116-XX (2019). https://www.intelligence.senate.gov/sites/default/files/documents/Report_Volume2.pdf

71 Lessig, Lawrence. *Code and Other Laws of Cyberspace* (New York: Basic Books, 1999).

72 Murphy, Brian. "This North Carolina city can't get Twitter to delete an imposter." *News & Observer* (June 6, 2018). https://www.newsobserver.com/news/politics-government/article212559284.html

Five

78 Di Iorio, A. "Meet at Pauper's Pub in T.O. for a beer and wings and talk all things Bitcoin." Meetup.com posting (November 3, 2012). https://www.meetup.com/decentral_ca/events/87122762/

Six

80 Kassam, Ashifa. "Spain's 'Robin Hood' swindled banks to help fight capitalism." *Guardian* (April 20, 2014). https://www.theguardian.com/world/2014/apr/20/spain-robin-hood-banks-capitalism-enric-duran

85 Gogulski, Mike. "BitLaundry re-launch!" BitcoinTalk forum post (May 19, 2011). https://bitcointalk.org/index.php?topic=9018.0

86 Wuille, Pieter. "Pieter Wuille – Bitcoin core developer" WeUseCoins web site biography (n.d.). https://www.weusecoins.com/pieter-wuille/

86   Hearn, Mike. "The resolution of the Bitcoin experiment." Medium (January 14, 2016). https://blog.plan99.net/the-resolution-of-the-bitcoin-experiment-dabb30201f7

86   Ricknäs, Mikael. "Pirate Bay case on its way to the court of appeal." *PC World* (April 21, 2009). https://www.pcworld.com/article/163492/pirate_bay_case_goes_to_court_of_appeal.html

86   Buterin, Vitalik. Email to friends and family (n.d.).

87   del Castillo, Michael. "Dark Wallet: A radical way to Bitcoin." *New Yorker* (September 24, 2013). https://www.newyorker.com/business/currency/dark-wallet-a-radical-way-to-bitcoin

87   Buterin, Vitalik. "Bitcoin conference in Amsterdam in two weeks." *Bitcoin Magazine* (September 14, 2013). https://bitcoinmagazine.com/articles/bitcoin-conference-in-amsterdam-in-two-weeks-1379177771

88   Branwen, Gwern. "Bitcoin is worse is better." Gwern Branwen website (May 27, 2011). https://www.gwern.net/Bitcoin-is-Worse-is-Better

89   Assia, Yoni, Buterin, Vitalik, Rosenfeld, Meni, et al. "Colored Coins white paper." (2013) https://docs.google.com/document/d/1AnkP_cVZTCMLI-zw4DvsW6M8Q2JC0lIzrTLuoWu2z1BE/edit

90   Buterin, Vitalik. "Ultimate scripting: A platform for generalized financial contracts on MasterCoin" (2013) via the WayBack Machine. https://web.archive.org/web/20150627031414/http://vbuterin.com/ultimatescripting.html

Nine

118   Eha, Brian Patrick. "This Bitcoin wallet service just added 3 major players to its roster." *Entrepreneur* (January 6, 2014). https://www.entrepreneur.com/article/230664

119   Buterin, Vitalik. "Shedding light on the Dark Wallet." *Bitcoin Magazine* (November 2, 2013). https://bitcoinmagazine.com/articles/shedding-light-on-the-dark-wallet-1383357523

119   Buterin, Vitalik. "KryptoKit: Easy-to-use, in-browser Bitcoin and messaging for the masses." *Bitcoin Magazine* (December 11, 2013). https://bitcoinmagazine.com/articles/kryptokit-easy-to-use-in-browser-bitcoin-and-messaging-for-the-masses-1386742599

121   Boase, Richard. "Bitcoin price skyrockets as senate hearing concludes." CoinDesk (November 19, 2013). https://www.coindesk.com/bitcoin-price-skyrockets-senate-hearing-concludes

121   Andreessen, Marc. "Why Bitcoin matters." *New York Times* (January 21, 2014). https://dealbook.nytimes.com/2014/01/21/why-bitcoin-matters/

122   Lubin, Joe. Keynote address. Ethereal SF 2017 conference via ConsenSys blog (2017). https://media.consensys.net/10-essential-ethereal-summit-talks-to-get-you-hyped-for-blockchain-week-9604f2f2b295

124   Peck, Morgen. "The uncanny mind that built Ethereum." *Wired* (June 13, 2016). https://www.wired.com/2016/06/the-uncanny-mind-that-built-ethereum/

130   Buterin, Vitalik. "Ethereum introduction – BTC Miami January 26, 2014."
       YouTube video (January 29, 2014). https://www.youtube.com/watch?v=tVPmv
       MBRRdQ

130   Larimer, Dan. "Dan Larimer and Vitalik Buterin at the North American
       Bitcoin conference in Miami." YouTube video (April 17, 2014). https://
       www.youtube.com/watch?time_continue=229&v=mP82XmUNgNM

Twelve

159   Kharif, Olga, and Dougherty, Carter. "Mt. Gox Bitcoins devalued as traders
       ponder insolvency." Bloomberg News (February 21, 2014).

159   WizSec. "The missing Mt. Gox Bitcoins [Mt. Gox investigation findings].
       WizSec blog (April 19, 2015). https://blog.wizsec.jp/2015/04/the-missing-
       mtgox-bitcoins.html

161   Castaldo, Joe, Posadzki, Alexandra, Leeder, Jessica, et al. "Crypto chaos: From
       Vancouver to Halifax, tracing the mystery of Quadriga's missing millions."
       Globe and Mail (February 8, 2019). https://www.theglobeandmail.com/busi-
       ness/article-crypto-chaos-from-vancouver-to-halifax-tracing-the-
       mystery-of/

161   Alexander, Doug. "'Questionable' death prompts call to exhume Quadriga
       CEO's body." Bloomberg News (December 13, 2019). https://www.bloomb-
       erg.com/news/articles/2019-12-13/-questionable-death-prompts-
       call-to-exhume-quadriga-ceo-s-body

163   De, Nikhilesh. "Lawyers ramp up pressure to exhume Quadriga CEO's body."
       CoinDesk (January 28, 2020). https://www.coindesk.com/lawyers-ramp-up-
       pressure-to-exhume-quadriga-ceos-body

163   Roberts, Jeff John, and Rapp, Nicolas. "Exclusive: Nearly 4 million Bitcoin
       lost forever, new study says." *Fortune* (November 25, 2017). https://fortune.
       com/2017/11/25/lost-bitcoins/

164   O'Brien, Will. "How 2014 became the year of multisig." CoinDesk (December
       29, 2014). https://www.coindesk.com/2014-became-year-multisig

Thirteen

178   Nakashima, Ellen. "Iran blamed for cyberattacks on US banks and compa-
       nies." *Washington Post* (September 21, 2012). https://www.washingtonpost.
       com/world/national-security/iran-blamed-for-cyberattacks/2012/09/21/
       afbe2be4-0412-11e2-9b24-ff730c7f6312_story.html

178   Leyden, John. "How mystery DDoSers tried to take down Bitcoin exchange
       with 100Gbps crapflood." *Register* (October 17, 2013). https://www.thereg-
       ister.co.uk/2013/10/17/bitcoin_exchange_ddos_flood/

180 Nakamoto, Satoshi. "Bitcoin P2P e-cash paper." Satoshi Nakamoto Institute, archive of email communication with Satoshi Nakamoto (November 17, 2008). https://satoshi.nakamotoinstitute.org/emails/cryptography/15/

181 Wood, Gavin. "Ethereum: A secure decentralised generalised transaction ledger." Gavin Wood website (2014). https://gavwood.com/paper.pdf

Fifteen

199 Buterin, Vitalik. "Launching the ether sale." Ethereum Foundation blog (July 22, 2014). https://blog.ethereum.org/2014/07/22/launching-the-ether-sale/

203 BNN Bloomberg. "Cryptocurrencies tycoon on his vision for Canada's biggest condo" (July 13, 2018). https://www.bnnbloomberg.ca/technology/video/cryptocurrencies-tycoon-on-his-vision-for-canada-s-biggest-condo~1438716

203 Shin, Laura. "How Joseph Lubin cofounded Ethereum and scored a billion-dollar fortune." *Forbes* (February 7, 2018). https://www.forbes.com/sites/laurashin/2018/02/07/joseph-lubin-ethereum-ether-consensys-crypto-cryptocurrency/#2cece6853575

Sixteen

212 karalabe. "DAO Wars 1.4.8." GitHub, Go-ethereum releases (June 29, 2016). https://github.com/ethereum/go-ethereum/releases?after=v1.4.14

213 Todd, Peter. "The Ethereum DAO bailout needs a coin vote." Peter Todd blog (June 23, 2016). https://petertodd.org/2016/ethereum-dao-bailout-vote

214 Wong, Joon Ian, and Kar, Ian. "Everything you need to know about the Ethereum 'hard fork.'" Quartz (July 18, 2016). https://qz.com/730004/everything-you-need-to-know-about-the-ethereum-hard-fork/

Seventeen

218 Buterin, Vitalik. "Ethereum Foundation open call re: Board selection." Ethereum Foundation blog (April 10, 2015). https://blog.ethereum.org/2015/04/10/ethereum-foundation-open-call-re-board-selection/

221 Karapetsas, Lefteris (@Lefteris JP). "Happy 4th birthday Ethereum." Twitter post [photo] (July 30, 2019). https://twitter.com/LefterisJP/status/1156224936840704000?s=20

Eighteen

229 Buterin, Vitalik. "DevCon is back!" Ethereum Foundation blog (September 24, 2015). https://blog.ethereum.org/2015/09/24/devcon-is-back/

229 Hallam, George. "Nick Szabo confirmed as keynote speaker at Ethereum's DevCon 1." Ethereum Foundation blog (October 22, 2015). https://blog. ethereum.org/2015/10/22/nick-szabo-confirmed-as-keynote-speaker-of-ethereums-devcon1/

230 Gray, Marley. "Ethereum Blockchain as a Service now on Azure." Microsoft blog (November 9, 2015). https://azure.microsoft.com/en-us/blog/ethereum-blockchain-as-a-service-now-on-azure/

232 Vigna, Paul. "BitBeat: Microsoft to offer Ethereum-based services on Azure." *Wall Street Journal* blog (October 28, 2015). https://blogs.wsj.com/moneybeat/2015/10/28/bitbeat-microsoft-to-offer-ethereum-based-services-on-azure/

233 Kelly, Jemima. "Microsoft launches cloud-based blockchain platform with Brooklyn startup." Reuters (November 10, 2015). https://www.reuters.com/article/microsoft-tech-blockchain/microsoft-launches-cloud-based-blockchain-platform-with-brooklyn-start-up-idUSL8N1354JE20151110

Nineteen

236 Bovaird, Charles. "Bitcoin prices stable as volatile Ethereum draws trader interest." CoinDesk (March 18, 2016). https://www.coindesk.com/bitcoin-prices-volatile-etherum-trader

236 Wong, Joon Ian. "The price of ether, a Bitcoin rival, is soaring because of a radical, $150 million experiment." Quartz (May 20, 2016). https://qz.com/688194/the-price-of-ether-a-bitcoin-rival-is-soaring-because-of-a-radical-150-million-experiment/

237 Zamfir, Vlad. "Dear Ethereum community." Medium (July 7, 2016). https://medium.com/@Vlad_Zamfir/dear-ethereum-community-acfa99a037c4#.outhcyspr

238 Carbon Vote. Vote: The DAO Hard Fork [result of ether holders "vote" on DAO hard fork] (n.d.). http://v1.carbonvote.com

241 Poloniex Exchange (@Poloniex). "ETC/BTC and ETC/ETH #Ethereum Classic markets added." Twitter post (July 24, 2016). https://twitter.com/Poloniex/status/757068619234803712

241 Rizzo, Pete. "Ethereum hard fork creates competing currencies." CoinDesk (July 24, 2016). https://www.coindesk.com/ethereum-hard-fork-creates-competing-currencies-support-ethereum-classic-rises

Twenty-two

270 World Economic Forum. "Central banks and distributed ledger technology: How are central banks exploring blockchain today?" World Economic Forum white paper (March 2019). http://www3.weforum.org/docs/WEF_Central_Bank_Activity_in_Blockchain_DLT.pdf

270 JPMorgan. "Largest number of banks to join live application of blockchain technology." JPMorgan website (n.d.). https://www.jpmorgan.com/global/treasury-services/IIN

271 Axoni. "Axoni distributed ledger network for equity swap processing goes live with leading market participants." Press release (February 6, 2020). https://axoni.com/press/axoni-distributed-ledger-network-for-equity-swap-processing-goes-live-with-leading-market-participants/

273 Securities and Exchange Commission. *Report of Investigation Pursuant to Section 21(a) of the Securities Exchange Act of 1934: The DAO.* Release No. 81207 (July 25, 2017). https://www.sec.gov/litigation/investreport/34-81207.pdf

274 Fairley, Peter. "Ethereum plans to cut its absurd energy consumption by 99 percent." *IEEE Spectrum* (January 2, 2019). https://spectrum.ieee.org/computing/networks/ethereum-plans-to-cut-its-absurd-energy-consumption-by-99-percent

278 Milano, Annaliese. "Ethereum is getting its first top-level domain name." CoinDesk (August 3, 2018). https://www.coindesk.com/ethereum-is-getting-its-first-top-level-domain-name

Appendix

Details of the 0x15def DAO hack on June 21, 2016
This is meant to be a more-detailed explanation for tech-savvy readers of how I used blockchain transactions and unidentified sources to piece together the DAO attack of July 21, 2016.

Bitcoin sent to Shape Shift, exchanged for ether, sent to address 0x4fae

https://shapeshift.io/txstat/1CFeDos3cf112WZWazMSu8TT8bZHazw89N

Bitcoin sent to Shape Shift, exchanged for DOA tokens, sent to address 0x4fae

https://shapeshift.io/txstat/12NBJ3KvMrdTkKxxJh2nACoLeBLyQu4HsD

Both of those withdrawals came from the Poloniex account of Tomoaki Sato, before being sent to Shape Shift, according to a source who asked not to be named.

Ethereum account 0x4fae created 6/19/16 17:34 (Sunday before attack)

https://etherscan.io/txs?a=0x4fae38ced4c4b1360d0535108bb1cbc376cb37a6

0x4fae funded account 0x35f on 6/20/16 at 10:56 (Monday)

https://etherscan.io/address/0x35f53e17adaad5cdd215792de55f 73ef67f7f3e4

33 minutes later, 0x35f funded account 0x15def on 6/20/16 at 11:29 (Monday)

https://etherscan.io/txs?a=0x15def77337168d707e47e68ab9f7f6c1 7126b562&p=3

0x15def used attack contract 0xe306 to attack the DAO beginning 6/21/16 at 8:08

https://etherscan.io/tx/0xb90183a0dc442d5cb8a3d0757d338832f c9b84e5c5e604df43bb234287a9f83c

attack contract 0xe306 sent stolen ETH to Dark DAO 101 0xf4c6

https://etherscan.io/txsInternal?a=0xf4c64518ea10f995918a45415 8c6b61407ea345c&p=18

0xf4c6 would come to hold 268,320 stolen ETH, the second largest DAO theft, according to Robin Hood Group records.

Acknowledgments

While I had no way of knowing it at the time, this book began in 2015 when I began writing about blockchain for *Bloomberg News*. I've been incredibly lucky to have been able to follow many of the big stories in this new part of computer science ever since, and I had a tremendous amount of help along the way.

None of this would have been possible without Joel Weber, the amazing editor of *Bloomberg Markets* in 2016, who came to me with the idea of a heist story. The way he allowed me to run with the reporting and writing of *The Ether Thief*, and the deft edit he gave the story, set a high-water mark for how beautifully collaborative this journalism thing can be. Along the way, other editors patiently came along with me as I tried my best to explain why this should matter to Wall Street. Rob Urban was there from the start, and spiked my first blockchain story, telling me it was too boring. It was, and he set the bar high for me ever since. Nick Baker helped me think through stories big and small and has a reporter's nose for where the story lies, which is a blessing in an editor. My colleagues Edgar Ortega, Sam Mamudi, John Detrixhe, Nina Mehta, and Annie Massa always made the market structure beat the best place to be in the newsroom. On the blockchain and crypto beat, it's been a pleasure to work with Lily Katz, Camila Russo, Olga Kharif, and Alastair Marsh, all under the benevolent leadership of Dave Liedtka. Kristin Powers was incredibly generous with granting me time off to write this book, and the enthusiasm and support I received from Alan Goldstein and Michael Moore as I was leaving them for many months meant a great deal to me.

I had given up hope of finding an agent for this project when Jeff Herman emailed me out of the blue many months after I'd stopped receiving rejections. His guidance and belief in me from the beginning were immense. Bill Falloon, my editor at John Wiley & Sons, provided a perfect blend of letting me run with this story as I went all over the world and keeping me focused on the people who made this story live and breathe. All the little things in the publishing process at Wiley were made so much easier with the help of Samantha Enders, Purvi Patel, Amy Laudicano, and Jean-Karl Martin. Missy Garnett, thank you for the thorough and justified copy edit.

Maybe the most terrifying moment for a writer is releasing your baby to early readers. But in my case, I was in expert hands. My wife Rebecca is by far the best editor I've ever known, she's as tough as they come and always right. Rob Dieterich convinced me to get more of my voice into the story, and it made the book so much better. To my dad, Jeff, thank you for the incisive tips and I'm glad you thought the story got going after a hundred pages. To Adam, my brother, sorry you didn't like it. Many thanks to Liam Vaughan and Nathaniel Popper for early advice on how to write a book.

As I hope came through in the text, the subjects of this story were wildly generous with their time. A few stand out. Vitalik was always willing to sit down with me, as long as I came to him. It was a pleasure getting to know him over the hours we spent together. His father Dmitry entrusted me with the Encyclopedia of Bunnies, which strange as it sounds really helped me understand his son. Griff Green gave me the prefect ending to this story with his Burning Man involvement, as well as help and guidance all along the way that was vital. Lefteris Karapetsas from the very beginning of my reporting contributed his insights and gave me immeasurable help. Alex Van de Sande did the same. Christoph Jentzsch kindly allowed me in his home to see where he suffered in his office on the day of the DAO attack, and generously put me up in

Mittweida when no hotels could be found. Emin Gün Sirer also graciously allowed me to visit his home, and along with Phil Daian gave a lot of their time to help me check my blockchain sleuthing. I was able, maybe, to get a bit more out of Joe Lubin for this book than usual, thanks for putting up with me, Joe. And Andrew Keys was always there to answer questions or help make a connection to someone I needed to speak with. Another early and instrumental source was Anthony Di Iorio, who gave me hours of his time, including a visit to his gorgeous Toronto condo. After much hounding, Gavin Wood and I exchanged long emails as he was in the midst of launching his latest blockchain project, Polkadot. Thank you, Gavin. Mihai and Roxana were always an absolute pleasure to speak with, and Roxana helped me "see" Calafou with the amazing photos she so kindly allowed me to use. Taylor Gerring did the same for the early days with his photographs and detailed recollections.

I couldn't have attended Burning Man without a camp, and I was very fortunate to be allowed into the Enclave. Thanks to Mark, Zach, Jewels, Melissa, and everyone else who made that week absolutely unforgettable. (Mark, we still need to talk blockchain, give me a call.) Ben Best made that introduction to the Enclave folks for me; thank you, Ben.

For their astute and ambitious public relations help I can't thank you enough Amanda Cassatt, Kelley Weaver, and Carissa Felger. Your kindness and generosity are amazing.

Lastly, my family have always been the rock underneath me during this project. To my boys, Noah and Nate, thank you for letting your dad disappear into the office for several months. To my mom, Tracy, your support and belief in me has never wavered and I'm the man I am because of you. Dad, thank you for showing me that it's possible to love your job. Rebecca, you beautiful thing, I do all of this for you.

Index